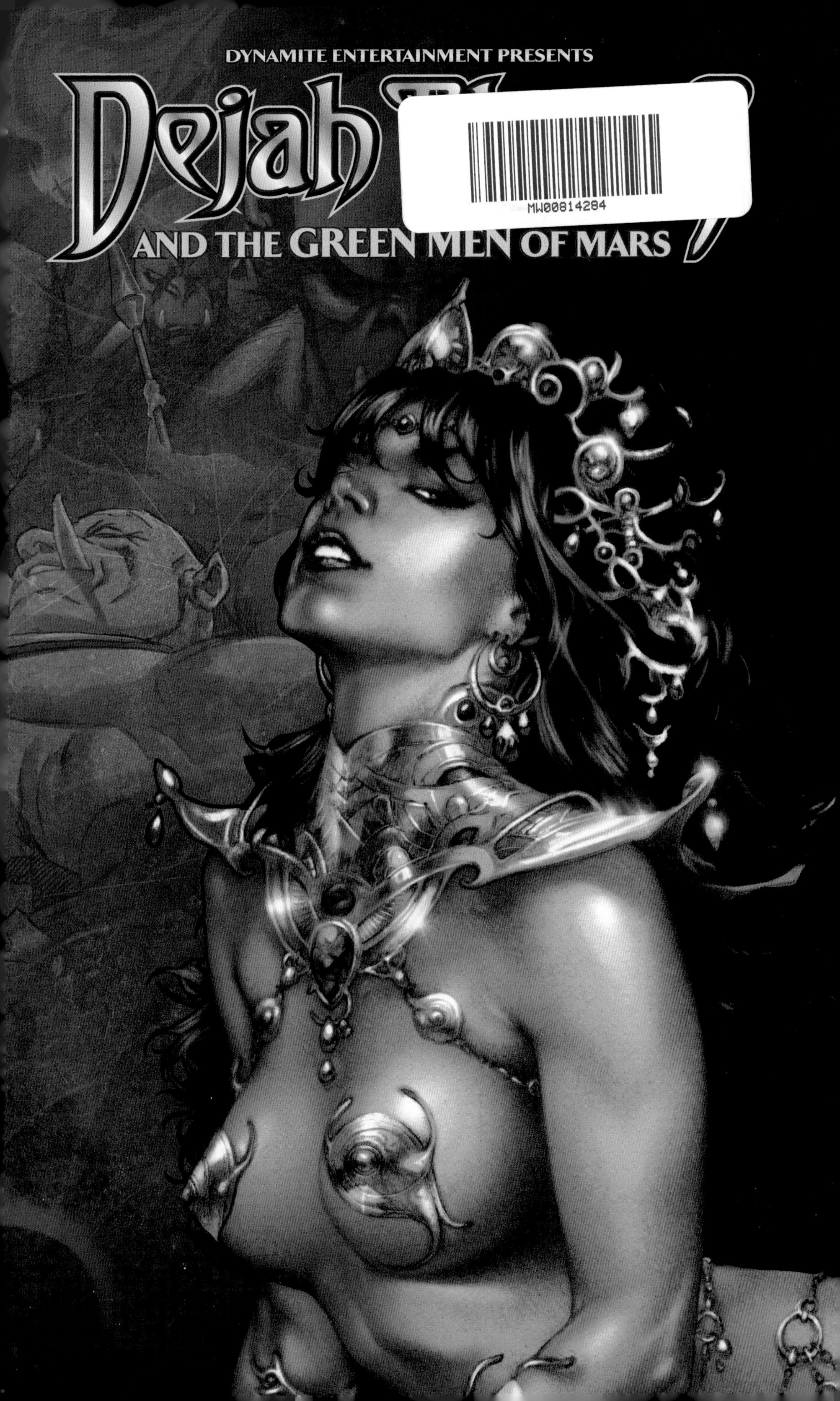
DYNAMITE ENTERTAINMENT PRESENTS
Dejah
AND THE GREEN MEN OF MARS

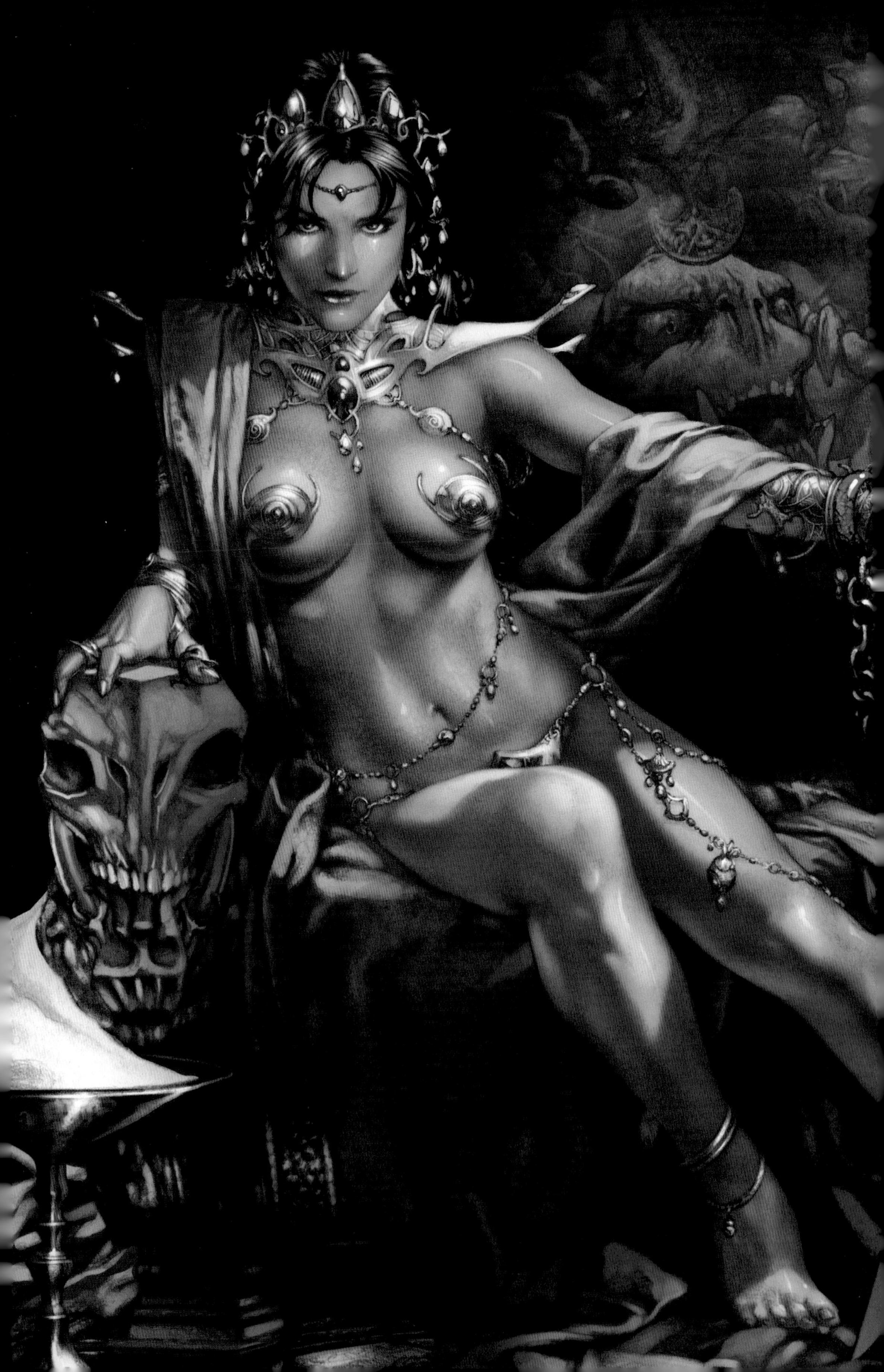

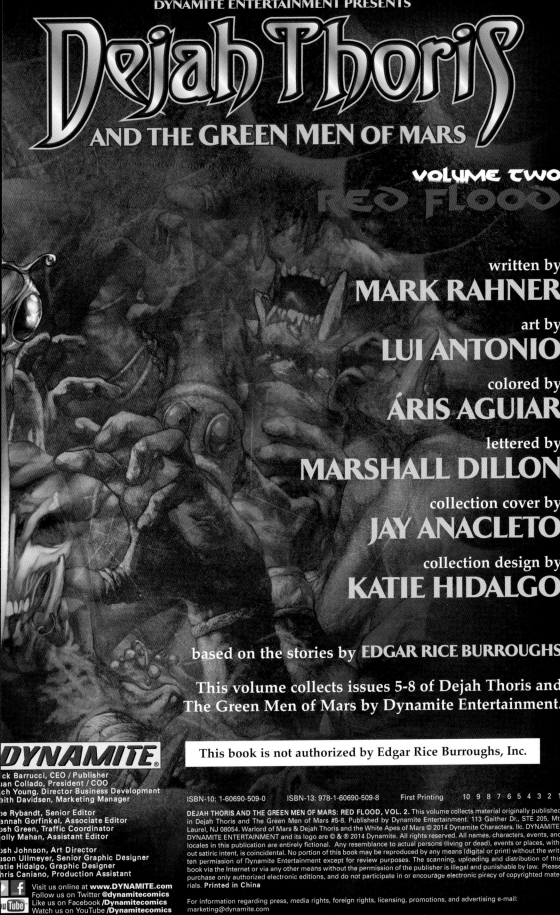

DYNAMITE ENTERTAINMENT PRESENTS

Dejah Thoris AND THE GREEN MEN OF MARS

VOLUME TWO
RED FLOOD

written by
MARK RAHNER

art by
LUI ANTONIO

colored by
ÁRIS AGUIAR

lettered by
MARSHALL DILLON

collection cover by
JAY ANACLETO

collection design by
KATIE HIDALGO

based on the stories by EDGAR RICE BURROUGHS

This volume collects issues 5-8 of Dejah Thoris and The Green Men of Mars by Dynamite Entertainment.

This book is not authorized by Edgar Rice Burroughs, Inc.

DYNAMITE®

ck Barrucci, CEO / Publisher
uan Collado, President / COO
ch Young, Director Business Development
eith Davidsen, Marketing Manager

oe Rybandt, Senior Editor
annah Gorfinkel, Associate Editor
osh Green, Traffic Coordinator
olly Mahan, Assistant Editor

osh Johnson, Art Director
ason Ullmeyer, Senior Graphic Designer
atie Hidalgo, Graphic Designer
hris Caniano, Production Assistant

Visit us online at **www.DYNAMITE.com**
Follow us on Twitter **@dynamitecomics**
Like us on Facebook **/Dynamitecomics**
Watch us on YouTube **/Dynamitecomics**

ISBN-10: 1-60690-509-0 ISBN-13: 978-1-60690-509-8 First Printing 10 9 8 7 6 5 4 3 2 1

DEJAH THORIS AND THE GREEN MEN OF MARS: RED FLOOD, VOL. 2. This volume collects material originally published in Dejah Thoris and The Green Men of Mars #5-8. Published by Dynamite Entertainment. 113 Gaither Dr., STE 205, Mt Laurel, NJ 08054. **Printed in China**

For information regarding press, media rights, foreign rights, licensing, promotions, and advertising e-mail:
marketing@dynamite.com

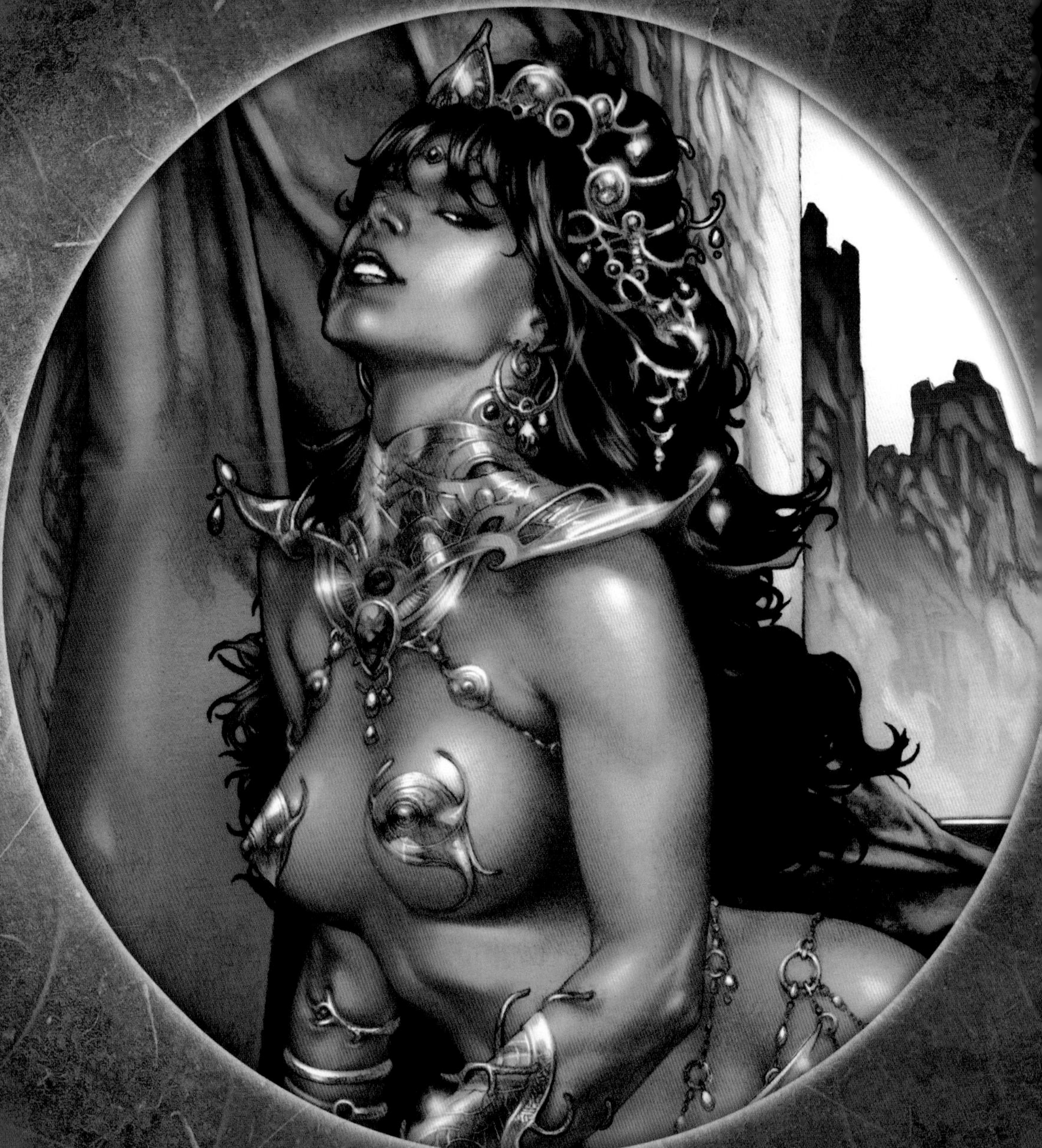

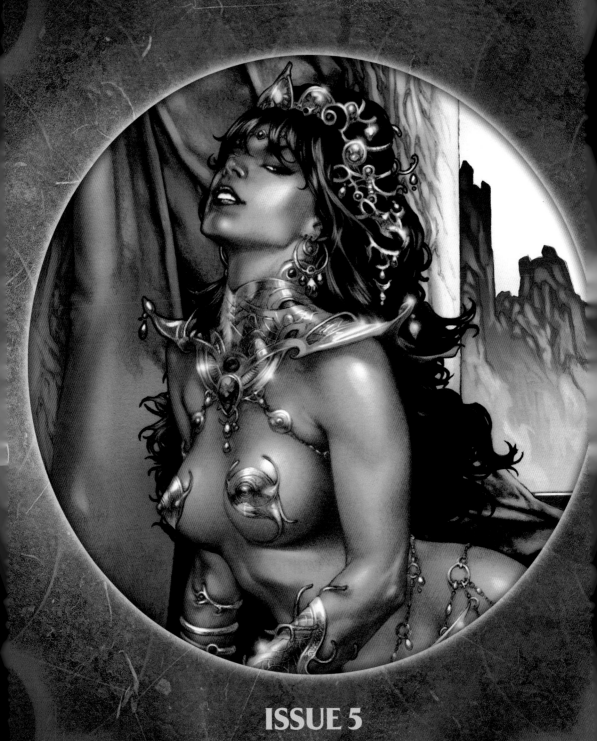

ISSUE 5

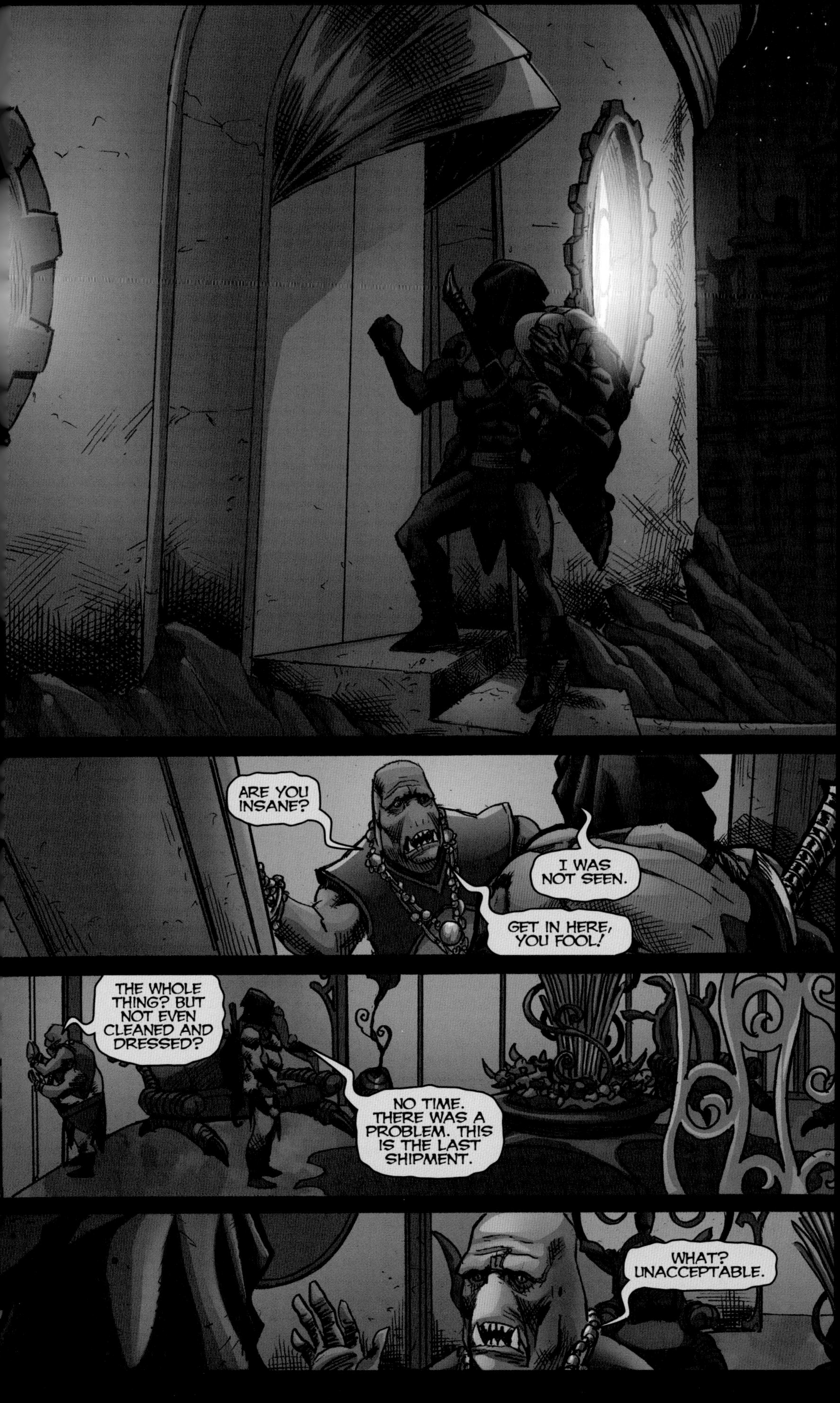

ARE YOU INSANE?
I WAS NOT SEEN.
GET IN HERE, YOU FOOL!
THE WHOLE THING? BUT NOT EVEN CLEANED AND DRESSED?
NO TIME. THERE WAS A PROBLEM. THIS IS THE LAST SHIPMENT.
WHAT? UNACCEPTABLE.

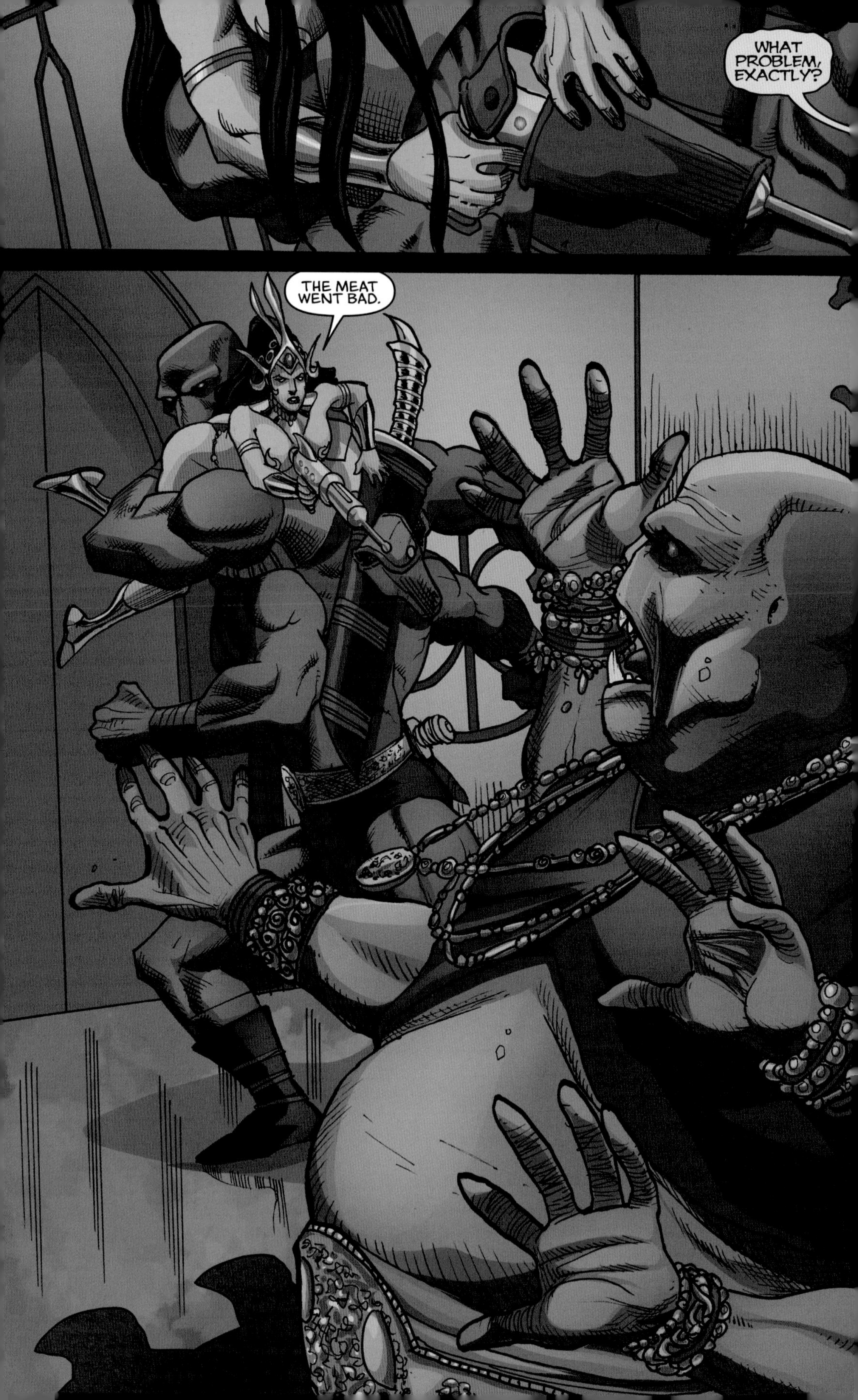
WHAT PROBLEM, EXACTLY?
THE MEAT WENT BAD.

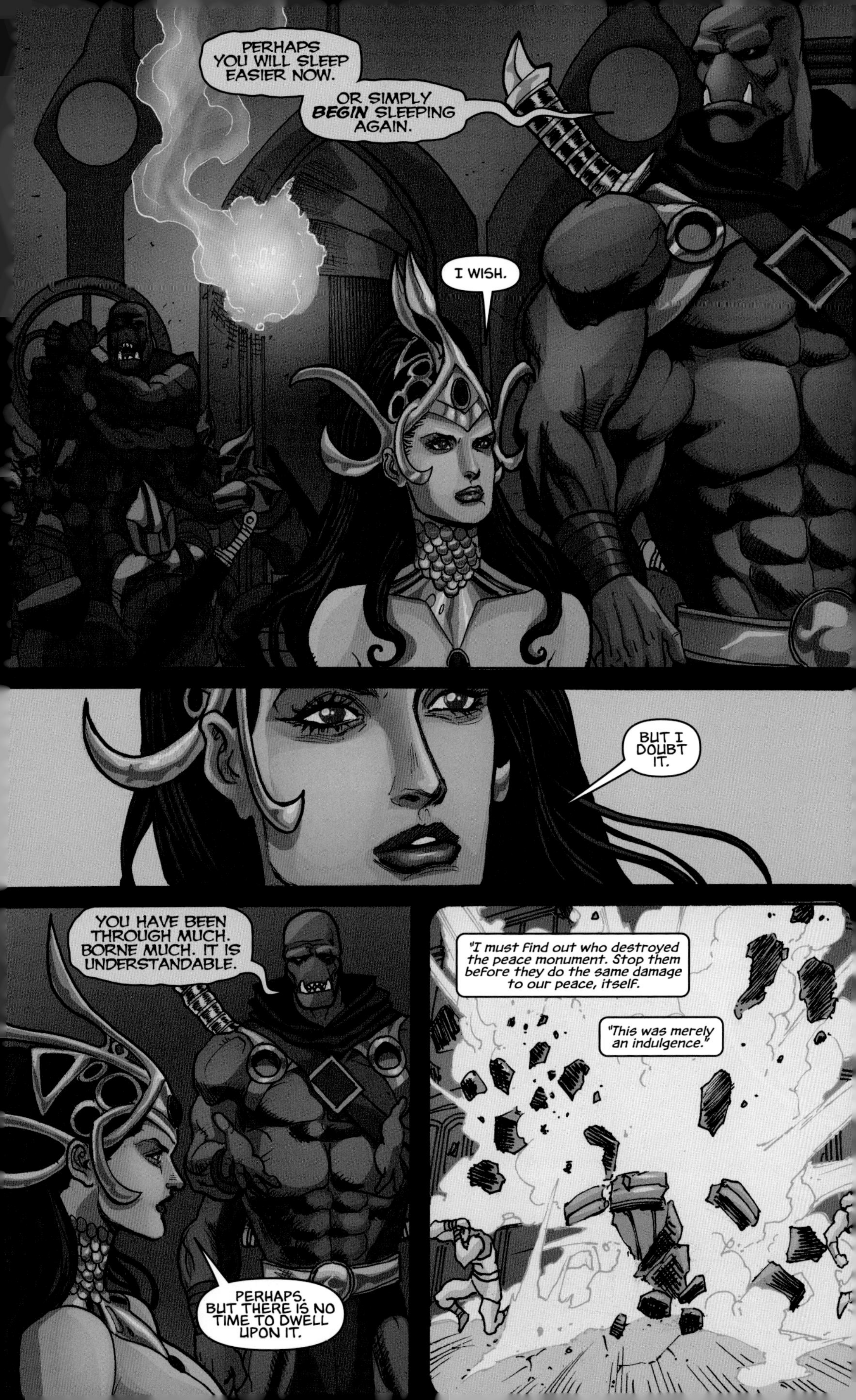
PERHAPS YOU WILL SLEEP EASIER NOW.
OR SIMPLY BEGIN SLEEPING AGAIN.
I WISH.
BUT I DOUBT IT.
YOU HAVE BEEN THROUGH MUCH. BORNE MUCH. IT IS UNDERSTANDABLE.
PERHAPS. BUT THERE IS NO TIME TO DWELL UPON IT.
"I must find out who destroyed the peace monument. Stop them before they do the same damage to our peace, itself.
"This was merely an indulgence."

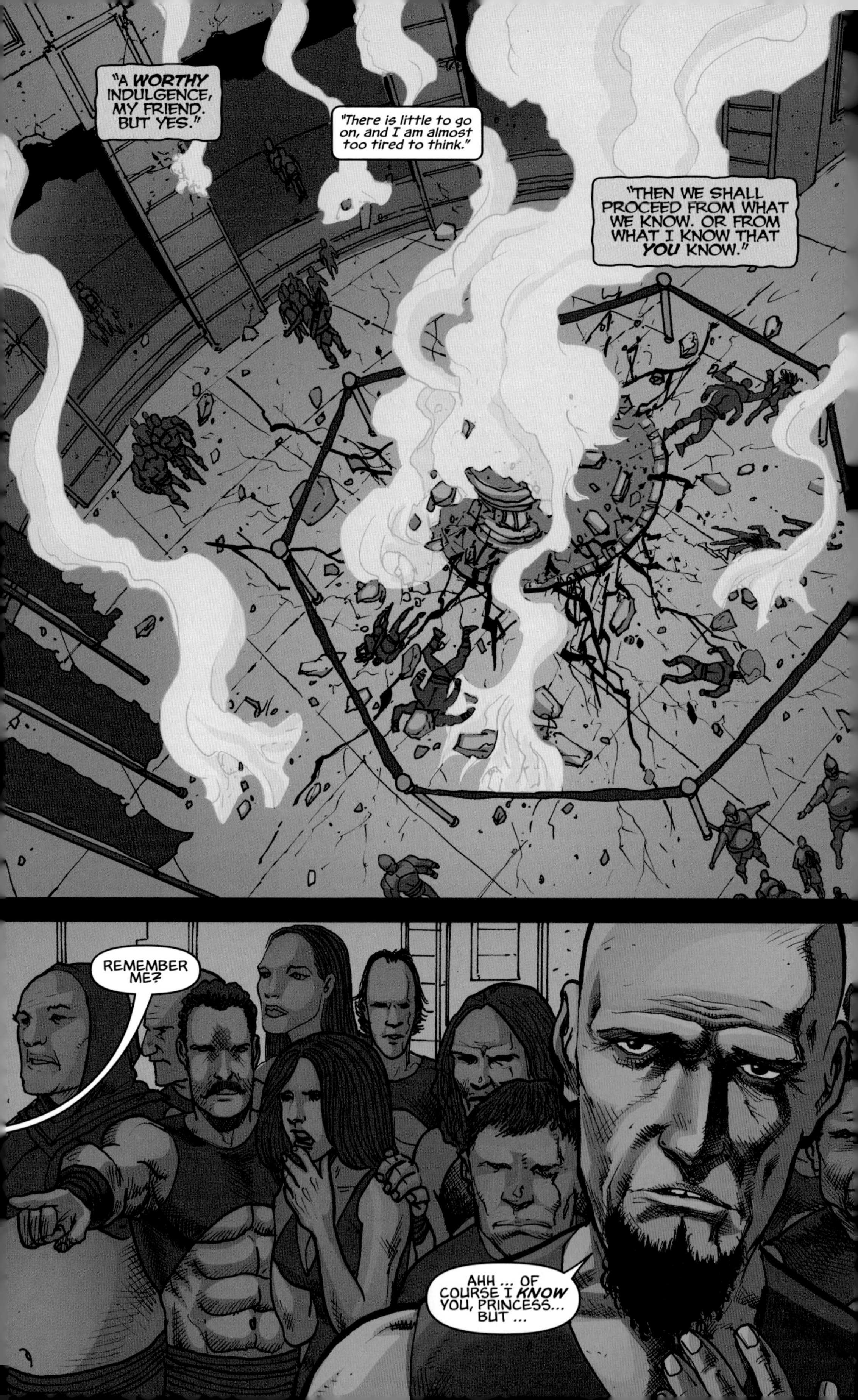
"A WORTHY INDULGENCE, MY FRIEND. BUT YES."
"There is little to go on, and I am almost too tired to think."
"THEN WE SHALL PROCEED FROM WHAT WE KNOW. OR FROM WHAT I KNOW THAT YOU KNOW."
REMEMBER ME?
AHH ... OF COURSE I KNOW YOU, PRINCESS... BUT ...

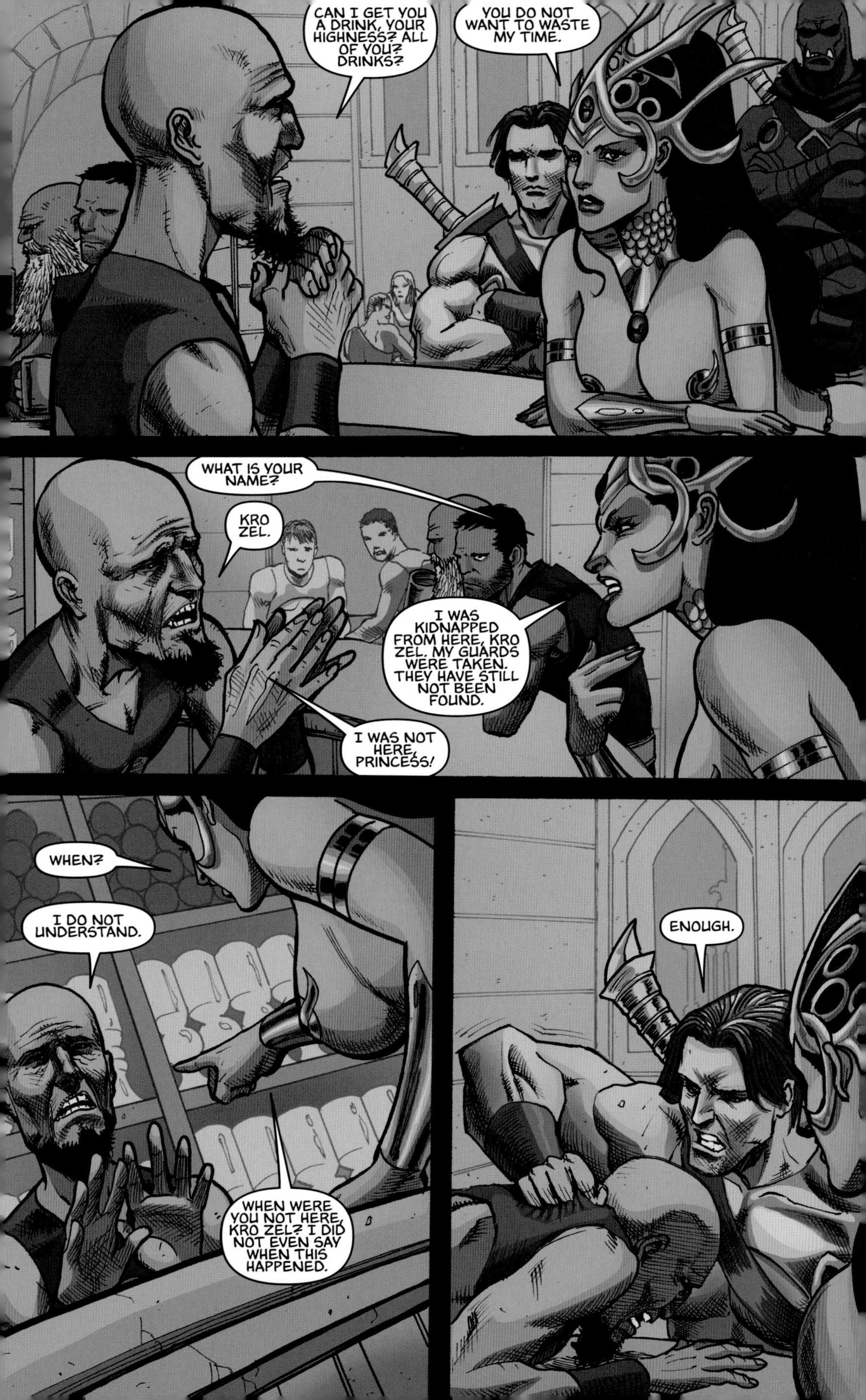
CAN I GET YOU A DRINK, YOUR HIGHNESS? ALL OF YOU? DRINKS?
YOU DO NOT WANT TO WASTE MY TIME.
WHAT IS YOUR NAME?
KRO ZEL.
I WAS KIDNAPPED FROM HERE, KRO ZEL. MY GUARDS WERE TAKEN. THEY HAVE STILL NOT BEEN FOUND.
I WAS NOT HERE, PRINCESS!
WHEN?
I DO NOT UNDERSTAND.
WHEN WERE YOU NOT HERE, KRO ZEL? I DID NOT EVEN SAY WHEN THIS HAPPENED.
ENOUGH.

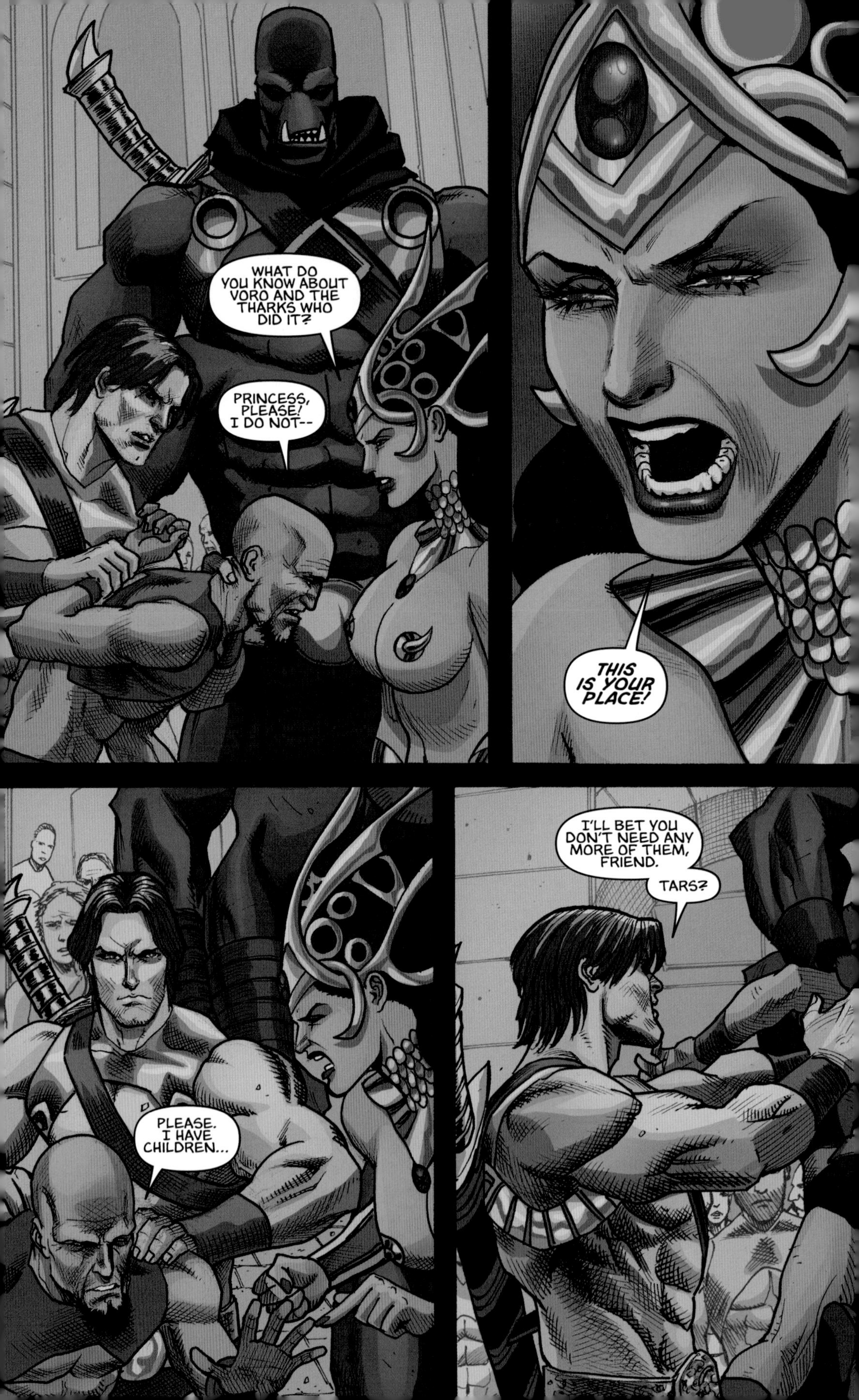
WHAT DO YOU KNOW ABOUT VORO AND THE THARKS WHO DID IT?
PRINCESS, PLEASE! I DO NOT--
THIS IS YOUR PLACE!
PLEASE. I HAVE CHILDREN...
I'LL BET YOU DON'T NEED ANY MORE OF THEM, FRIEND.
TARS?

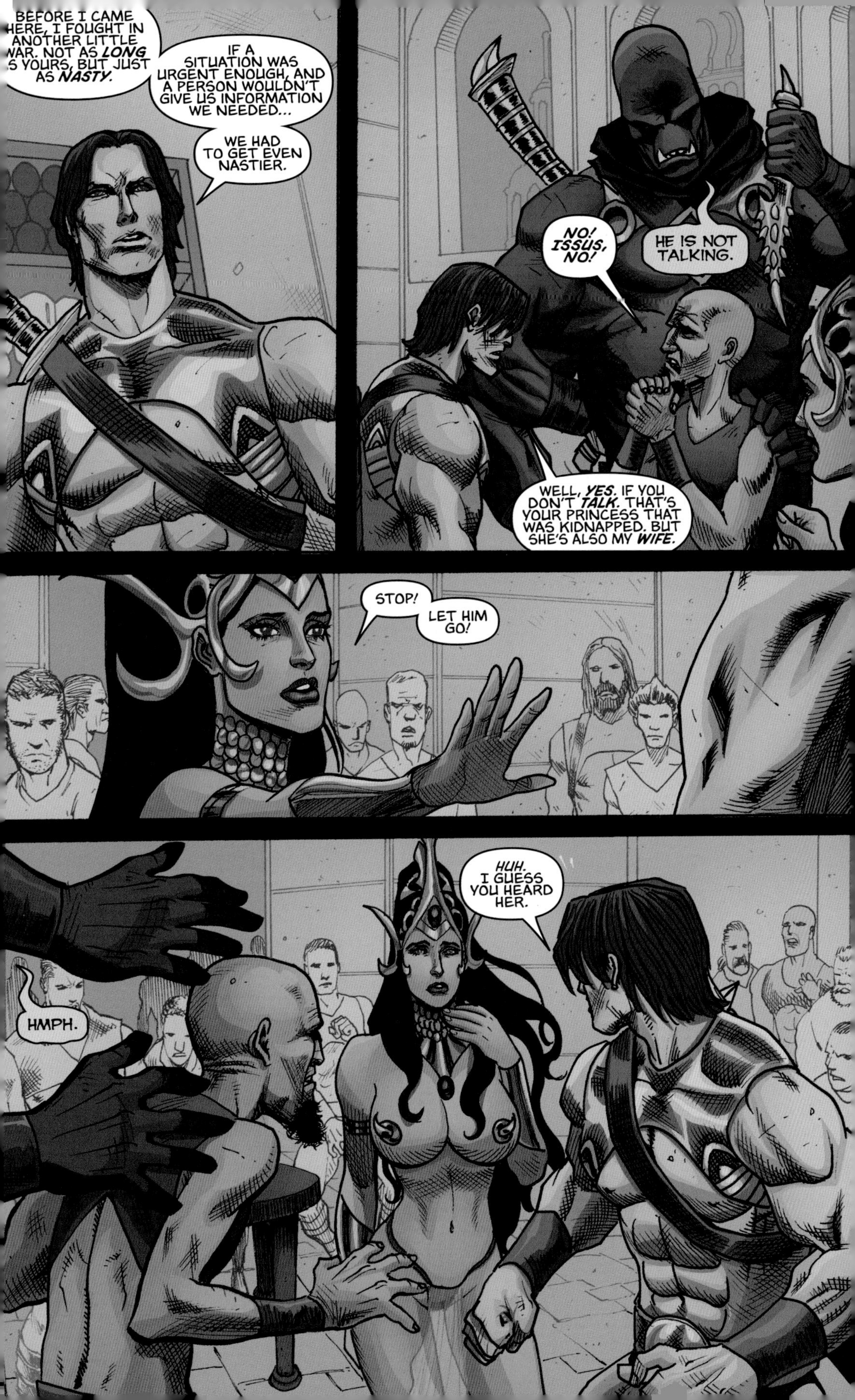
BEFORE I CAME HERE, I FOUGHT IN ANOTHER LITTLE WAR. NOT AS LONG AS YOURS, BUT JUST AS NASTY.
IF A SITUATION WAS URGENT ENOUGH, AND A PERSON WOULDN'T GIVE US INFORMATION WE NEEDED...
WE HAD TO GET EVEN NASTIER.
NO! ISSUS, NO!
HE IS NOT TALKING.
WELL, YES. IF YOU DON'T TALK. THAT'S YOUR PRINCESS THAT WAS KIDNAPPED. BUT SHE'S ALSO MY WIFE.
STOP!
LET HIM GO!
HUH. I GUESS YOU HEARD HER.
HMPH.

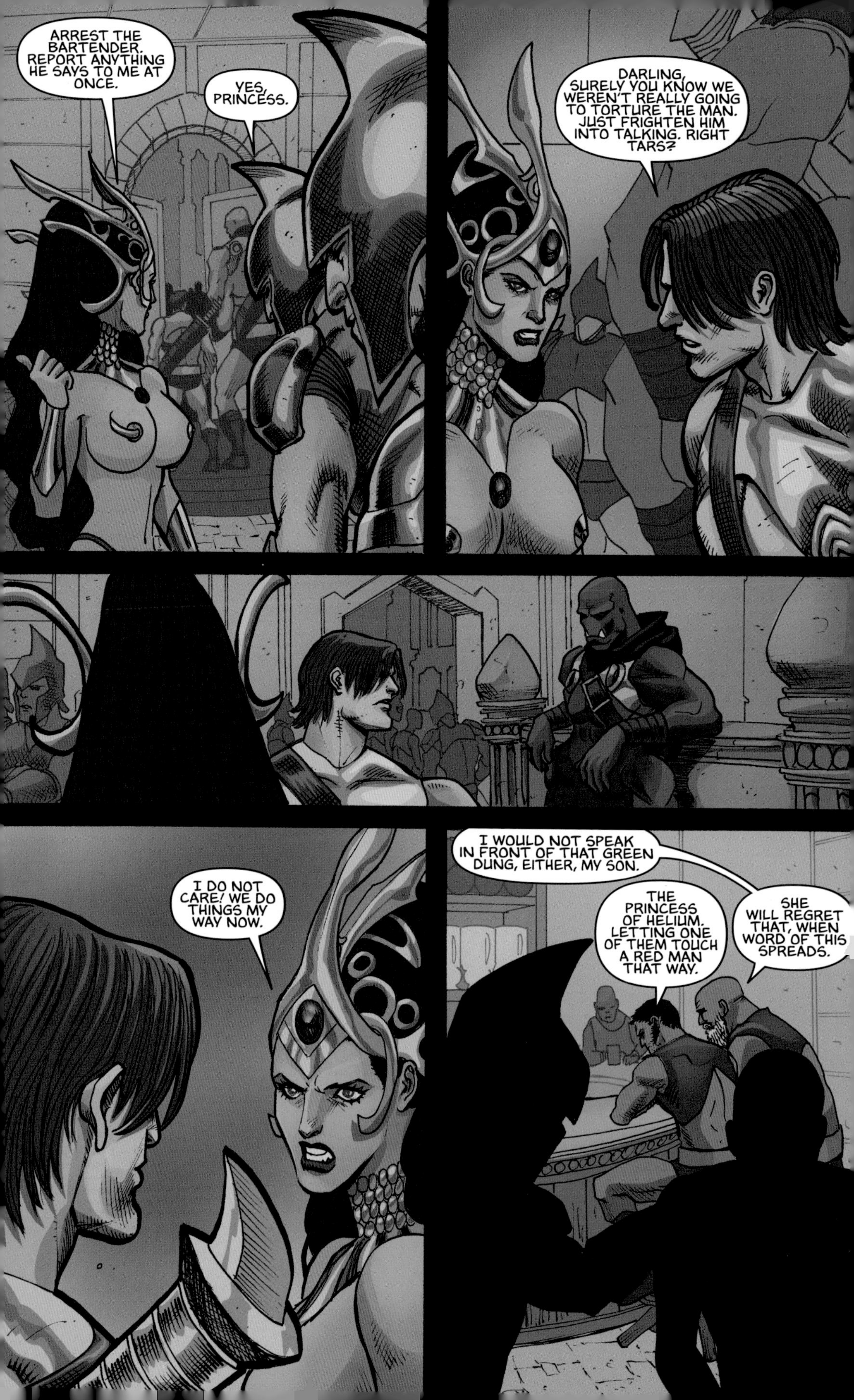
ARREST THE BARTENDER. REPORT ANYTHING HE SAYS TO ME AT ONCE.
YES, PRINCESS.
DARLING, SURELY YOU KNOW WE WEREN'T REALLY GOING TO TORTURE THE MAN. JUST FRIGHTEN HIM INTO TALKING. RIGHT TARS?
I DO NOT CARE! WE DO THINGS MY WAY NOW.
I WOULD NOT SPEAK IN FRONT OF THAT GREEN DUNG, EITHER, MY SON.
THE PRINCESS OF HELIUM. LETTING ONE OF THEM TOUCH A RED MAN THAT WAY.
SHE WILL REGRET THAT, WHEN WORD OF THIS SPREADS.

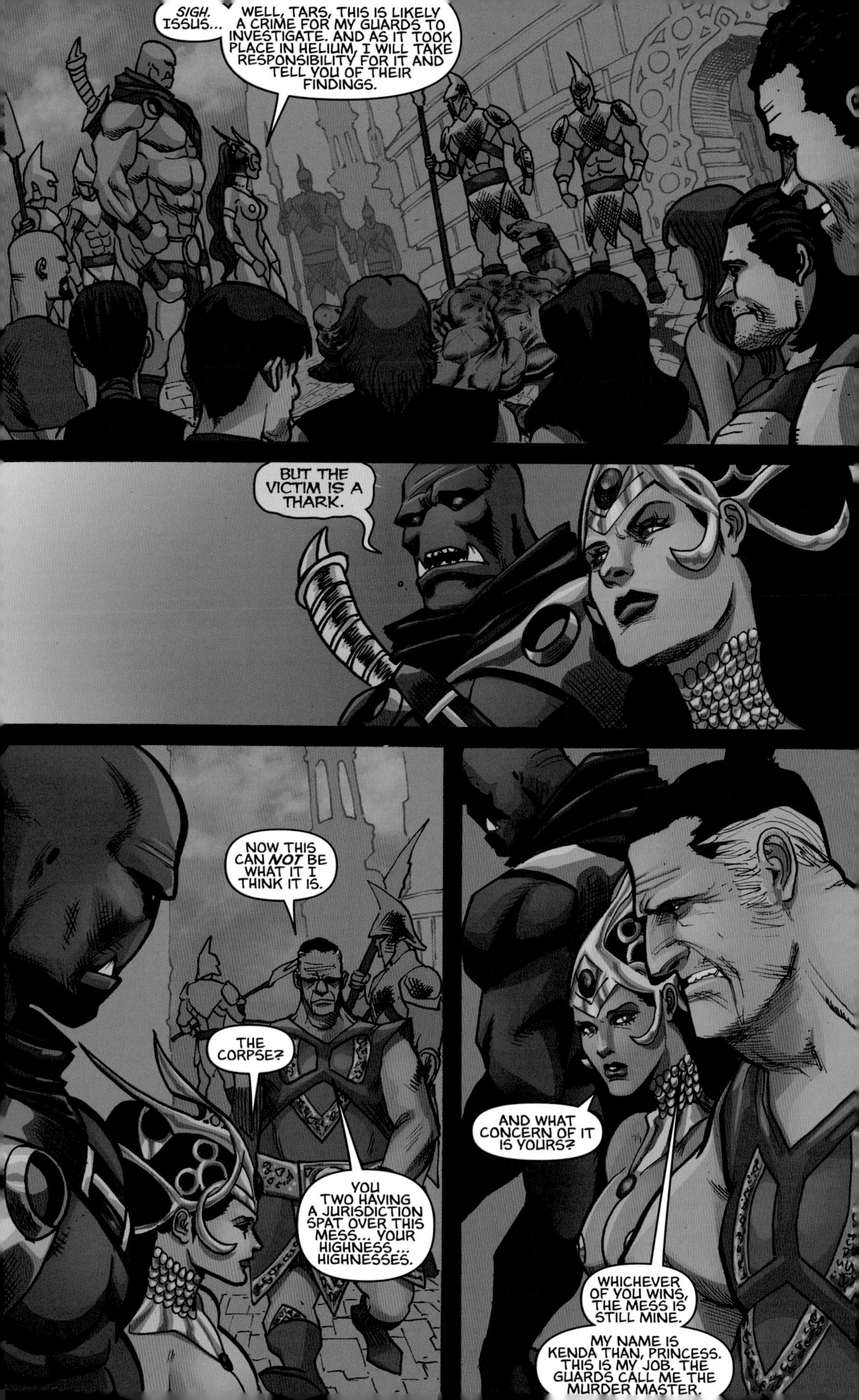
SIGH. ISSUS...
WELL, TARS, THIS IS LIKELY A CRIME FOR MY GUARDS TO INVESTIGATE. AND AS IT TOOK PLACE IN HELIUM, I WILL TAKE RESPONSIBILITY FOR IT AND TELL YOU OF THEIR FINDINGS.
BUT THE VICTIM IS A THARK.
NOW THIS CAN *NOT* BE WHAT IT I THINK IT IS.
THE CORPSE?
YOU TWO HAVING A JURISDICTION SPAT OVER THIS MESS... YOUR HIGHNESS ... HIGHNESSES.
AND WHAT CONCERN OF IT IS YOURS?
WHICHEVER OF YOU WINS, THE MESS IS STILL MINE.
MY NAME IS KENDA THAN, PRINCESS. THIS IS MY JOB. THE GUARDS CALL ME THE MURDER MASTER.

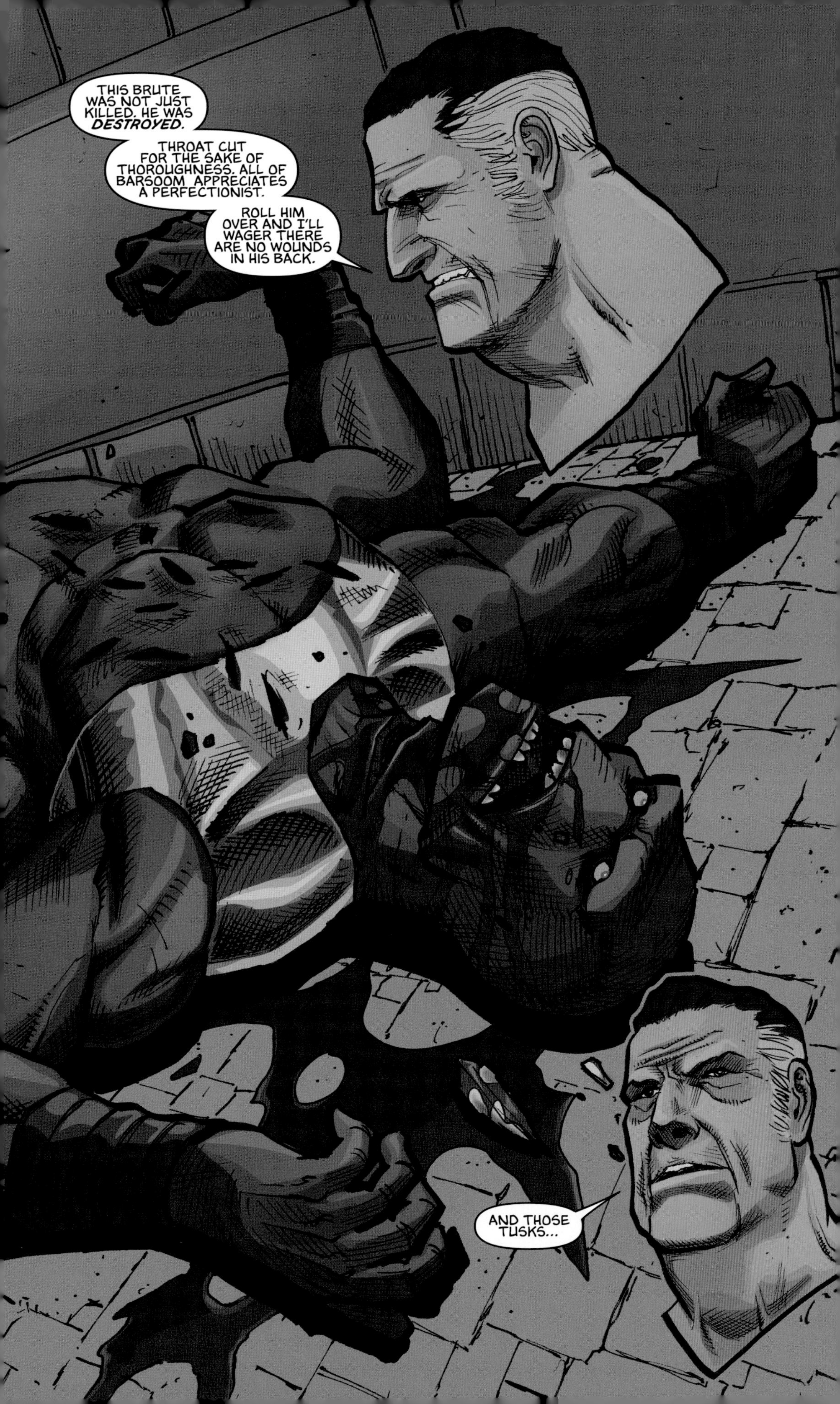
THIS BRUTE WAS NOT JUST KILLED. HE WAS ***DESTROYED***.
THROAT CUT FOR THE SAKE OF THOROUGHNESS. ALL OF BARSOOM APPRECIATES A PERFECTIONIST.
ROLL HIM OVER AND I'LL WAGER THERE ARE NO WOUNDS IN HIS BACK.
AND THOSE TUSKS...

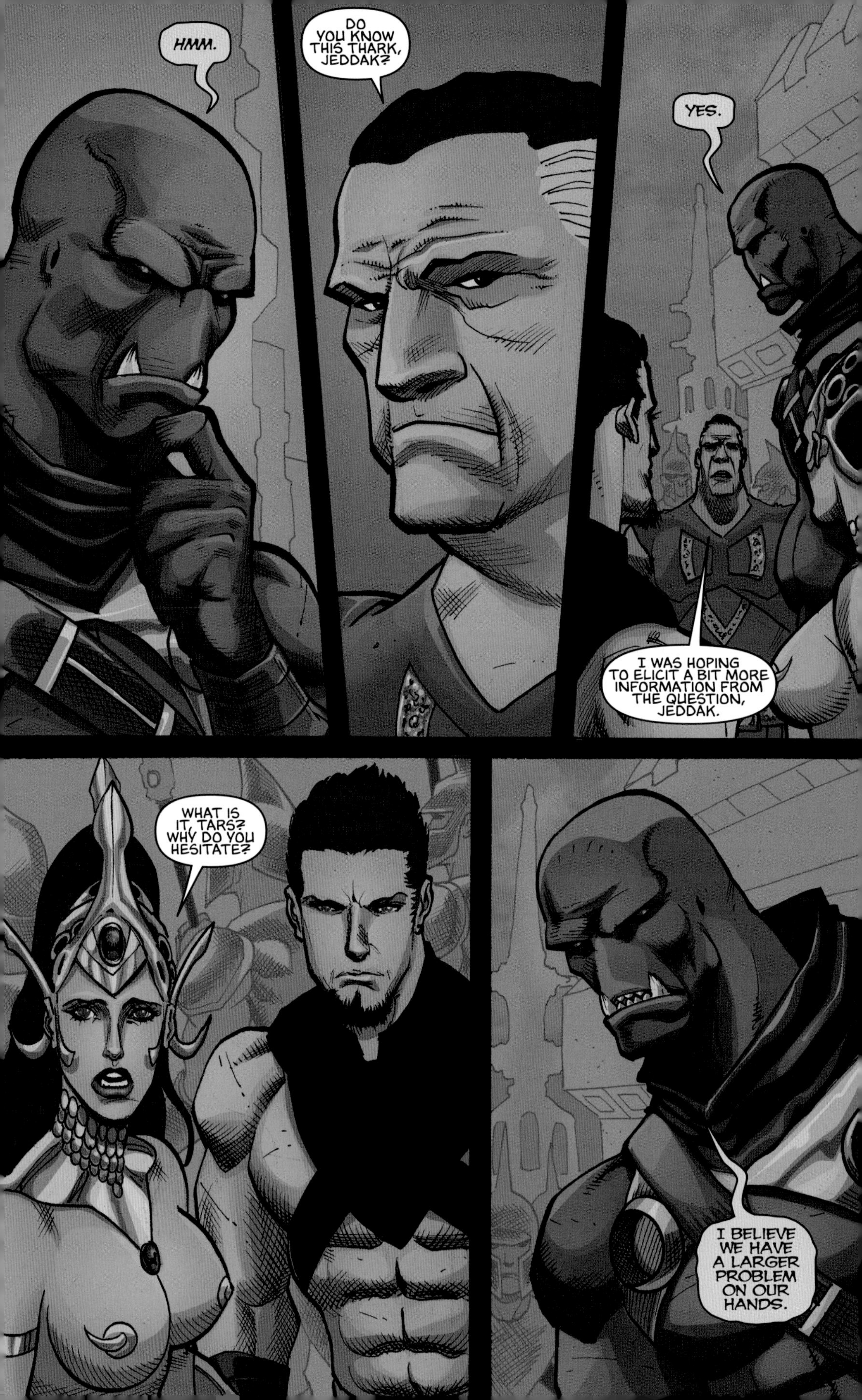
HMM.
DO YOU KNOW THIS THARK, JEDDAK?
YES.
I WAS HOPING TO ELICIT A BIT MORE INFORMATION FROM THE QUESTION, JEDDAK.
WHAT IS IT, TARS? WHY DO YOU HESITATE?
I BELIEVE WE HAVE A LARGER PROBLEM ON OUR HANDS.

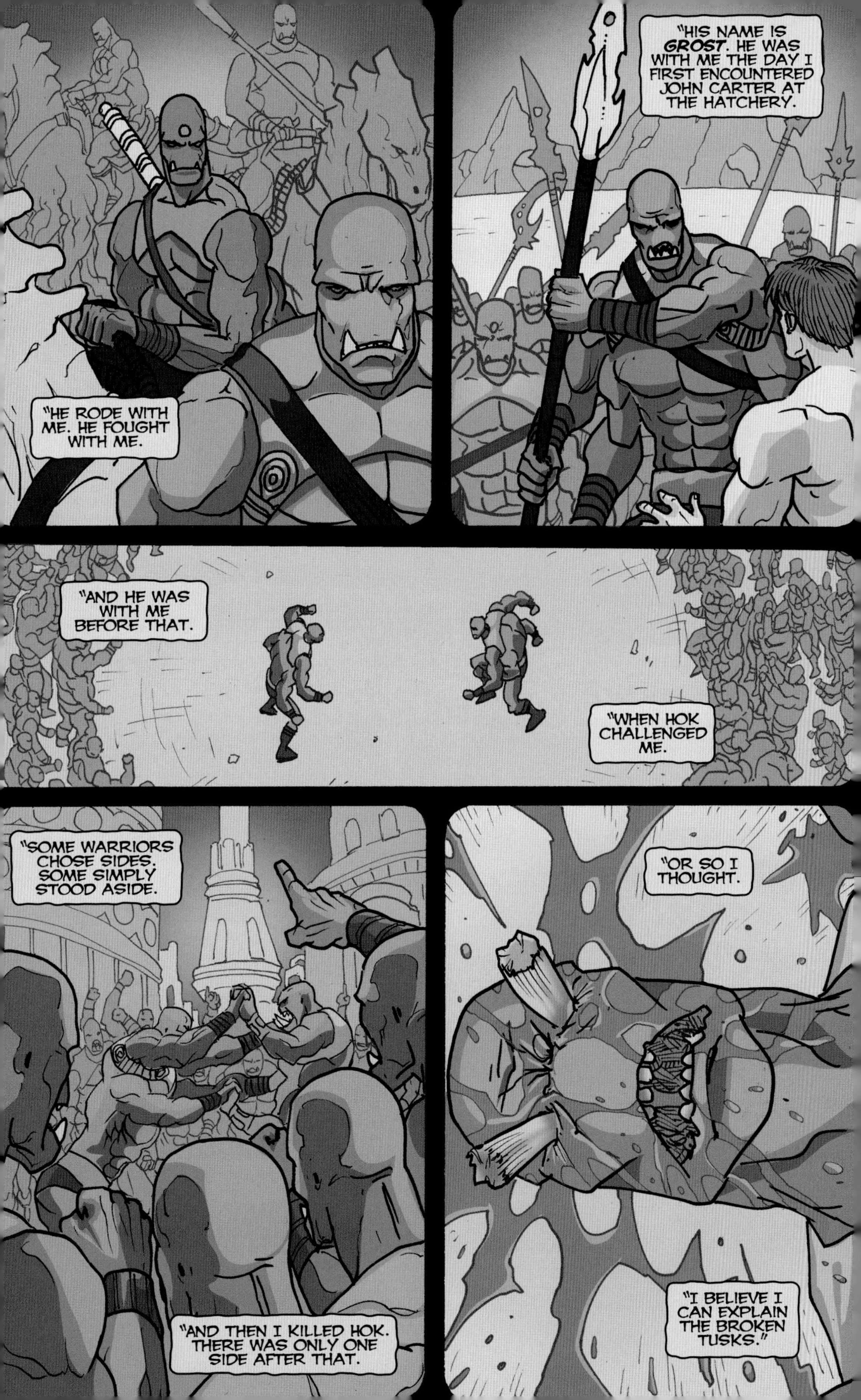
"HE RODE WITH ME. HE FOUGHT WITH ME.
"HIS NAME IS GROST. HE WAS WITH ME THE DAY I FIRST ENCOUNTERED JOHN CARTER AT THE HATCHERY.
"AND HE WAS WITH ME BEFORE THAT.
"WHEN HOK CHALLENGED ME.
"SOME WARRIORS CHOSE SIDES. SOME SIMPLY STOOD ASIDE.
"AND THEN I KILLED HOK. THERE WAS ONLY ONE SIDE AFTER THAT.
"OR SO I THOUGHT.
"I BELIEVE I CAN EXPLAIN THE BROKEN TUSKS."

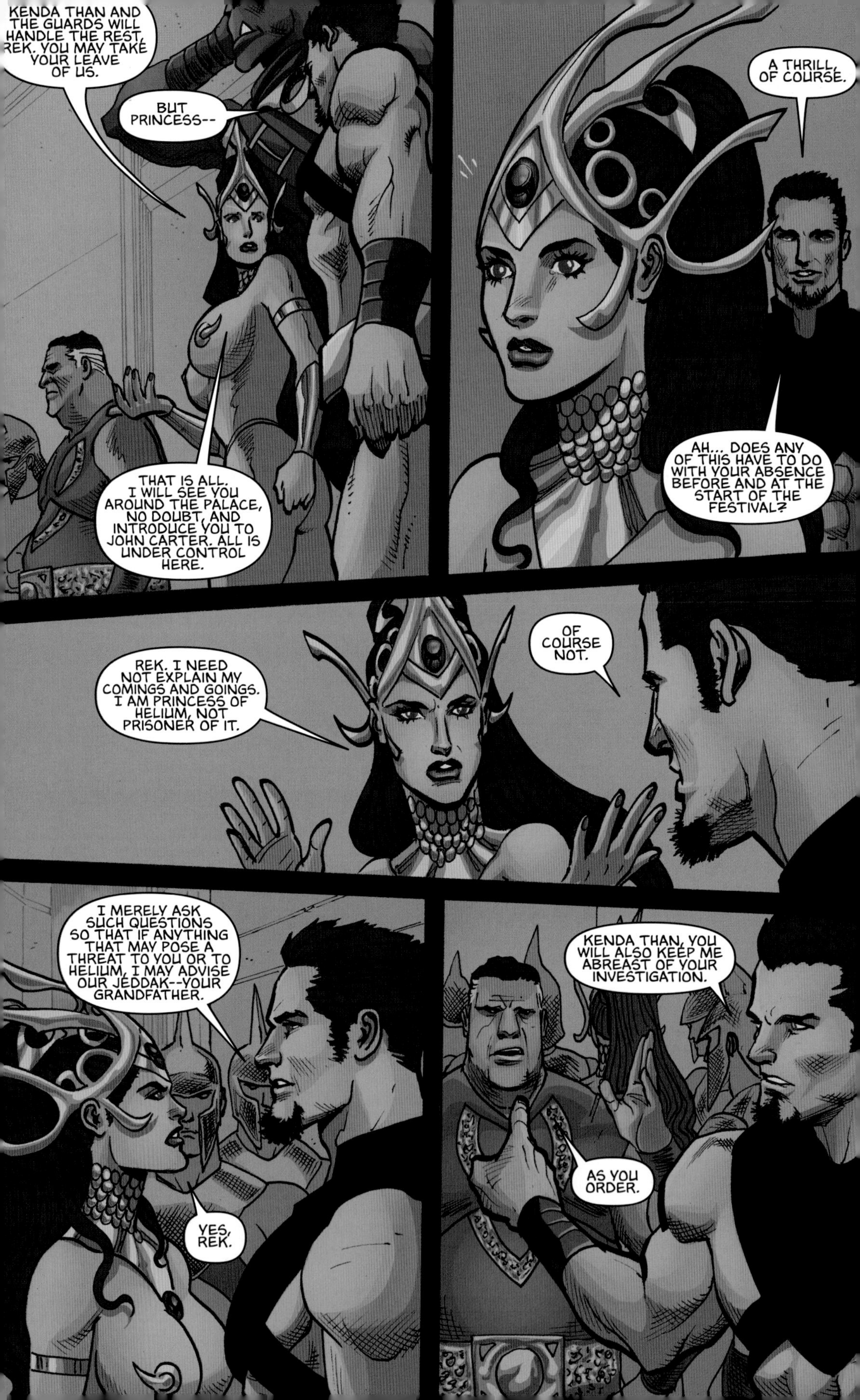
KENDA THAN AND THE GUARDS WILL HANDLE THE REST, REK. YOU MAY TAKE YOUR LEAVE OF US.
BUT PRINCESS--
THAT IS ALL. I WILL SEE YOU AROUND THE PALACE, NO DOUBT, AND INTRODUCE YOU TO JOHN CARTER. ALL IS UNDER CONTROL HERE.
A THRILL, OF COURSE.
AH... DOES ANY OF THIS HAVE TO DO WITH YOUR ABSENCE BEFORE AND AT THE START OF THE FESTIVAL?
REK. I NEED NOT EXPLAIN MY COMINGS AND GOINGS. I AM PRINCESS OF HELIUM, NOT PRISONER OF IT.
OF COURSE NOT.
I MERELY ASK SUCH QUESTIONS SO THAT IF ANYTHING THAT MAY POSE A THREAT TO YOU OR TO HELIUM, I MAY ADVISE OUR JEDDAK--YOUR GRANDFATHER.
YES, REK.
KENDA THAN, YOU WILL ALSO KEEP ME ABREAST OF YOUR INVESTIGATION.
AS YOU ORDER.

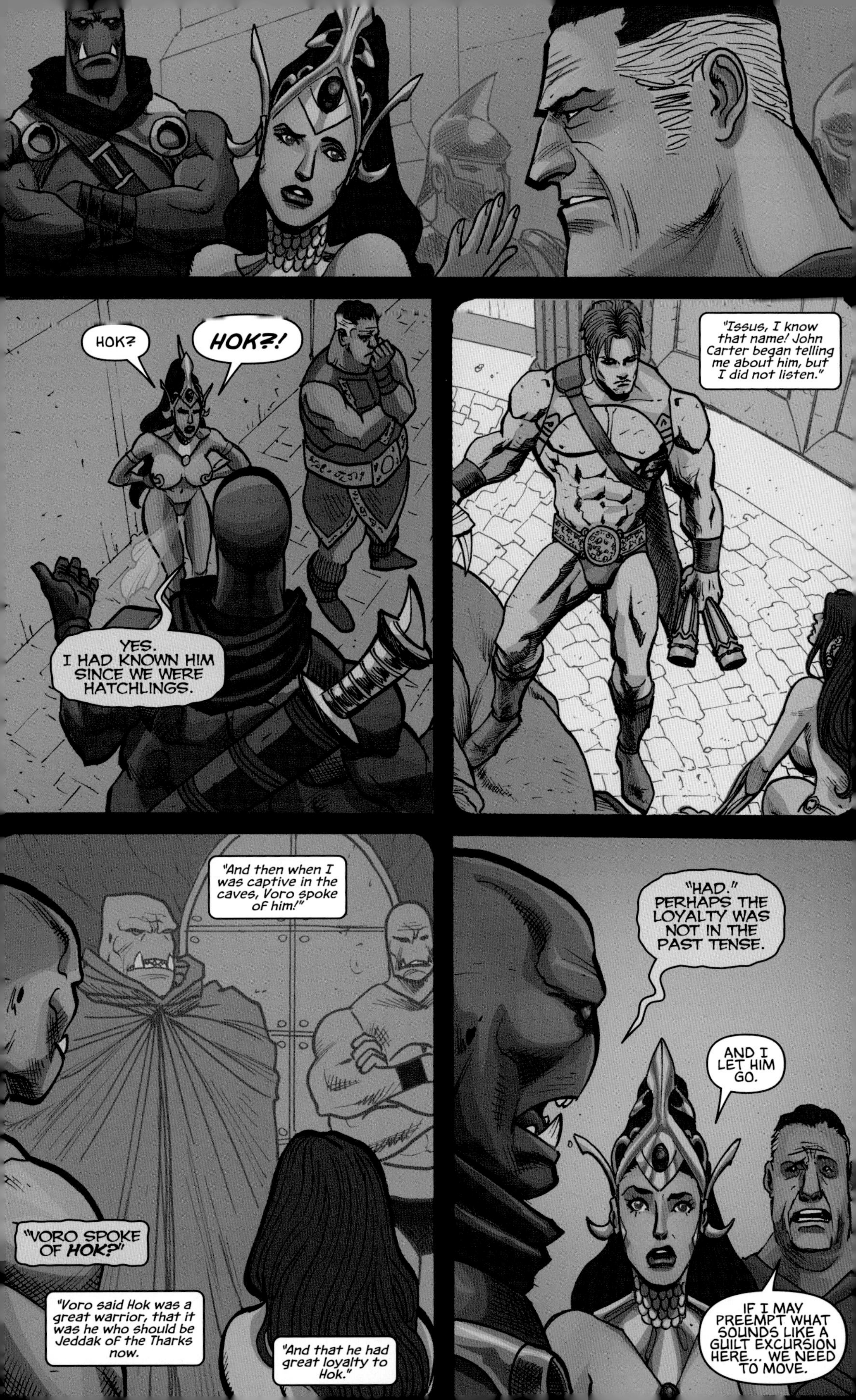

HOK?
HOK?!
YES. I HAD KNOWN HIM SINCE WE WERE HATCHLINGS.
"Issus, I know that name! John Carter began telling me about him, but I did not listen."
"And then when I was captive in the caves, Voro spoke of him!"
"VORO SPOKE OF HOK?"
"Voro said Hok was a great warrior, that it was he who should be Jeddak of the Tharks now.
"And that he had great loyalty to Hok."
"HAD." PERHAPS THE LOYALTY WAS NOT IN THE PAST TENSE.
AND I LET HIM GO.
IF I MAY PREEMPT WHAT SOUNDS LIKE A GUILT EXCURSION HERE... WE NEED TO MOVE.

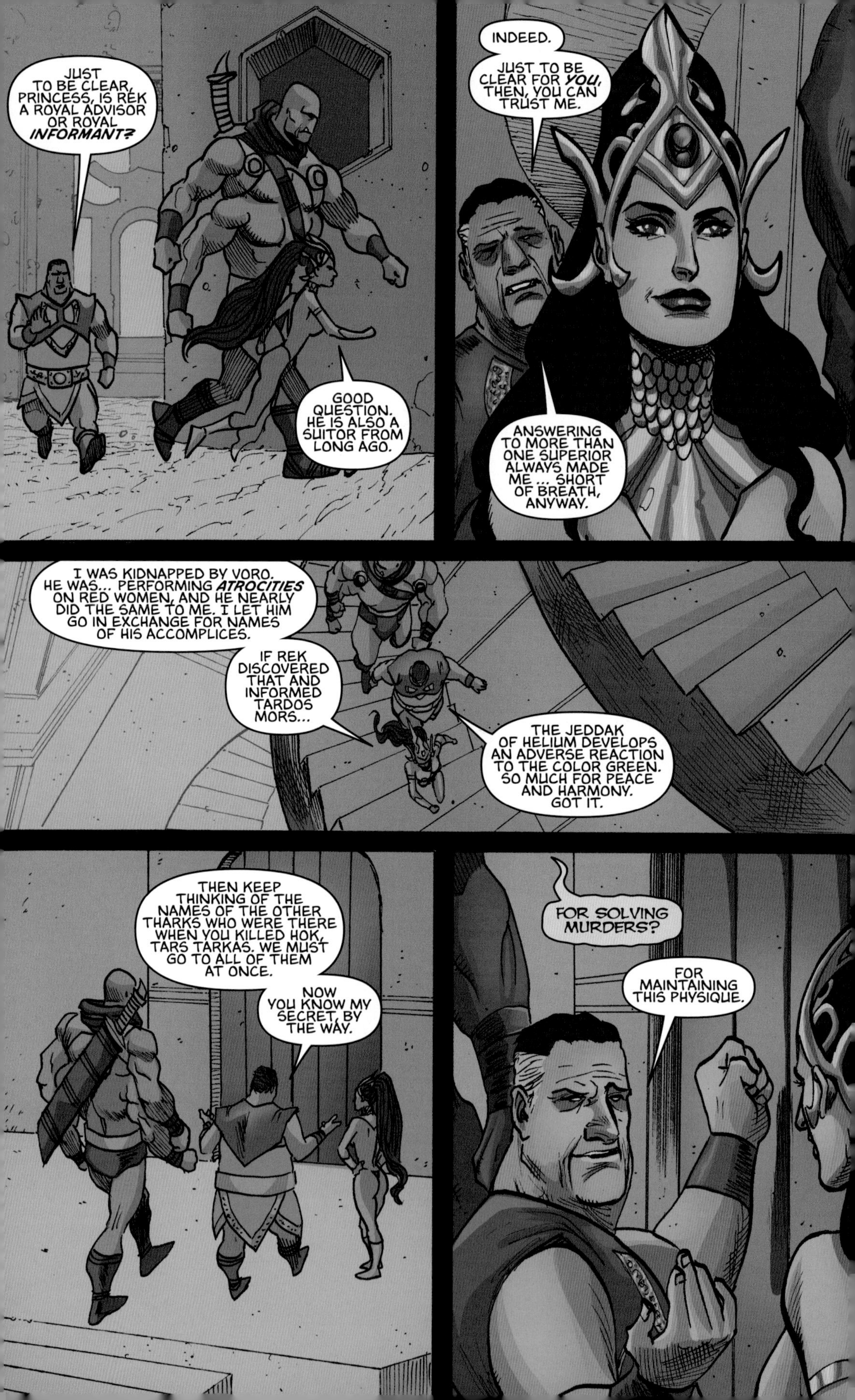
JUST TO BE CLEAR, PRINCESS, IS REK A ROYAL ADVISOR OR ROYAL INFORMANT?
GOOD QUESTION. HE IS ALSO A SUITOR FROM LONG AGO.
INDEED.
JUST TO BE CLEAR FOR YOU, THEN, YOU CAN TRUST ME.
ANSWERING TO MORE THAN ONE SUPERIOR ALWAYS MADE ME ... SHORT OF BREATH, ANYWAY.
I WAS KIDNAPPED BY VORO. HE WAS... PERFORMING ATROCITIES ON RED WOMEN, AND HE NEARLY DID THE SAME TO ME. I LET HIM GO IN EXCHANGE FOR NAMES OF HIS ACCOMPLICES.
IF REK DISCOVERED THAT AND INFORMED TARDOS MORS...
THE JEDDAK OF HELIUM DEVELOPS AN ADVERSE REACTION TO THE COLOR GREEN. SO MUCH FOR PEACE AND HARMONY. GOT IT.
THEN KEEP THINKING OF THE NAMES OF THE OTHER THARKS WHO WERE THERE WHEN YOU KILLED HOK, TARS TARKAS. WE MUST GO TO ALL OF THEM AT ONCE.
NOW YOU KNOW MY SECRET, BY THE WAY.
FOR SOLVING MURDERS?
FOR MAINTAINING THIS PHYSIQUE.

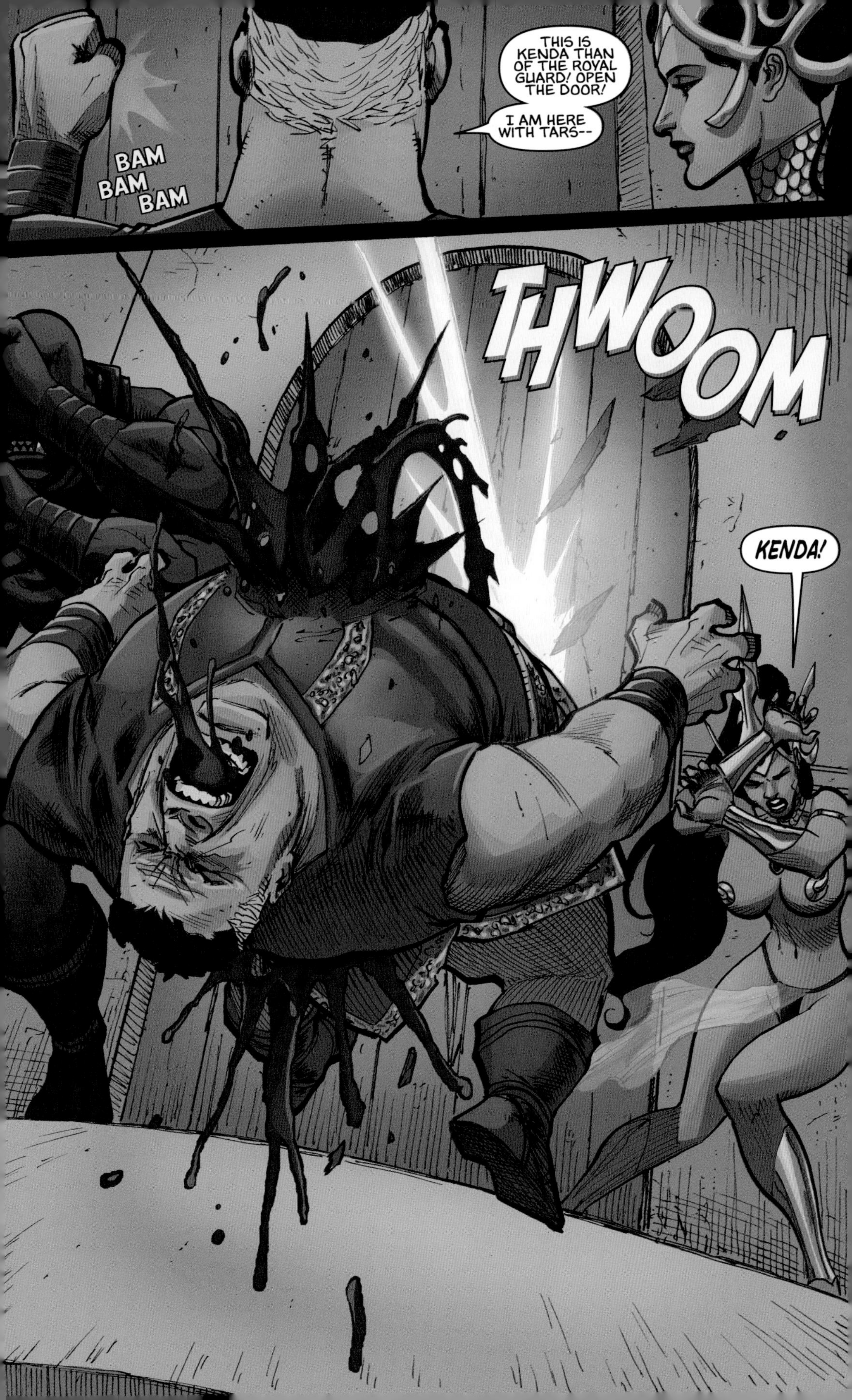
BAM
BAM BAM
THIS IS KENDA THAN OF THE ROYAL GUARD! OPEN THE DOOR!
I AM HERE WITH TARS--
THWOOM
KENDA!

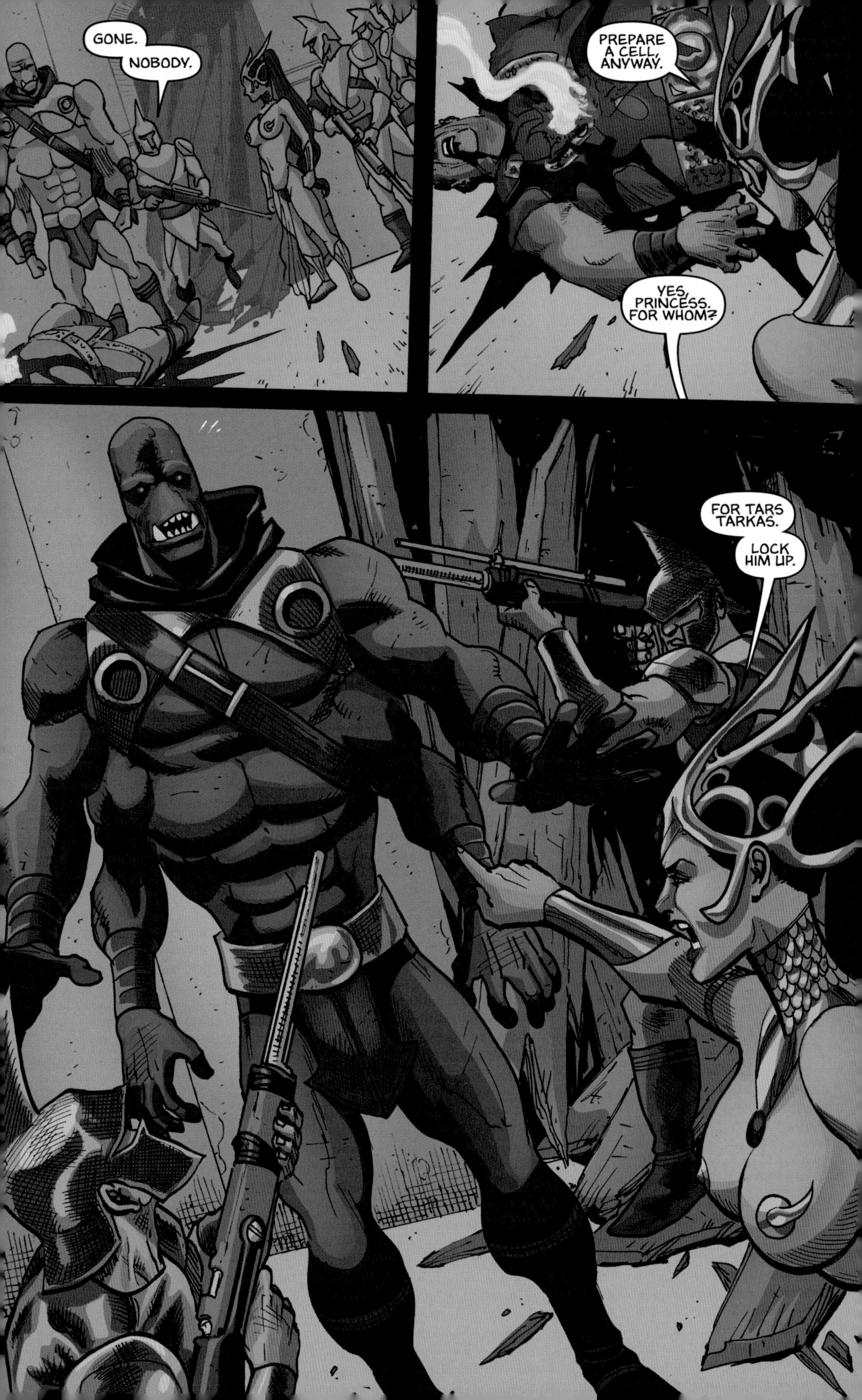
GONE.
NOBODY.
PREPARE A CELL, ANYWAY.
YES, PRINCESS. FOR WHOM?
FOR TARS TARKAS.
LOCK HIM UP.

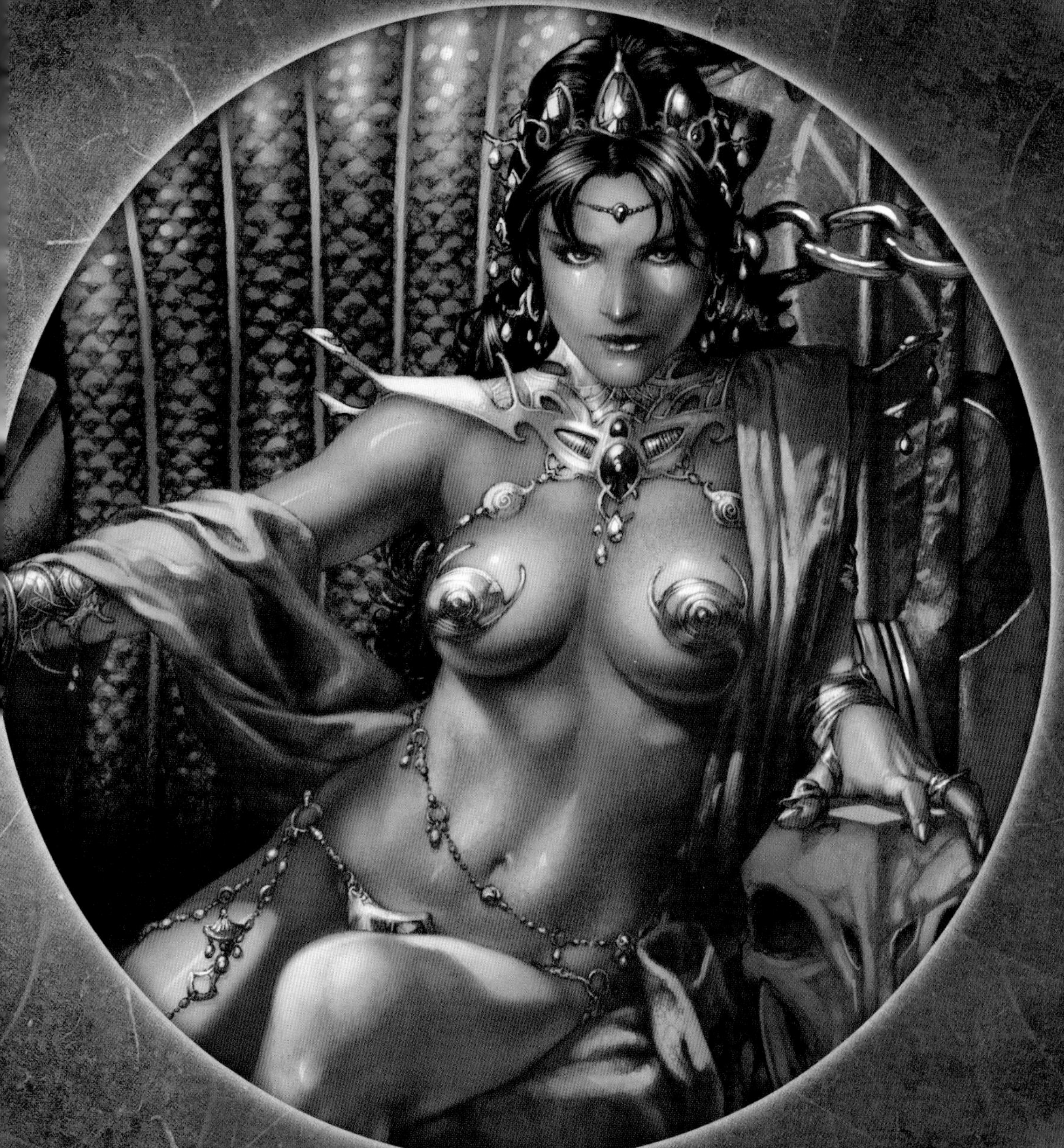

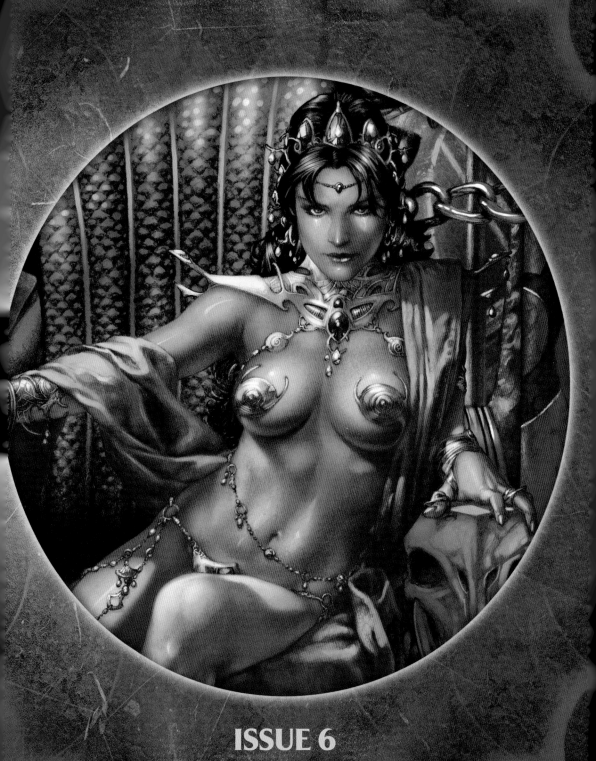

ISSUE 6

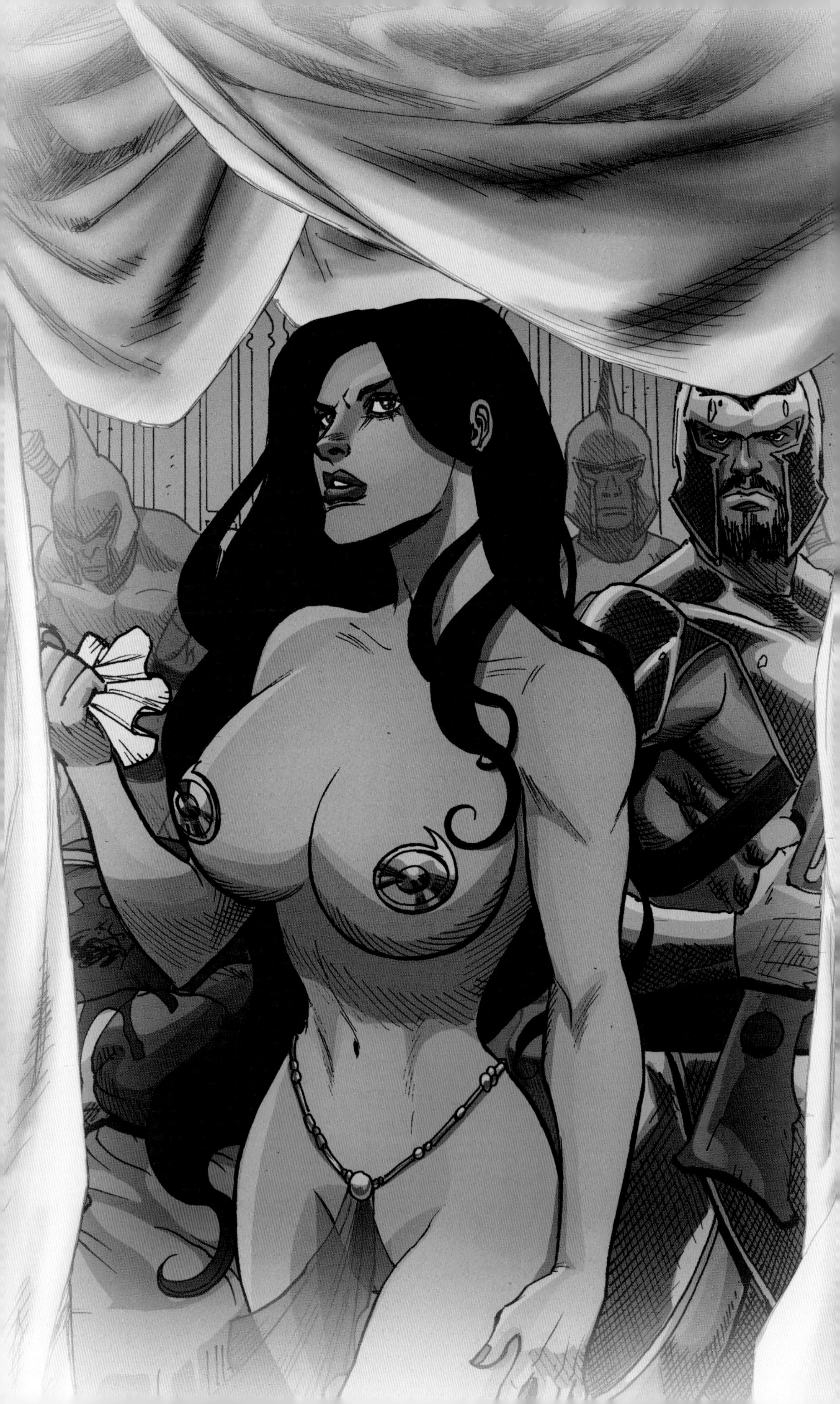

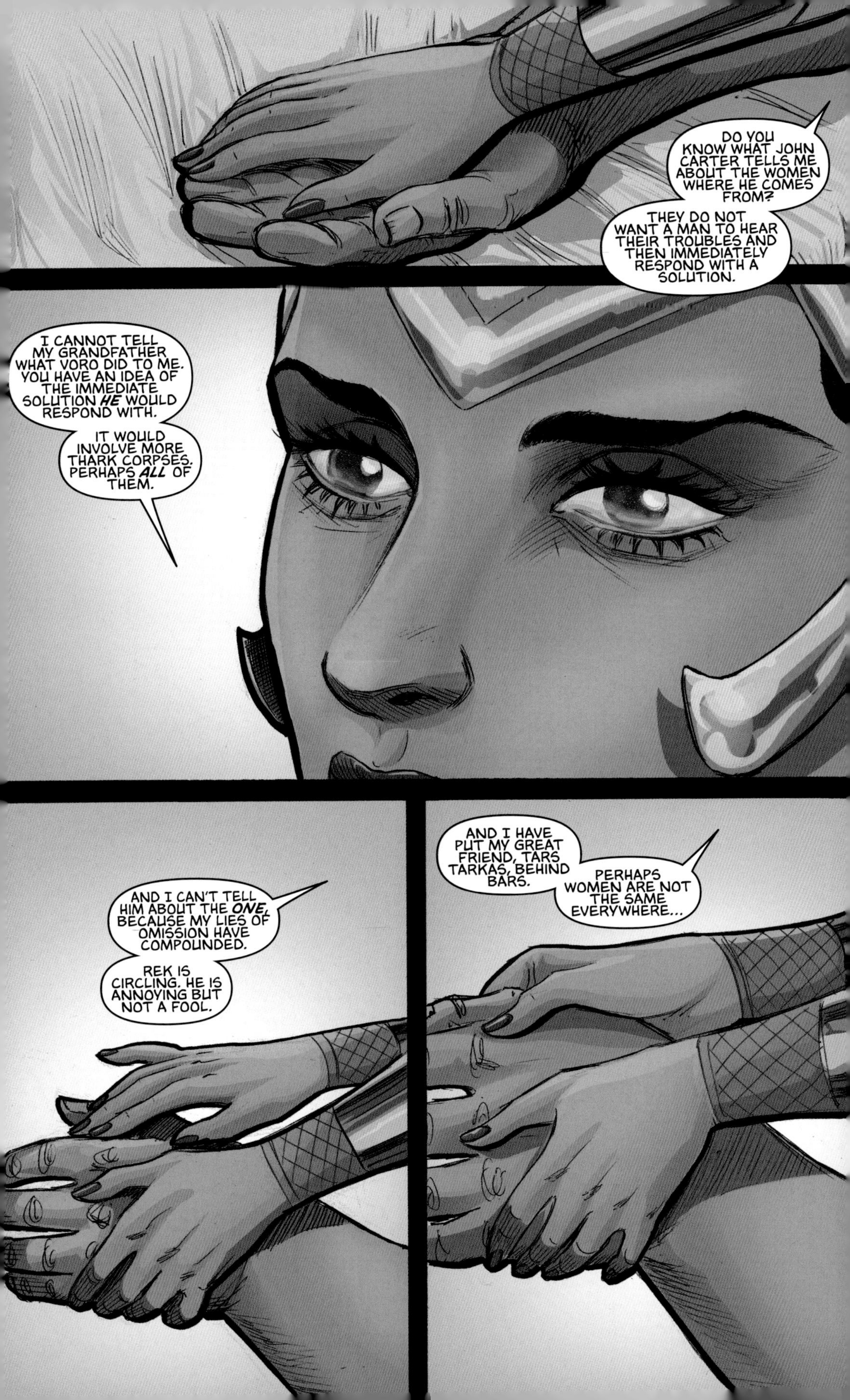
DO YOU KNOW WHAT JOHN CARTER TELLS ME ABOUT THE WOMEN WHERE HE COMES FROM?
THEY DO NOT WANT A MAN TO HEAR THEIR TROUBLES AND THEN IMMEDIATELY RESPOND WITH A SOLUTION.
I CANNOT TELL MY GRANDFATHER WHAT VORO DID TO ME. YOU HAVE AN IDEA OF THE IMMEDIATE SOLUTION *HE* WOULD RESPOND WITH.
IT WOULD INVOLVE MORE THARK CORPSES. PERHAPS *ALL* OF THEM.
AND I CAN'T TELL HIM ABOUT THE *ONE*, BECAUSE MY LIES OF OMISSION HAVE COMPOUNDED.
REK IS CIRCLING. HE IS ANNOYING BUT NOT A FOOL.
AND I HAVE PUT MY GREAT FRIEND, TARS TARKAS, BEHIND BARS.
PERHAPS WOMEN ARE NOT THE SAME EVERYWHERE...

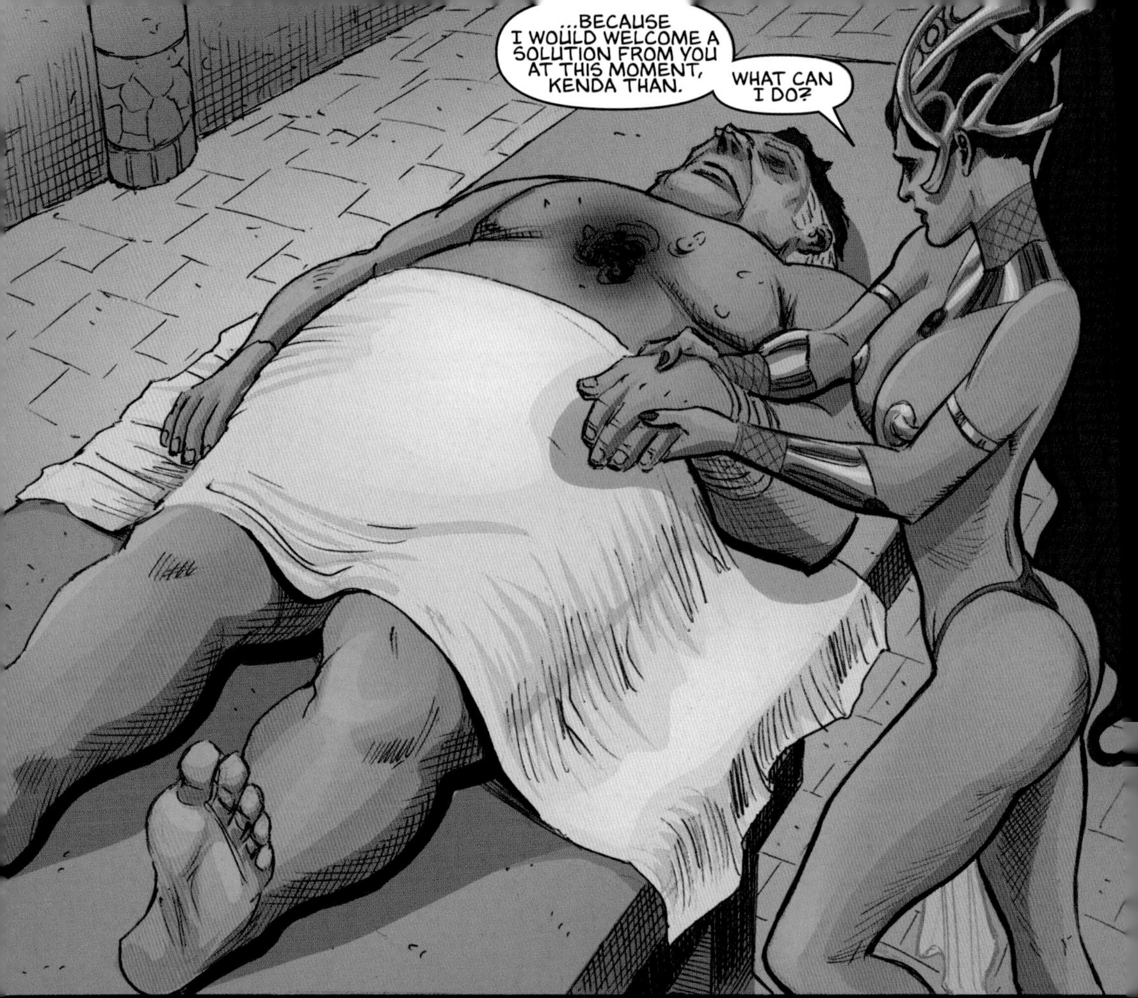
...BECAUSE I WOULD WELCOME A SOLUTION FROM YOU AT THIS MOMENT, KENDA THAN.
WHAT CAN I DO?

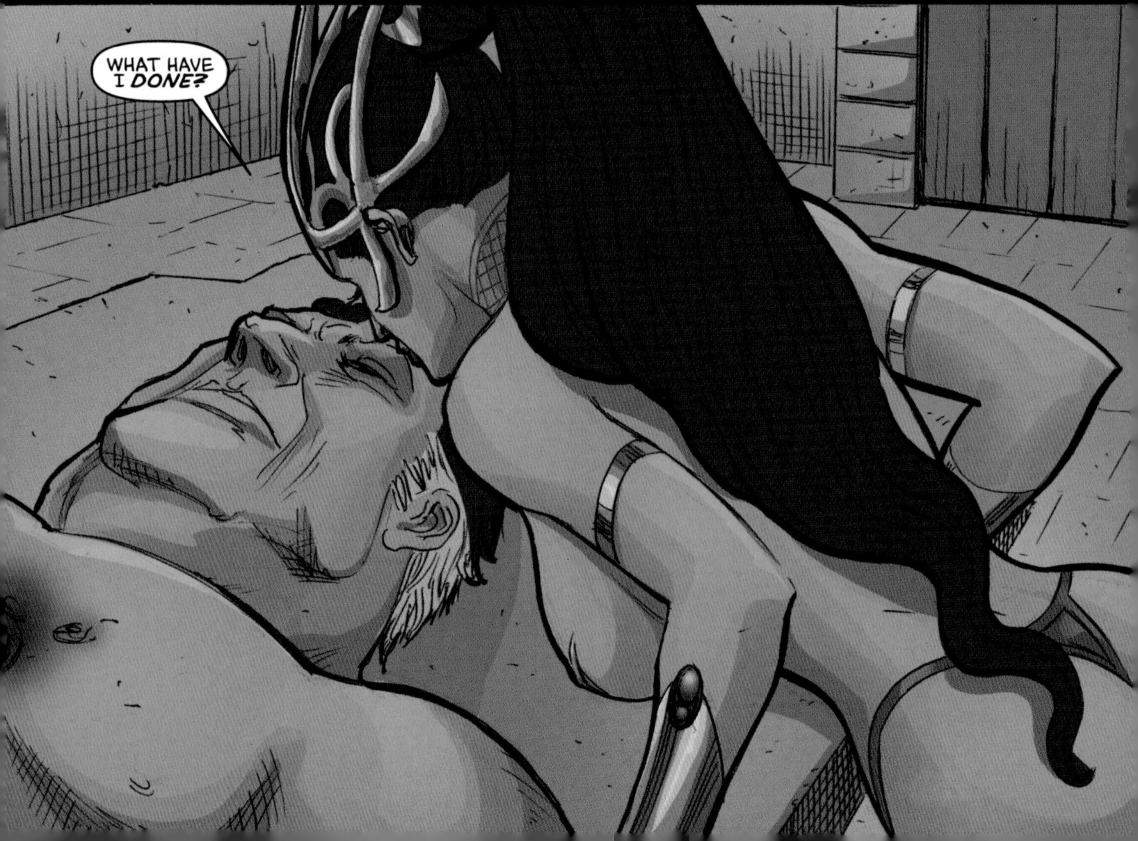
WHAT HAVE I *DONE?*

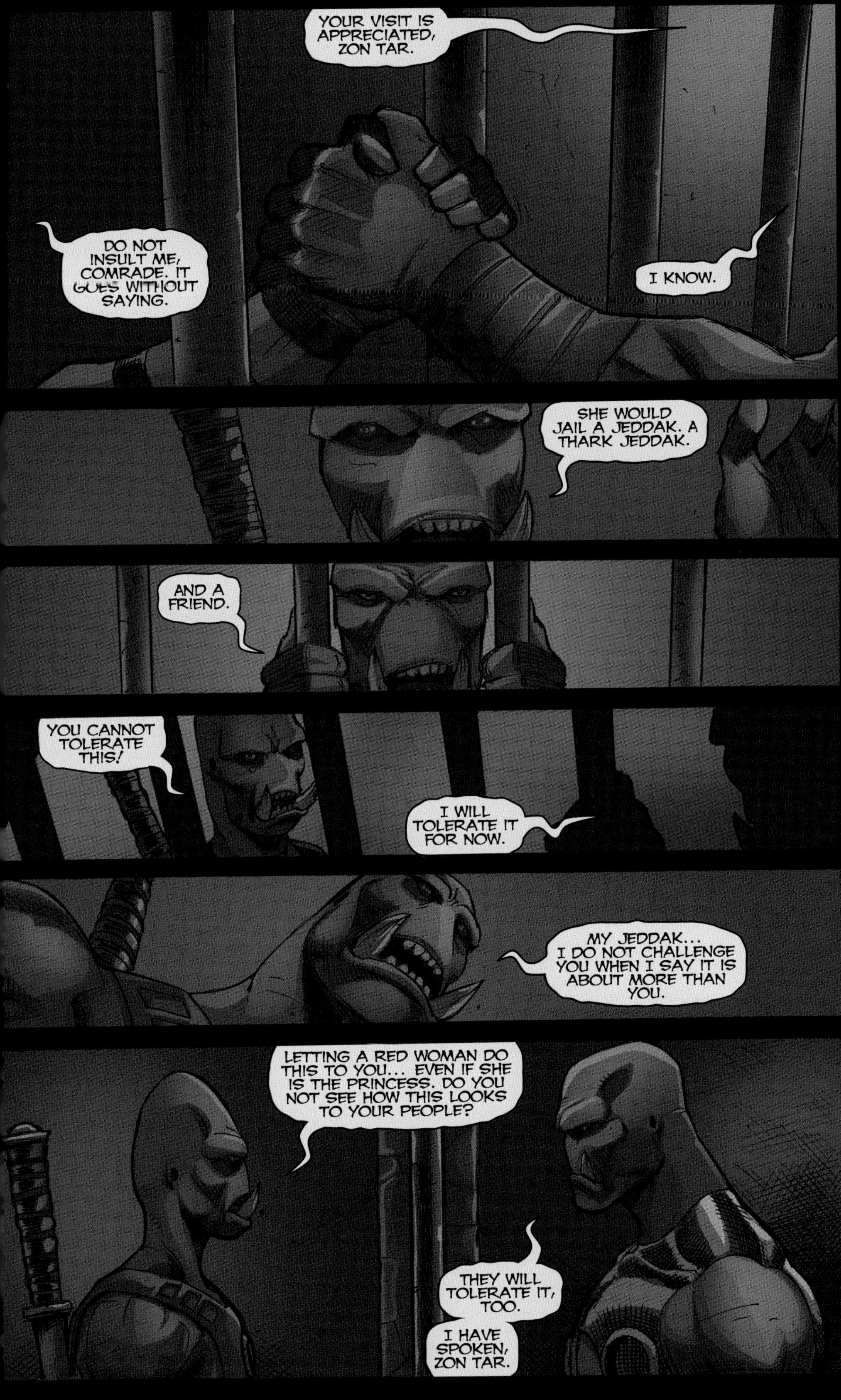
YOUR VISIT IS APPRECIATED, ZON TAR.
DO NOT INSULT ME, COMRADE. IT GOES WITHOUT SAYING.
I KNOW.
SHE WOULD JAIL A JEDDAK. A THARK JEDDAK.
AND A FRIEND.
YOU CANNOT TOLERATE THIS!
I WILL TOLERATE IT FOR NOW.
MY JEDDAK... I DO NOT CHALLENGE YOU WHEN I SAY IT IS ABOUT MORE THAN YOU.
LETTING A RED WOMAN DO THIS TO YOU... EVEN IF SHE IS THE PRINCESS. DO YOU NOT SEE HOW THIS LOOKS TO YOUR PEOPLE?
THEY WILL TOLERATE IT, TOO.
I HAVE SPOKEN, ZON TAR.

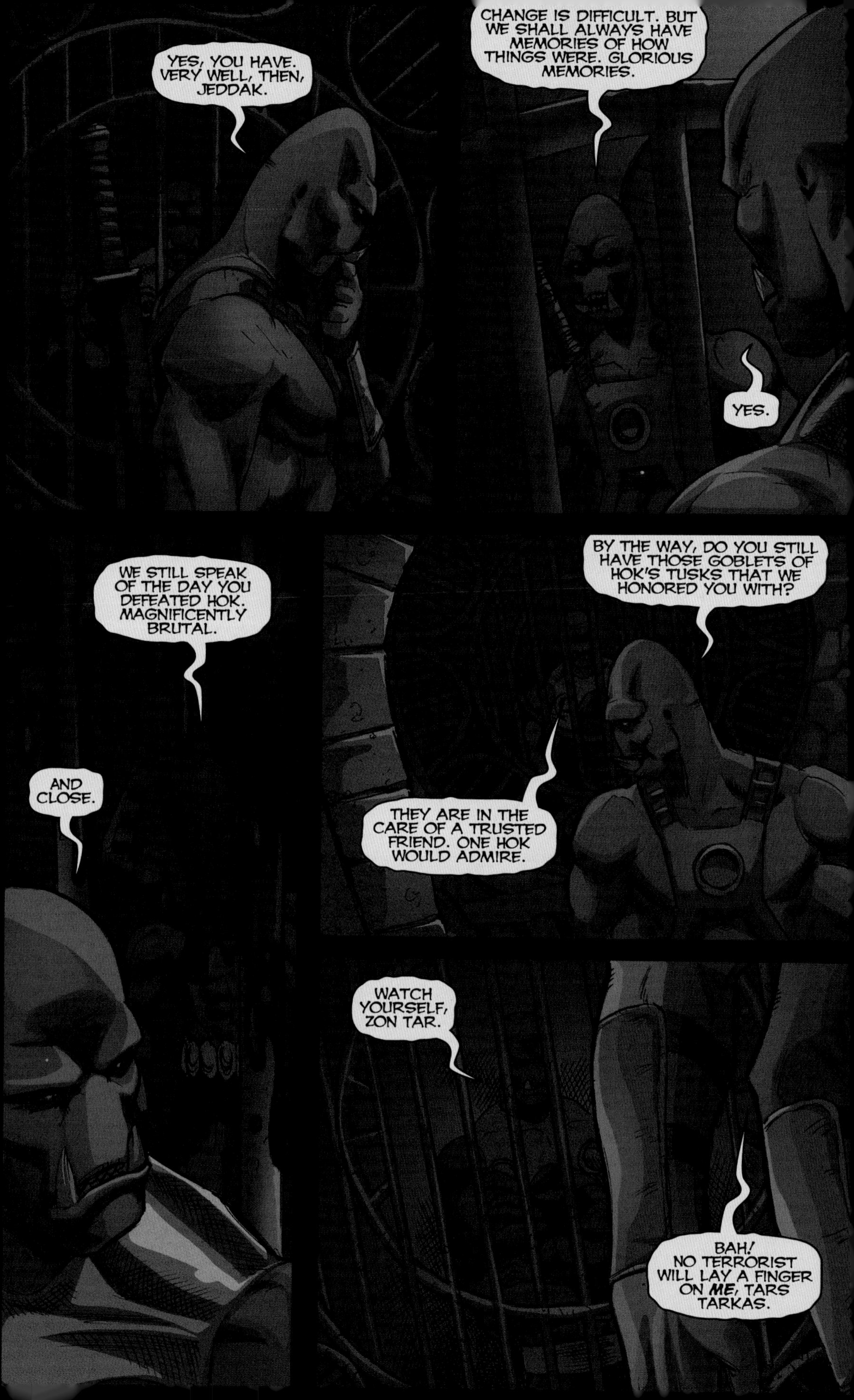
YES, YOU HAVE. VERY WELL, THEN, JEDDAK.
CHANGE IS DIFFICULT. BUT WE SHALL ALWAYS HAVE MEMORIES OF HOW THINGS WERE. GLORIOUS MEMORIES.
YES.
WE STILL SPEAK OF THE DAY YOU DEFEATED HOK. MAGNIFICENTLY BRUTAL.
AND CLOSE.
BY THE WAY, DO YOU STILL HAVE THOSE GOBLETS OF HOK'S TUSKS THAT WE HONORED YOU WITH?
THEY ARE IN THE CARE OF A TRUSTED FRIEND. ONE HOK WOULD ADMIRE.
WATCH YOURSELF, ZON TAR.
BAH! NO TERRORIST WILL LAY A FINGER ON *ME*, TARS TARKAS.

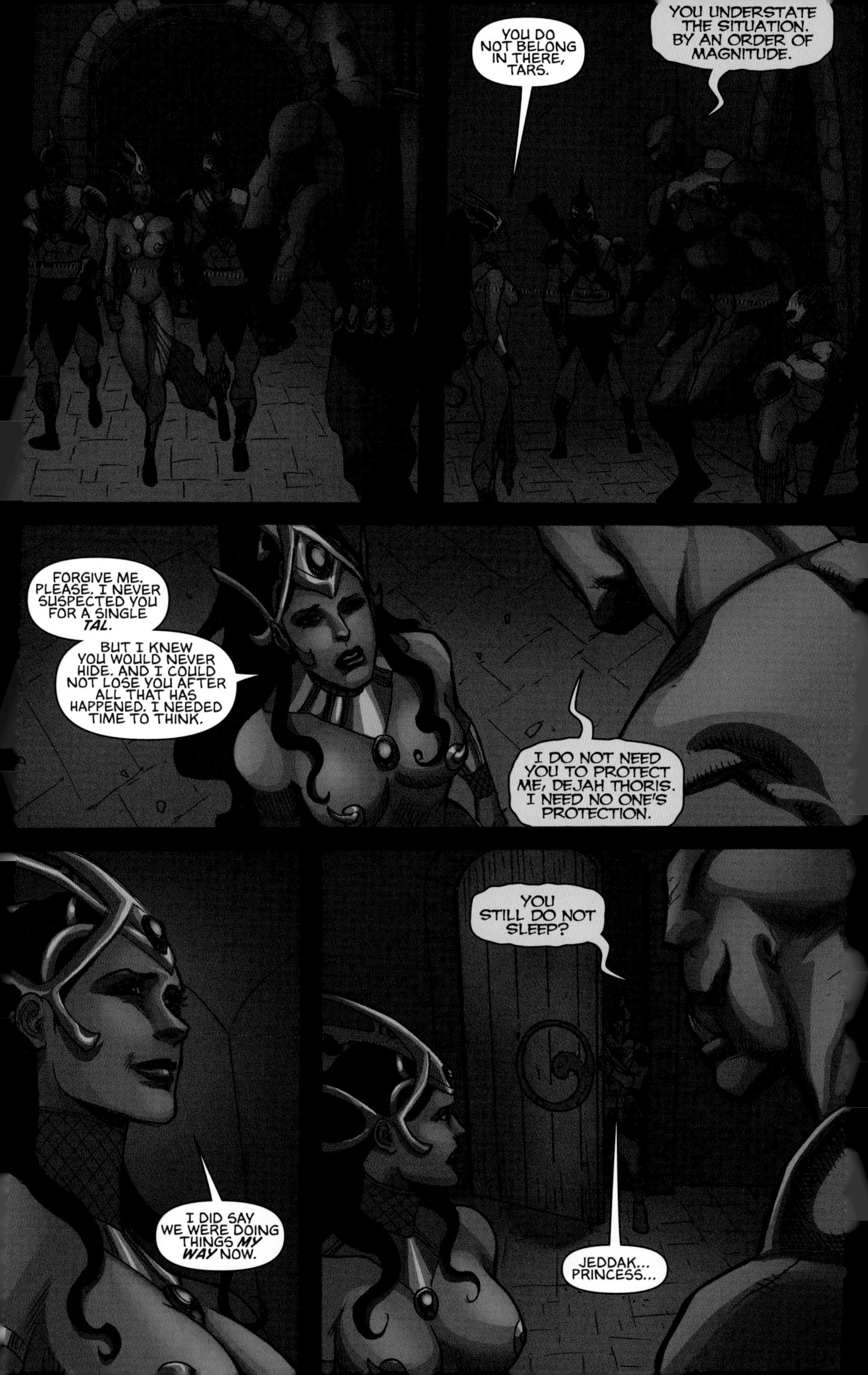
YOU DO NOT BELONG IN THERE, TARS.
YOU UNDERSTATE THE SITUATION. BY AN ORDER OF MAGNITUDE.
FORGIVE ME. PLEASE. I NEVER SUSPECTED YOU FOR A SINGLE *TAL*.
BUT I KNEW YOU WOULD NEVER HIDE. AND I COULD NOT LOSE YOU AFTER ALL THAT HAS HAPPENED. I NEEDED TIME TO THINK.
I DO NOT NEED YOU TO PROTECT ME, DEJAH THORIS. I NEED NO ONE'S PROTECTION.
I DID SAY WE WERE DOING THINGS *MY WAY* NOW.
YOU STILL DO NOT SLEEP?
JEDDAK... PRINCESS...

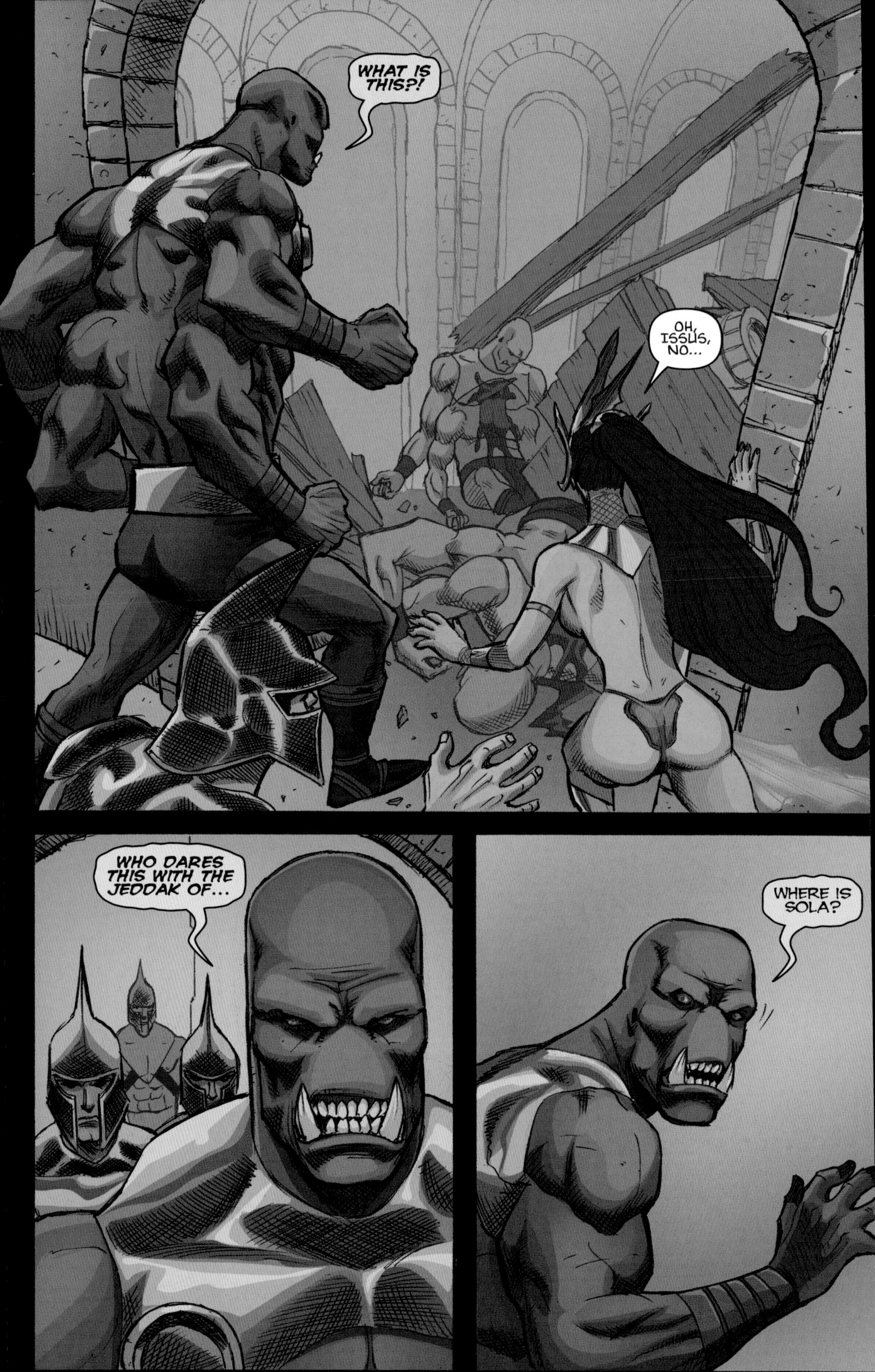
WHAT IS THIS?!
OH, ISSUS, NO...
WHO DARES THIS WITH THE JEDDAK OF...
WHERE IS SOLA?

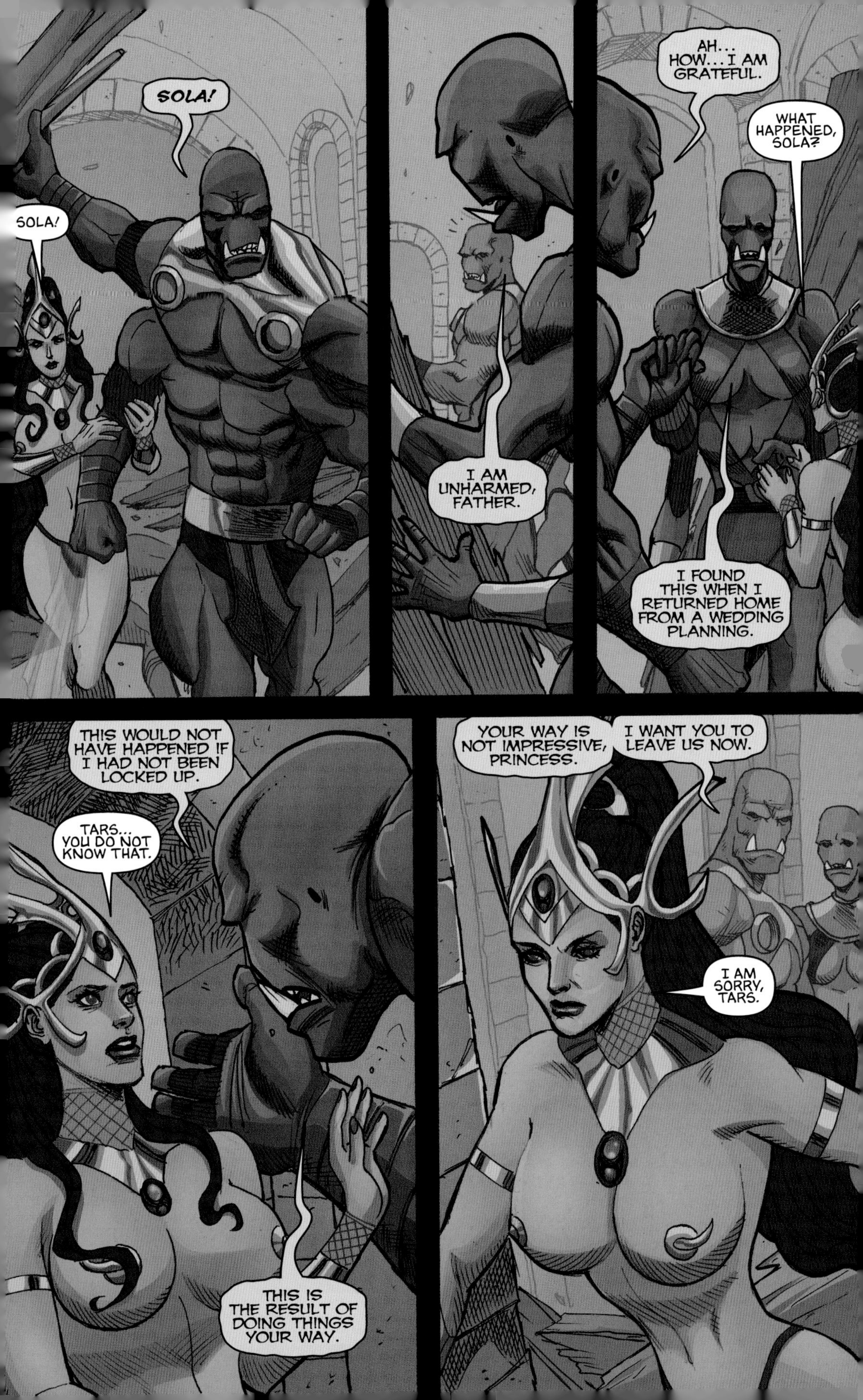
SOLA!
SOLA!
I AM UNHARMED, FATHER.
AH... HOW... I AM GRATEFUL.
WHAT HAPPENED, SOLA?
I FOUND THIS WHEN I RETURNED HOME FROM A WEDDING PLANNING.
THIS WOULD NOT HAVE HAPPENED IF I HAD NOT BEEN LOCKED UP.
TARS... YOU DO NOT KNOW THAT.
THIS IS THE RESULT OF DOING THINGS YOUR WAY.
YOUR WAY IS NOT IMPRESSIVE, PRINCESS.
I WANT YOU TO LEAVE US NOW.
I AM SORRY, TARS.

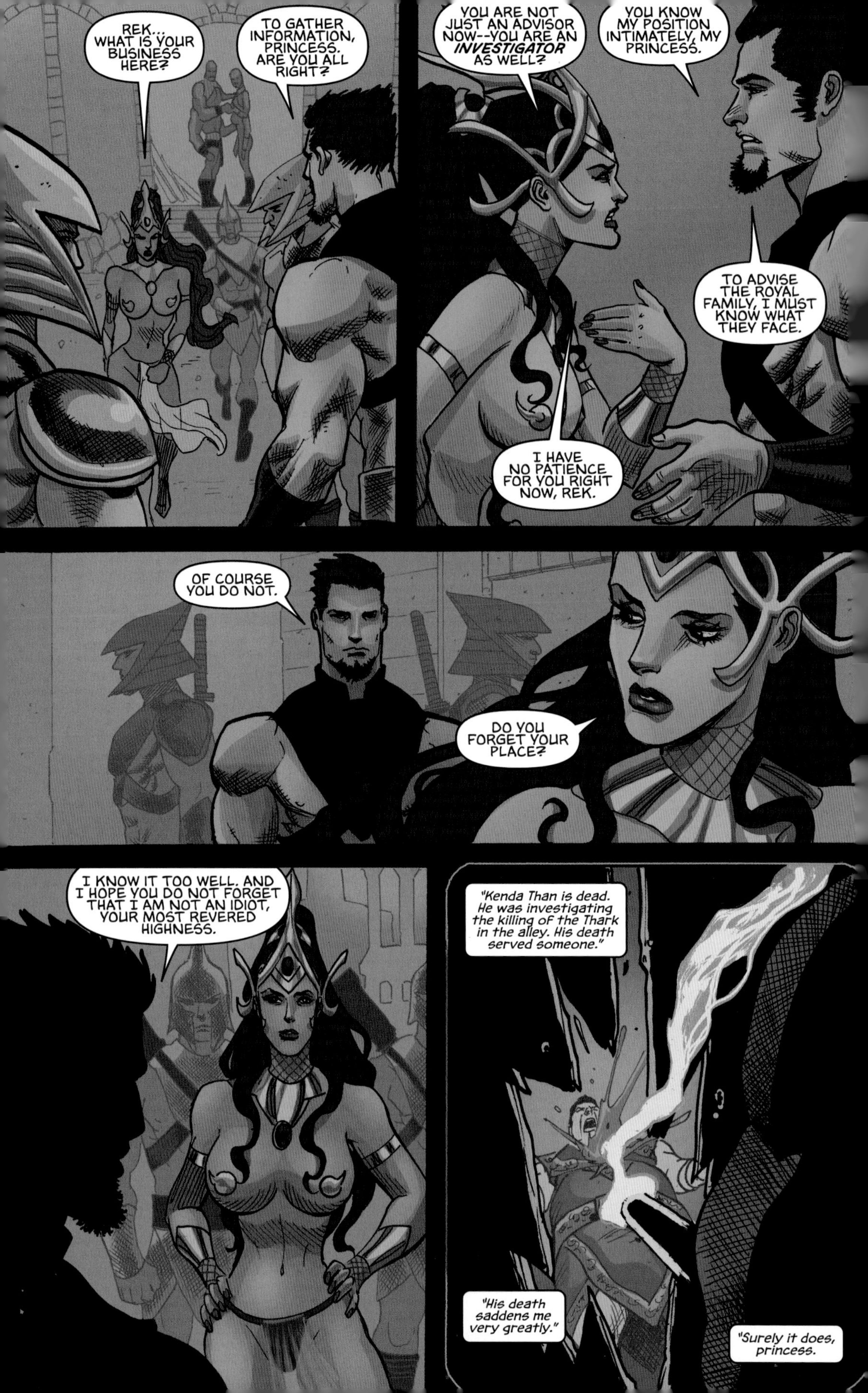
REK... WHAT IS YOUR BUSINESS HERE?
TO GATHER INFORMATION, PRINCESS. ARE YOU ALL RIGHT?
YOU ARE NOT JUST AN ADVISOR NOW--YOU ARE AN *INVESTIGATOR* AS WELL?
YOU KNOW MY POSITION INTIMATELY, MY PRINCESS.
TO ADVISE THE ROYAL FAMILY, I MUST KNOW WHAT THEY FACE.
I HAVE NO PATIENCE FOR YOU RIGHT NOW, REK.
OF COURSE YOU DO NOT.
DO YOU FORGET YOUR PLACE?
I KNOW IT TOO WELL. AND I HOPE YOU DO NOT FORGET THAT I AM NOT AN IDIOT, YOUR MOST REVERED HIGHNESS.
"Kenda Than is dead. He was investigating the killing of the Thark in the alley. His death served someone."
"His death saddens me very greatly."
"Surely it does, princess.

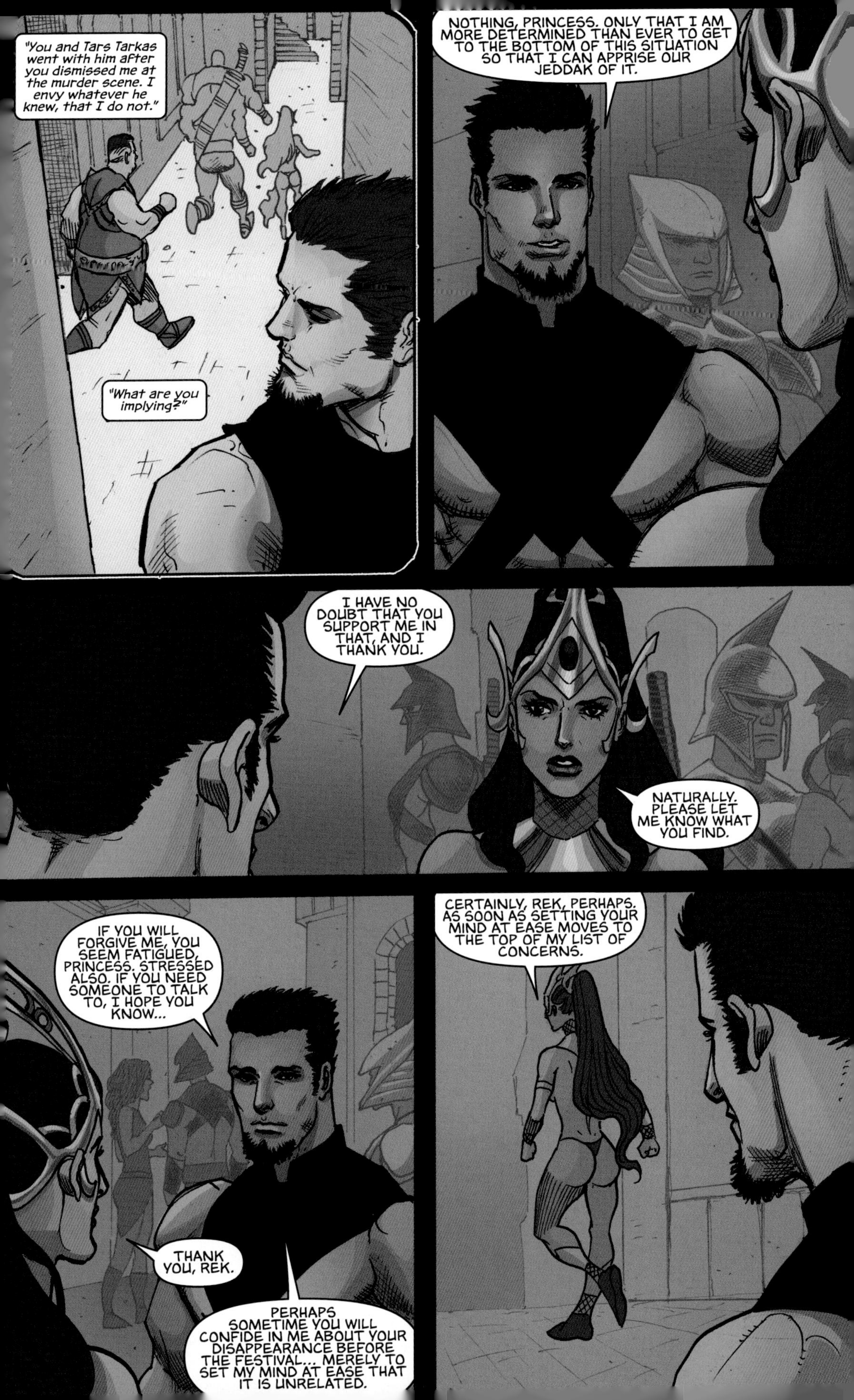
"You and Tars Tarkas went with him after you dismissed me at the murder scene. I envy whatever he knew, that I do not."
"What are you implying?"
NOTHING, PRINCESS. ONLY THAT I AM MORE DETERMINED THAN EVER TO GET TO THE BOTTOM OF THIS SITUATION SO THAT I CAN APPRISE OUR JEDDAK OF IT.
I HAVE NO DOUBT THAT YOU SUPPORT ME IN THAT, AND I THANK YOU.
NATURALLY. PLEASE LET ME KNOW WHAT YOU FIND.
IF YOU WILL FORGIVE ME, YOU SEEM FATIGUED, PRINCESS. STRESSED ALSO. IF YOU NEED SOMEONE TO TALK TO, I HOPE YOU KNOW...
THANK YOU, REK.
PERHAPS SOMETIME YOU WILL CONFIDE IN ME ABOUT YOUR DISAPPEARANCE BEFORE THE FESTIVAL... MERELY TO SET MY MIND AT EASE THAT IT IS UNRELATED.
CERTAINLY, REK, PERHAPS. AS SOON AS SETTING YOUR MIND AT EASE MOVES TO THE TOP OF MY LIST OF CONCERNS.

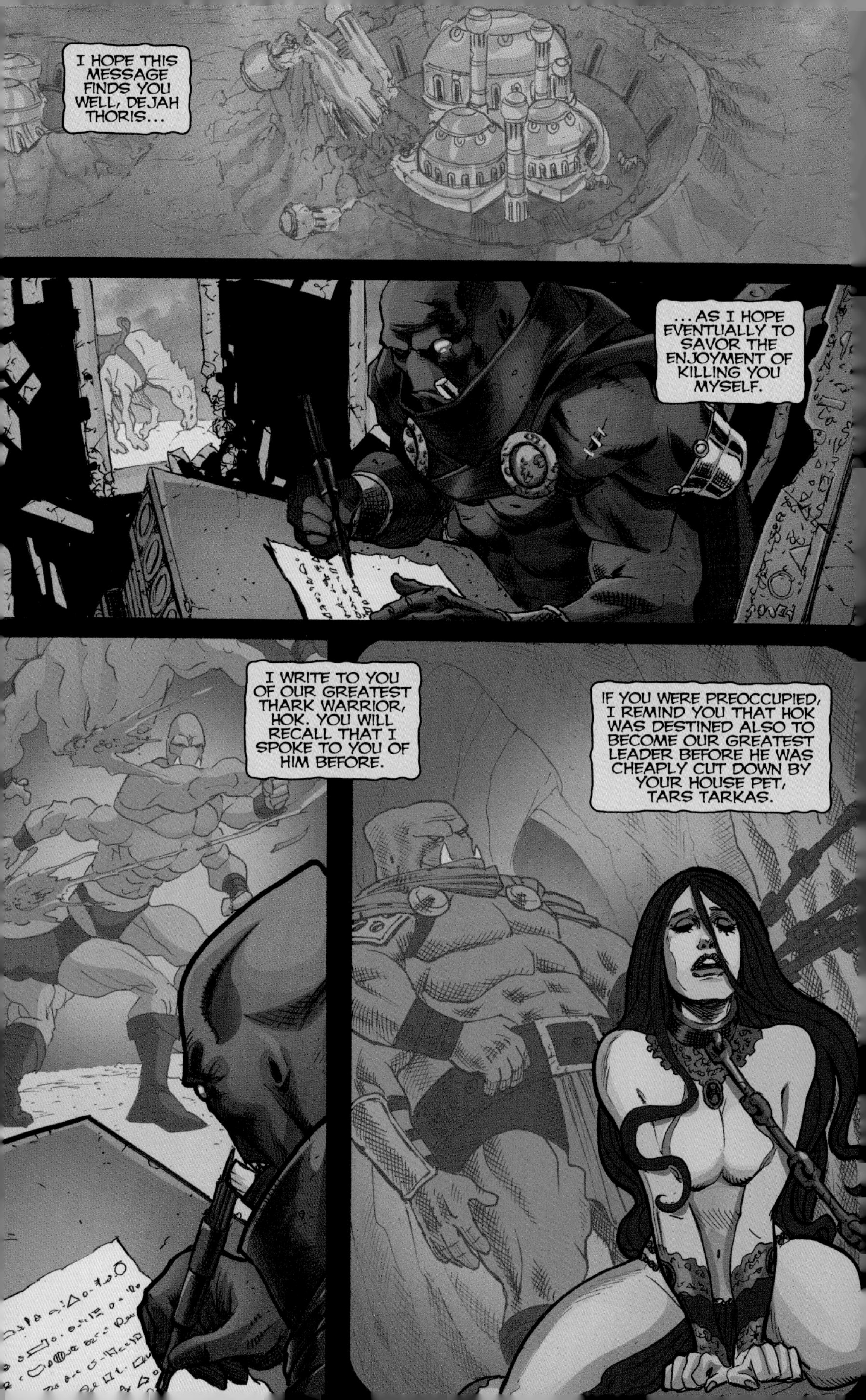
I HOPE THIS MESSAGE FINDS YOU WELL, DEJAH THORIS...
...AS I HOPE EVENTUALLY TO SAVOR THE ENJOYMENT OF KILLING YOU MYSELF.
I WRITE TO YOU OF OUR GREATEST THARK WARRIOR, HOK. YOU WILL RECALL THAT I SPOKE TO YOU OF HIM BEFORE.
IF YOU WERE PREOCCUPIED, I REMIND YOU THAT HOK WAS DESTINED ALSO TO BECOME OUR GREATEST LEADER BEFORE HE WAS CHEAPLY CUT DOWN BY YOUR HOUSE PET, TARS TARKAS.

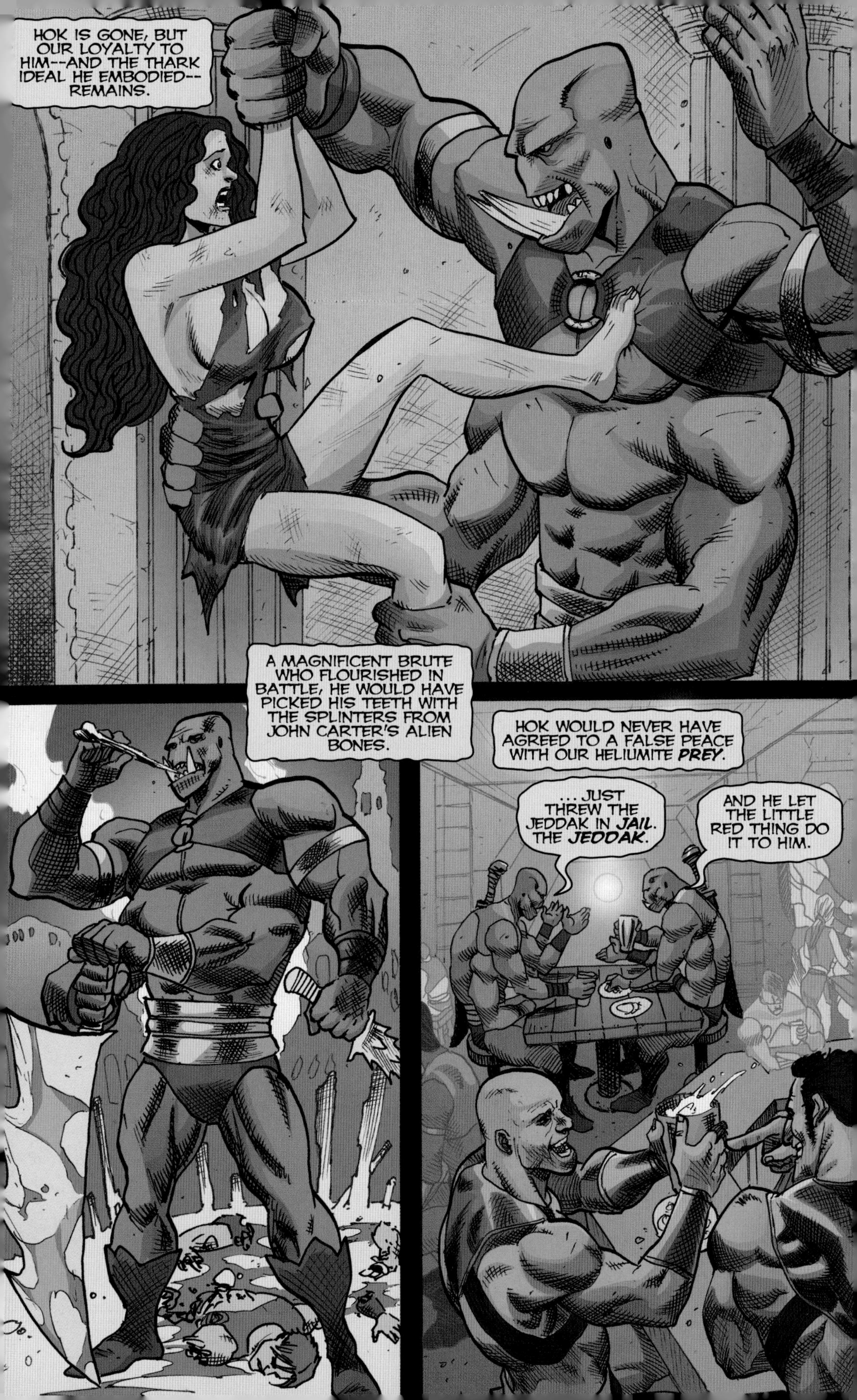

HOK IS GONE, BUT OUR LOYALTY TO HIM--AND THE THARK IDEAL HE EMBODIED--REMAINS.
A MAGNIFICENT BRUTE WHO FLOURISHED IN BATTLE, HE WOULD HAVE PICKED HIS TEETH WITH THE SPLINTERS FROM JOHN CARTER'S ALIEN BONES.
HOK WOULD NEVER HAVE AGREED TO A FALSE PEACE WITH OUR HELIUMITE ***PREY***.
...JUST THREW THE JEDDAK IN ***JAIL***. THE ***JEDDAK***.
AND HE LET THE LITTLE RED THING DO IT TO HIM.

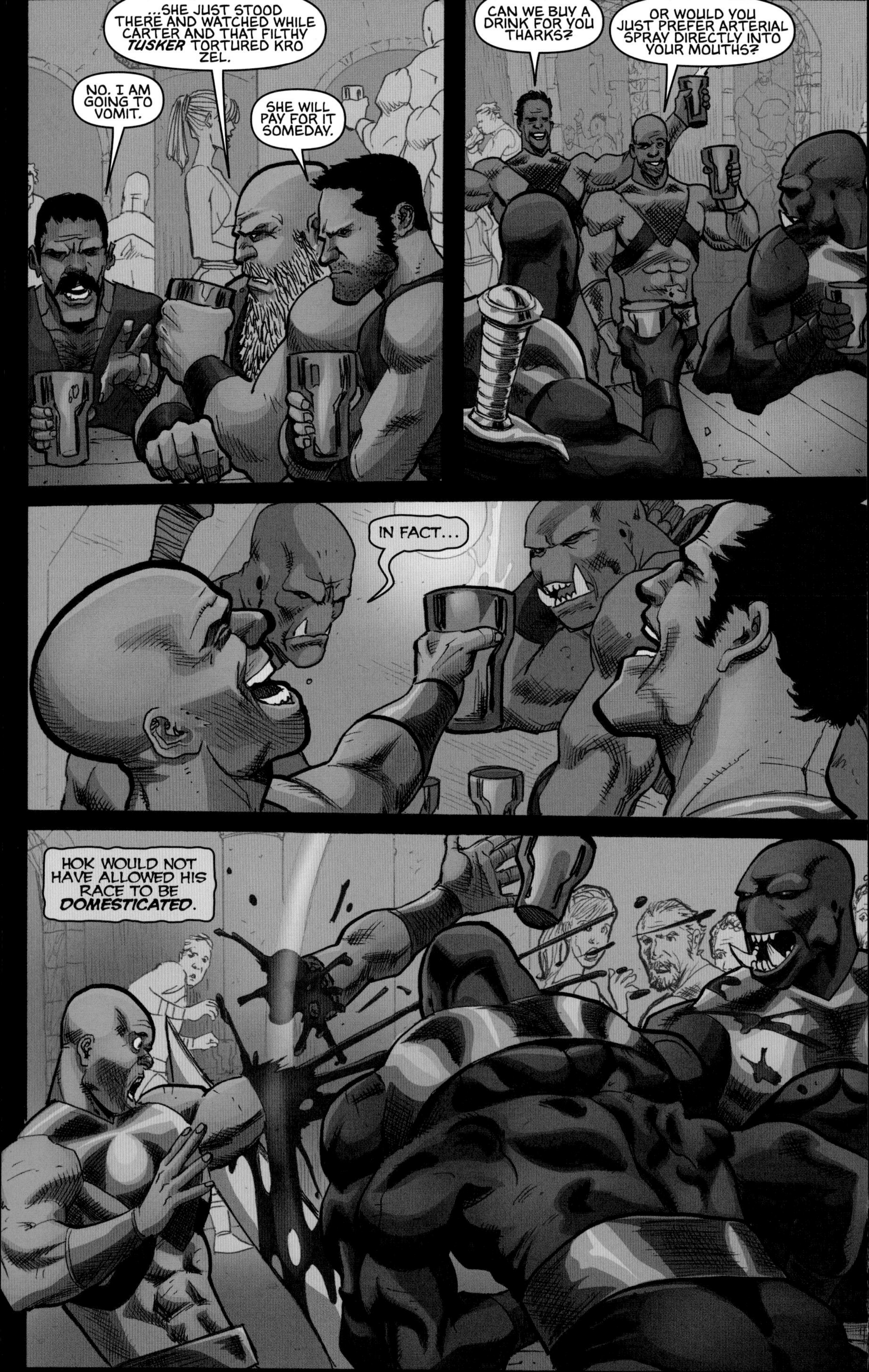
...SHE JUST STOOD THERE AND WATCHED WHILE CARTER AND THAT FILTHY TUSKER TORTURED KRO ZEL.
NO. I AM GOING TO VOMIT.
SHE WILL PAY FOR IT SOMEDAY.
CAN WE BUY A DRINK FOR YOU THARKS?
OR WOULD YOU JUST PREFER ARTERIAL SPRAY DIRECTLY INTO YOUR MOUTHS?
IN FACT...
HOK WOULD NOT HAVE ALLOWED HIS RACE TO BE DOMESTICATED.

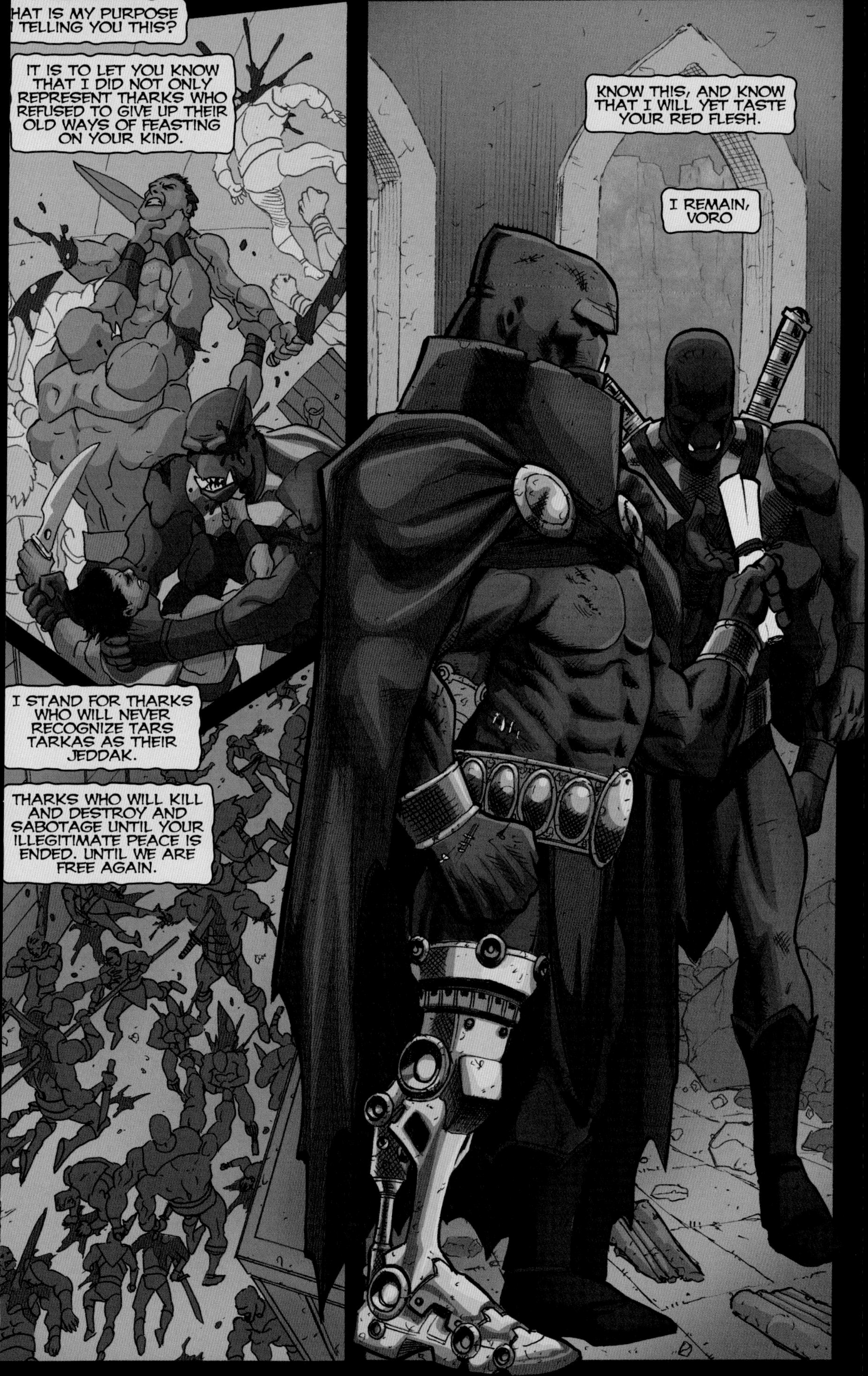
HAT IS MY PURPOSE
I TELLING YOU THIS?
IT IS TO LET YOU KNOW THAT I DID NOT ONLY REPRESENT THARKS WHO REFUSED TO GIVE UP THEIR OLD WAYS OF FEASTING ON YOUR KIND.
I STAND FOR THARKS WHO WILL NEVER RECOGNIZE TARS TARKAS AS THEIR JEDDAK.
THARKS WHO WILL KILL AND DESTROY AND SABOTAGE UNTIL YOUR ILLEGITIMATE PEACE IS ENDED. UNTIL WE ARE FREE AGAIN.
KNOW THIS, AND KNOW THAT I WILL YET TASTE YOUR RED FLESH.
I REMAIN, VORO

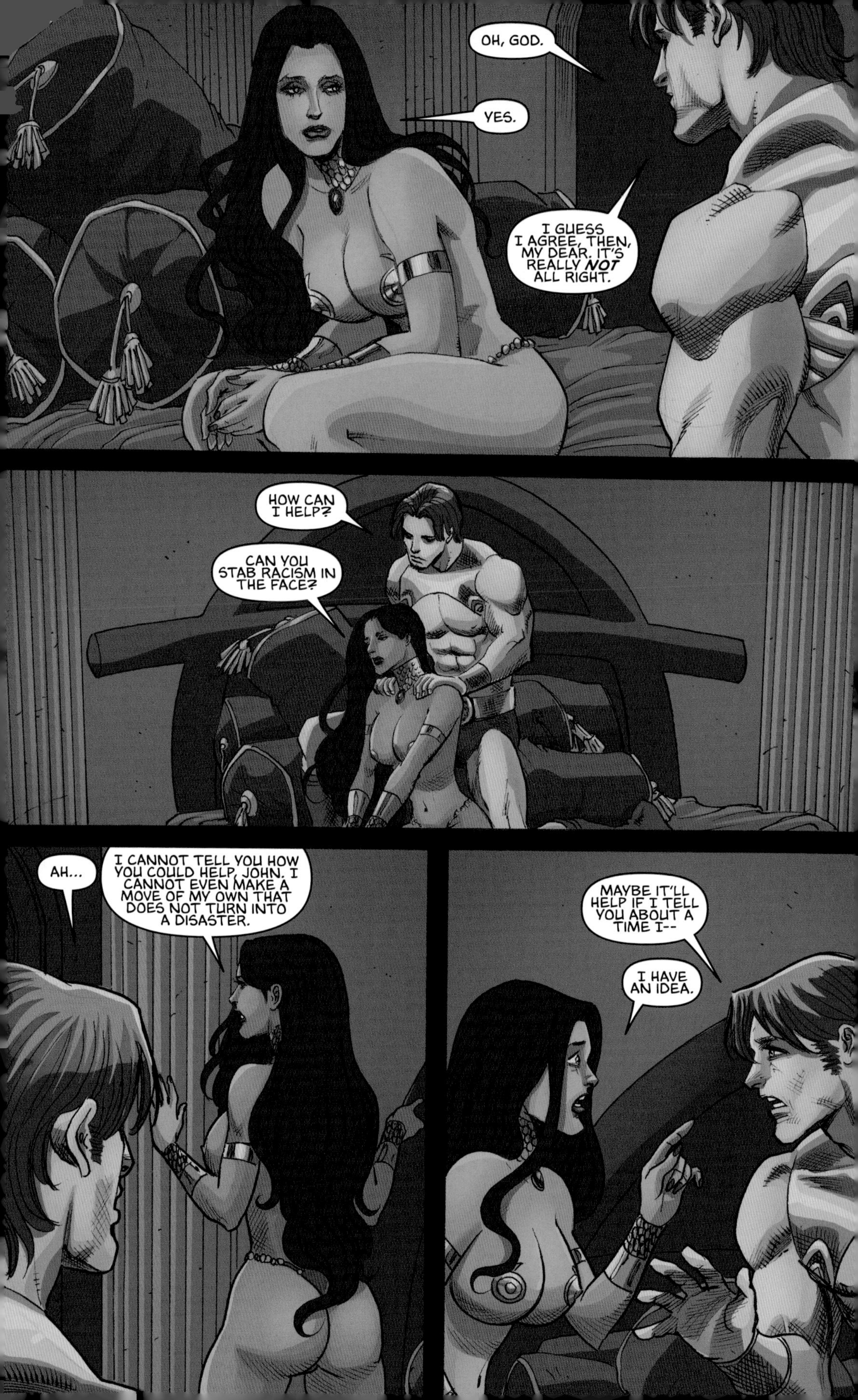
OH, GOD.
YES.
I GUESS I AGREE, THEN, MY DEAR. IT'S REALLY *NOT* ALL RIGHT.
HOW CAN I HELP?
CAN YOU STAB RACISM IN THE FACE?
AH...
I CANNOT TELL YOU HOW YOU COULD HELP, JOHN. I CANNOT EVEN MAKE A MOVE OF MY OWN THAT DOES NOT TURN INTO A DISASTER.
MAYBE IT'LL HELP IF I TELL YOU ABOUT A TIME I--
I HAVE AN IDEA.

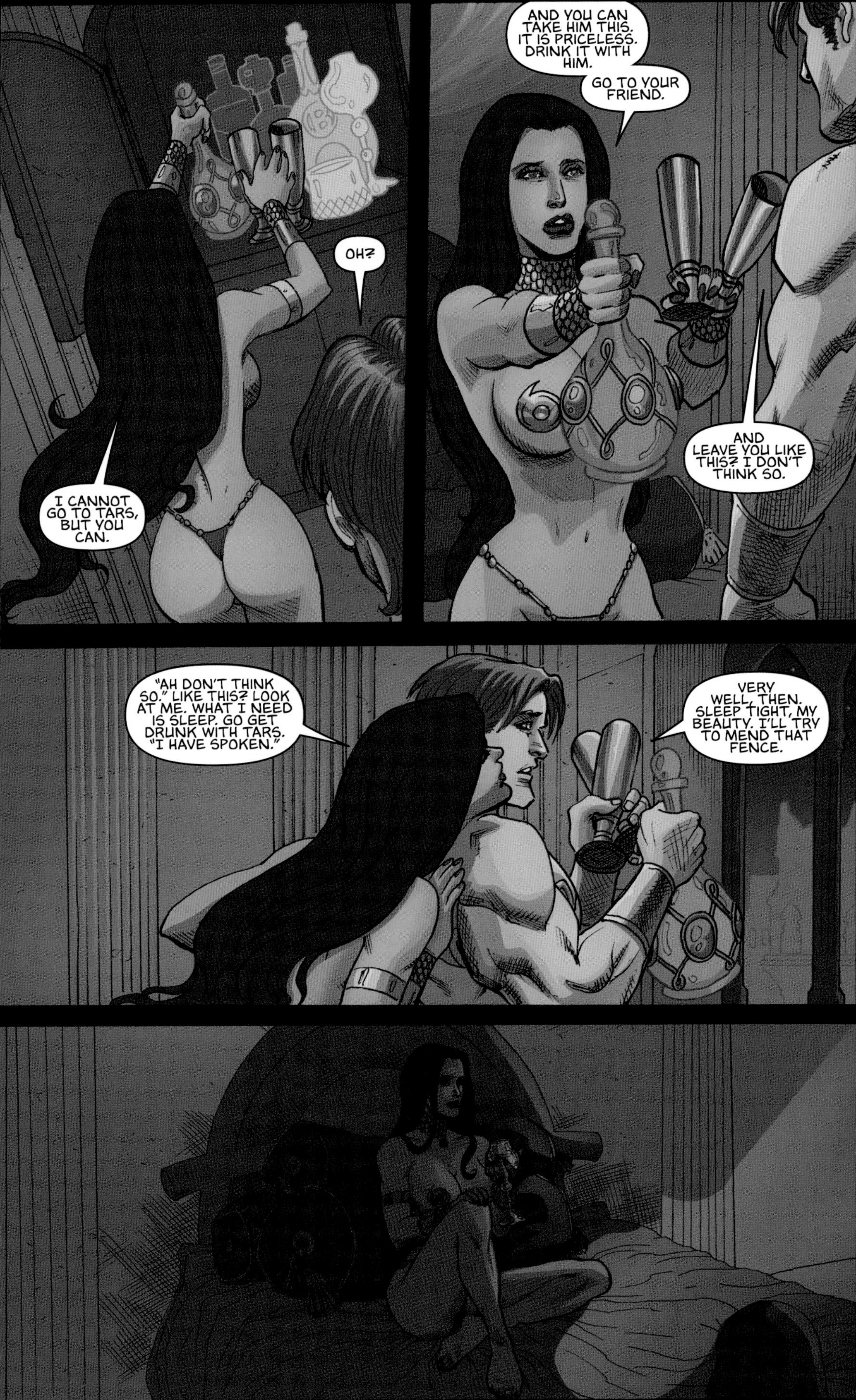
OH?
I CANNOT GO TO TARS, BUT YOU CAN.
AND YOU CAN TAKE HIM THIS. IT IS PRICELESS. DRINK IT WITH HIM.
GO TO YOUR FRIEND.
AND LEAVE YOU LIKE THIS? I DON'T THINK SO.
"AH DON'T THINK SO." LIKE THIS? LOOK AT ME. WHAT I NEED IS SLEEP. GO GET DRUNK WITH TARS. "I HAVE SPOKEN."
VERY WELL, THEN. SLEEP TIGHT, MY BEAUTY. I'LL TRY TO MEND THAT FENCE.

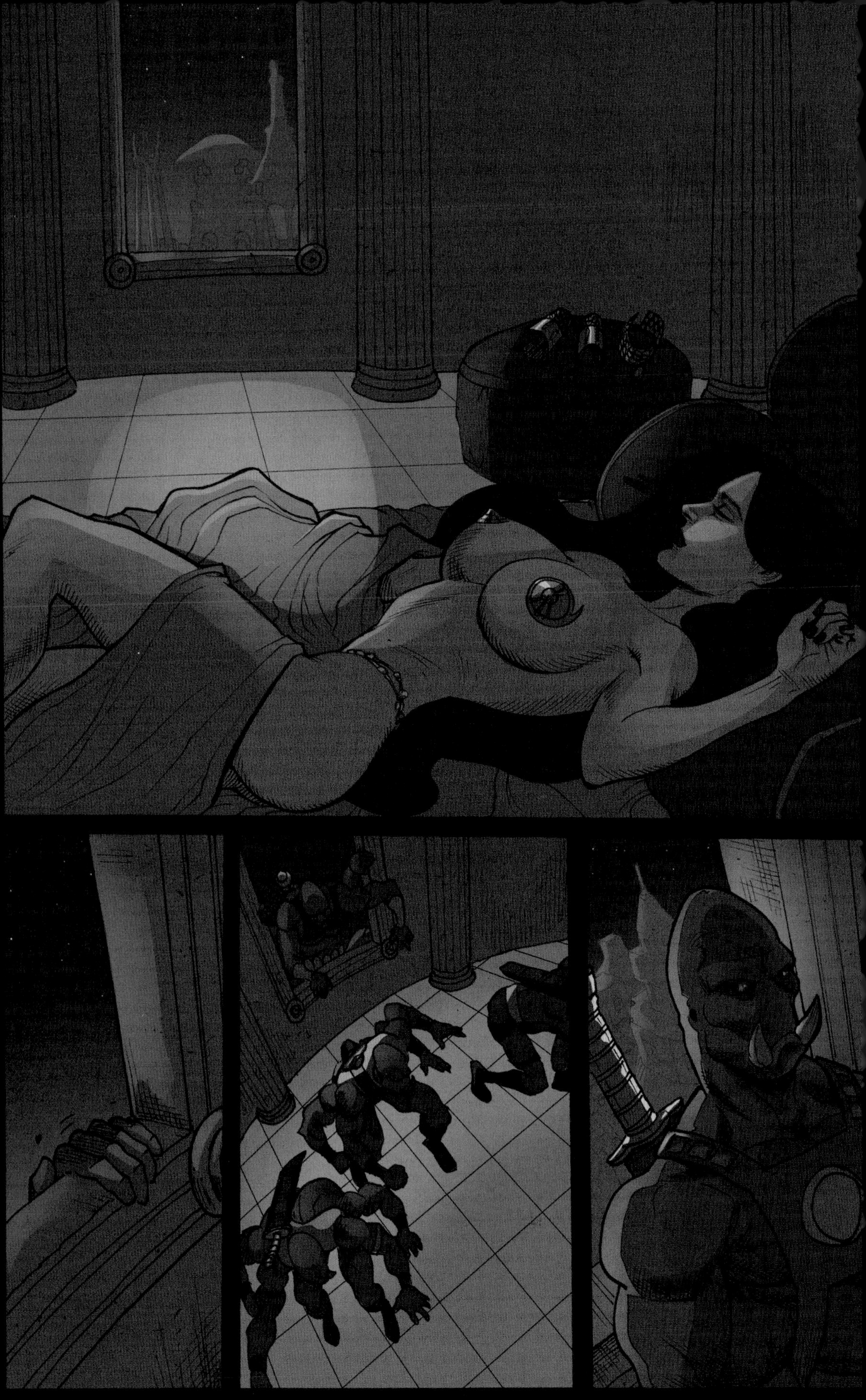

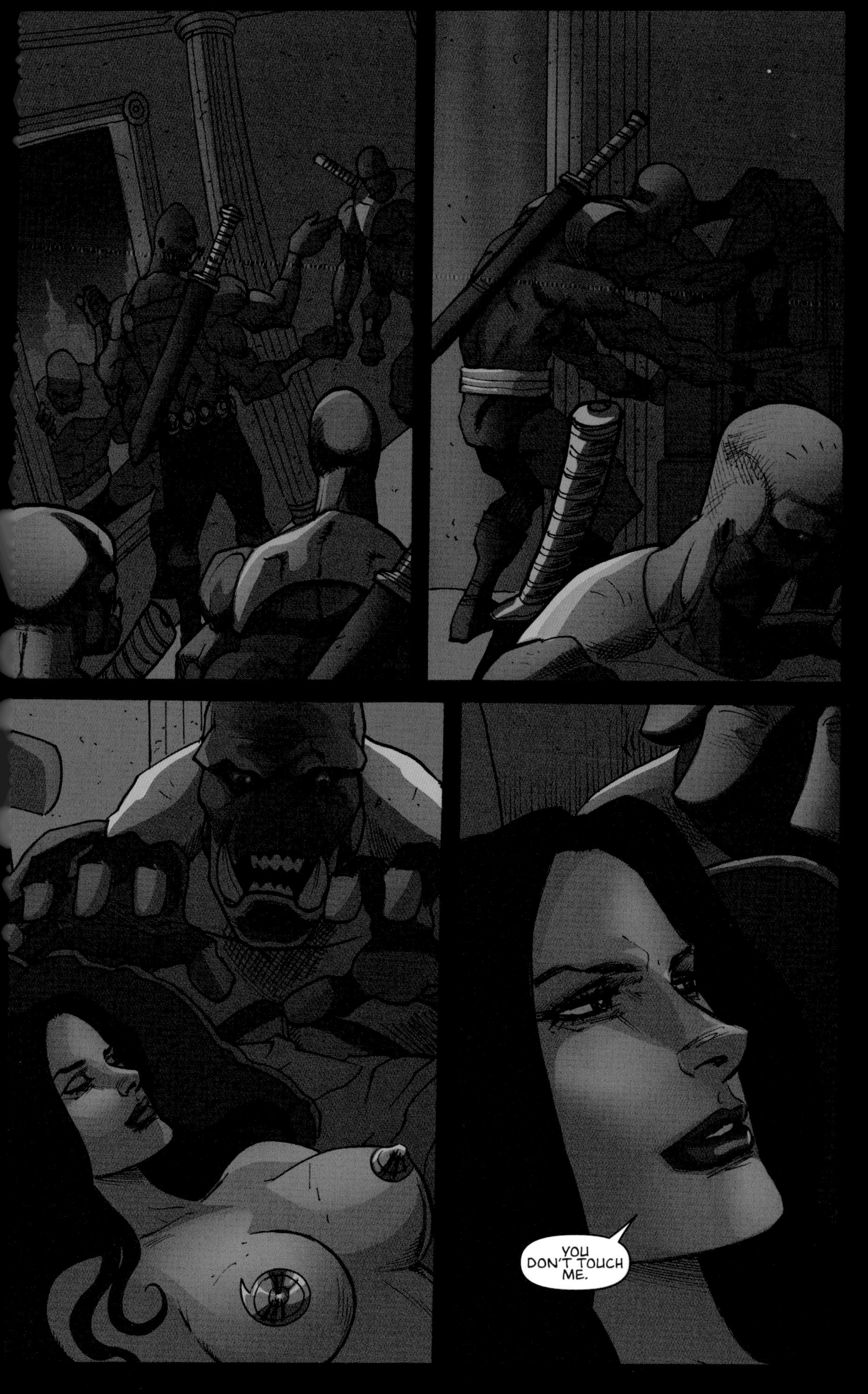
YOU DON'T TOUCH ME.

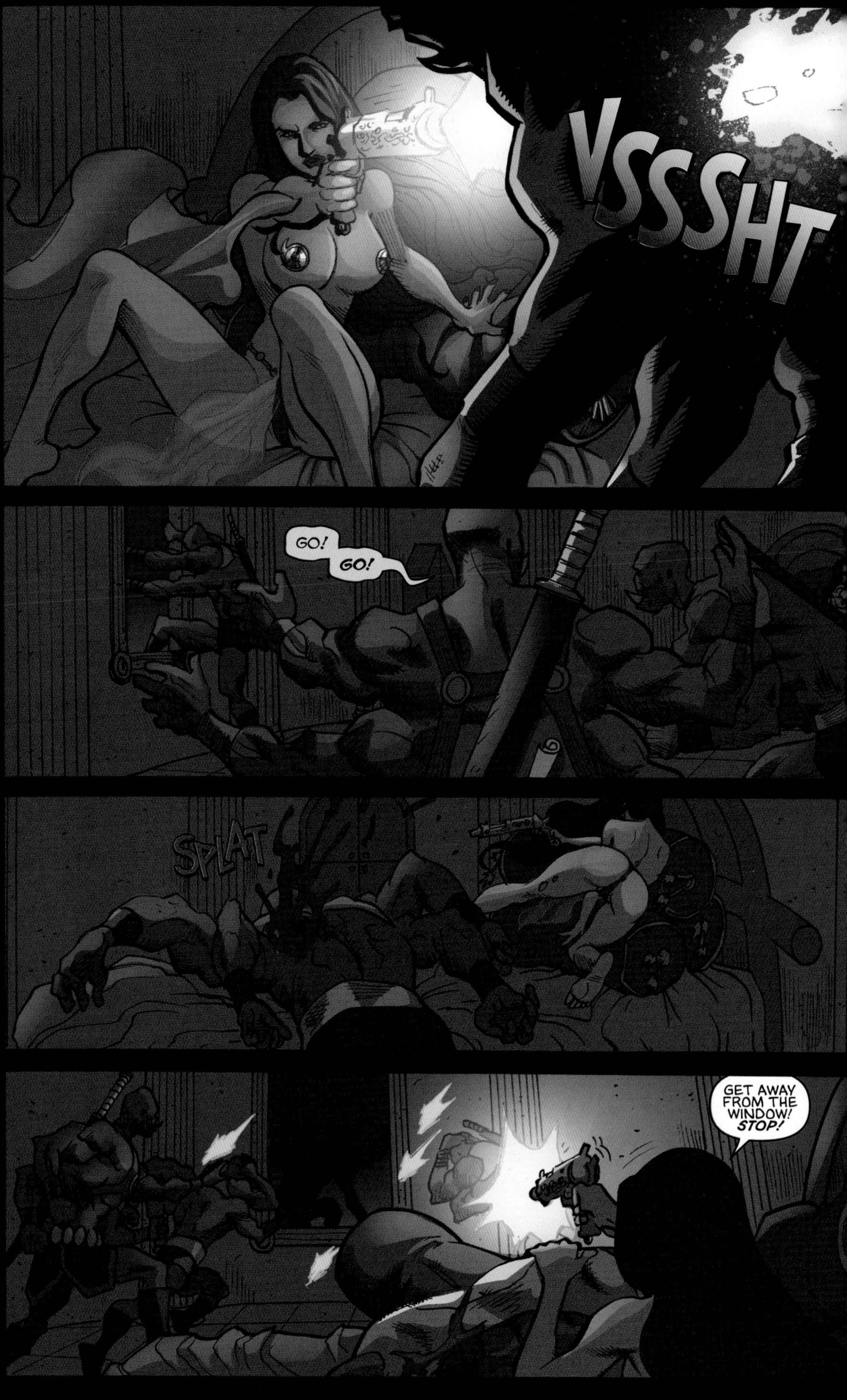
VSSSHT
GO!
GO!
SPLAT
GET AWAY FROM THE WINDOW! STOP!

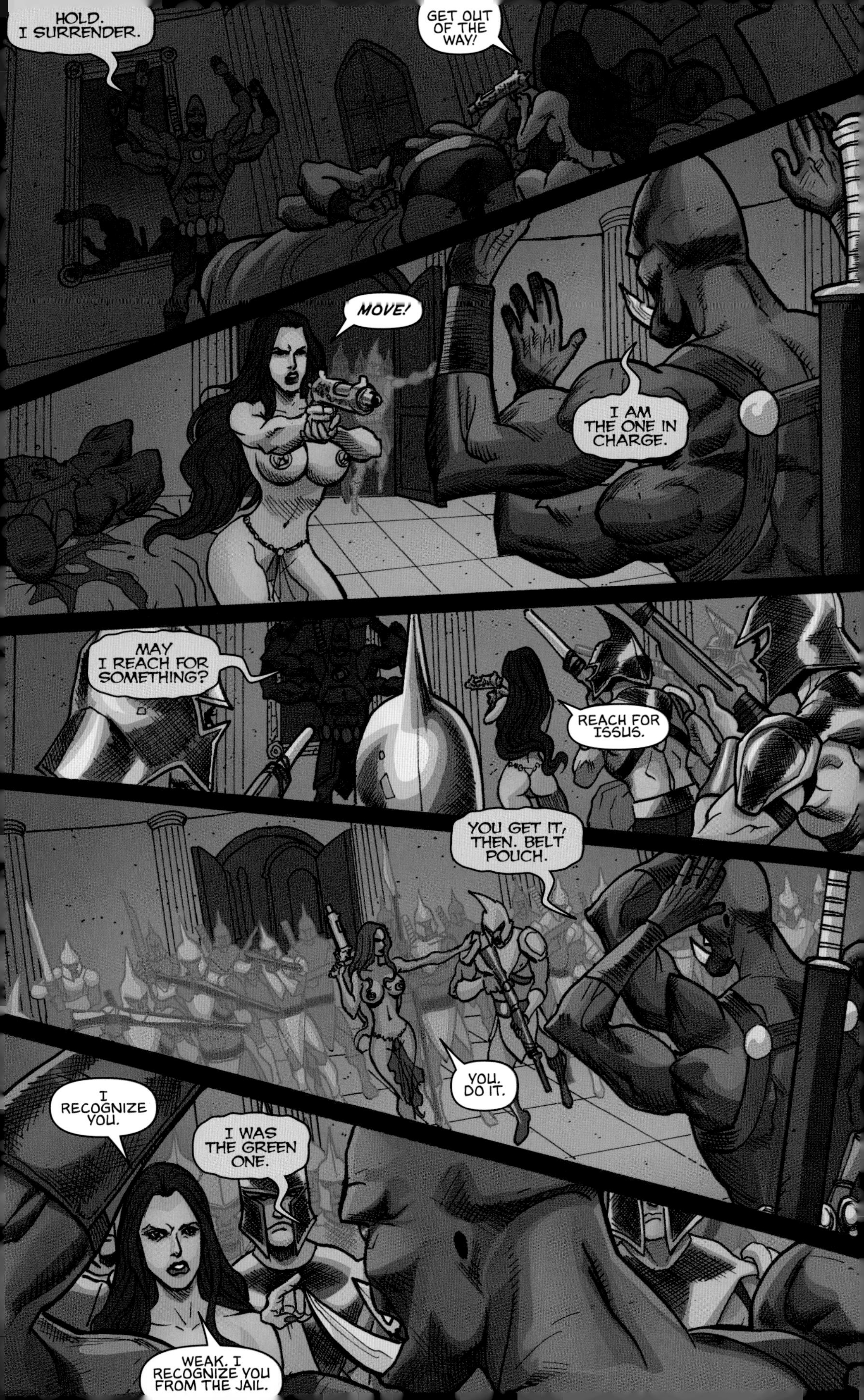
HOLD. I SURRENDER.
GET OUT OF THE WAY!
MOVE!
I AM THE ONE IN CHARGE.
MAY I REACH FOR SOMETHING?
REACH FOR ISSUS.
YOU GET IT, THEN. BELT POUCH.
YOU. DO IT.
I RECOGNIZE YOU.
I WAS THE GREEN ONE.
WEAK. I RECOGNIZE YOU FROM THE JAIL.

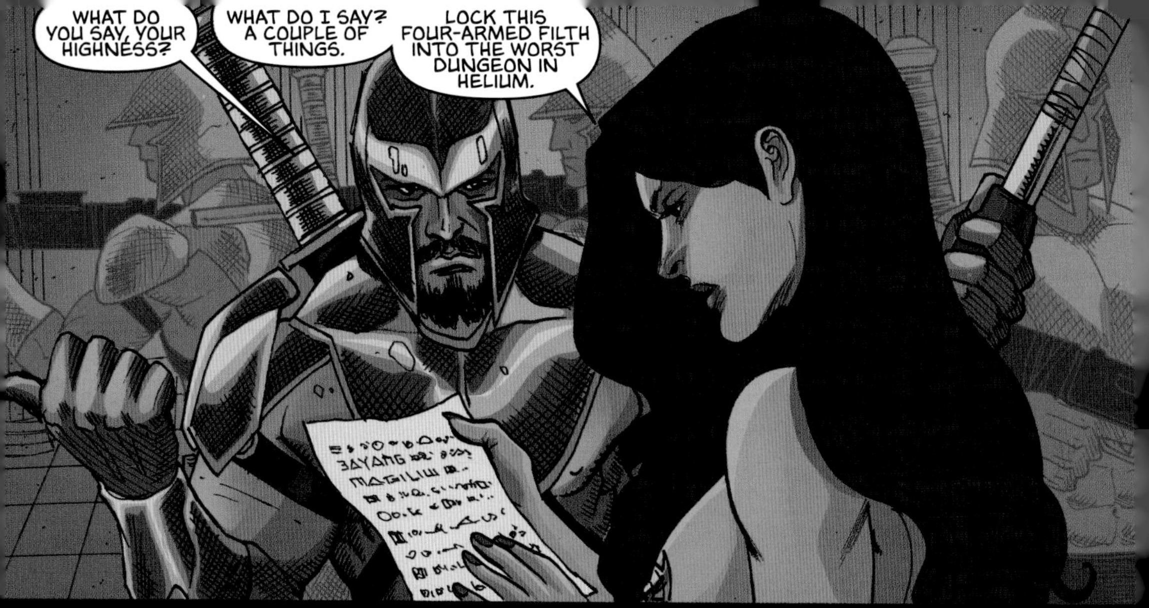
WHAT DO YOU SAY, YOUR HIGHNESS?
WHAT DO I SAY? A COUPLE OF THINGS.
LOCK THIS FOUR-ARMED FILTH INTO THE WORST DUNGEON IN HELIUM.
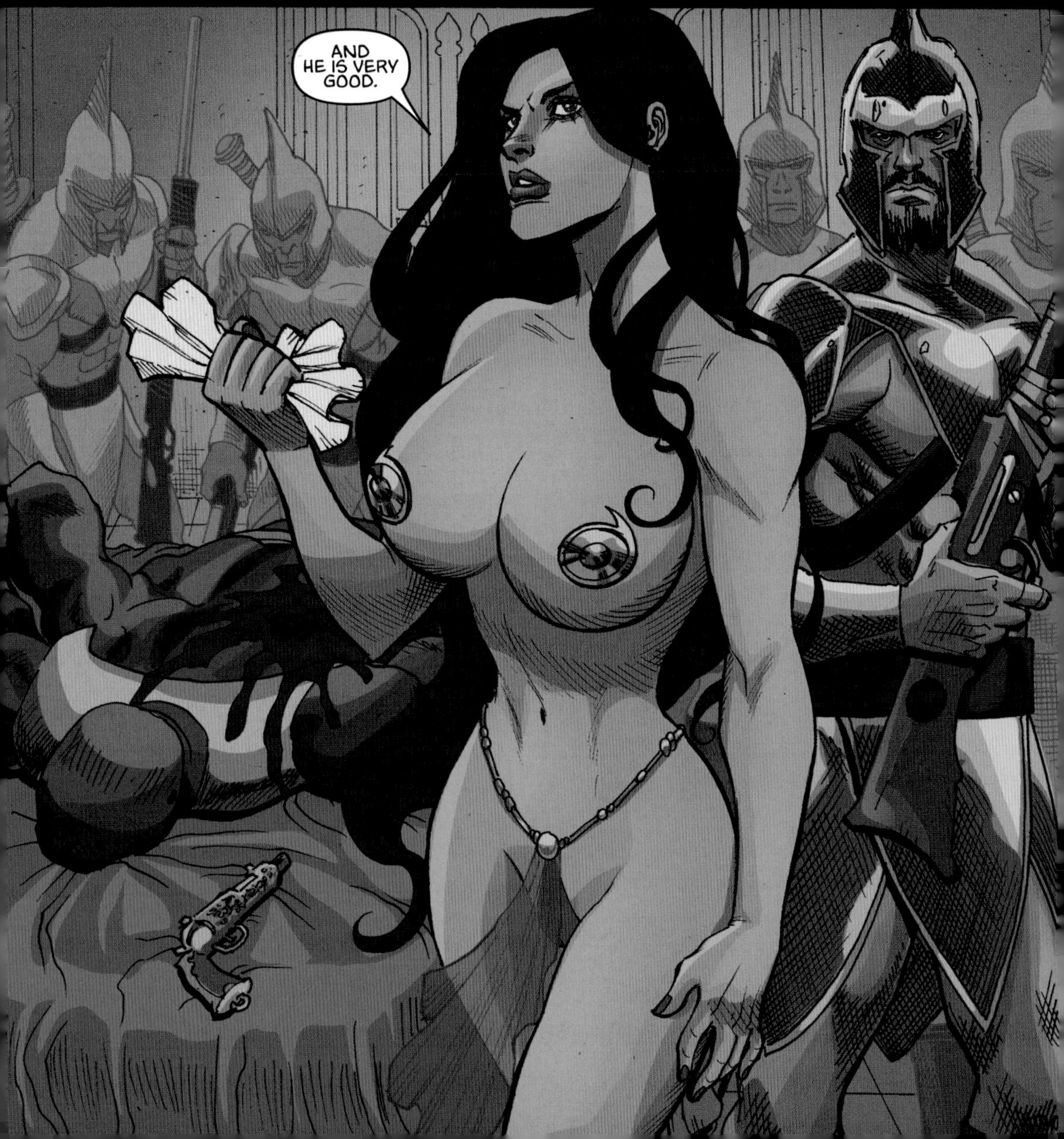
AND HE IS VERY GOOD.

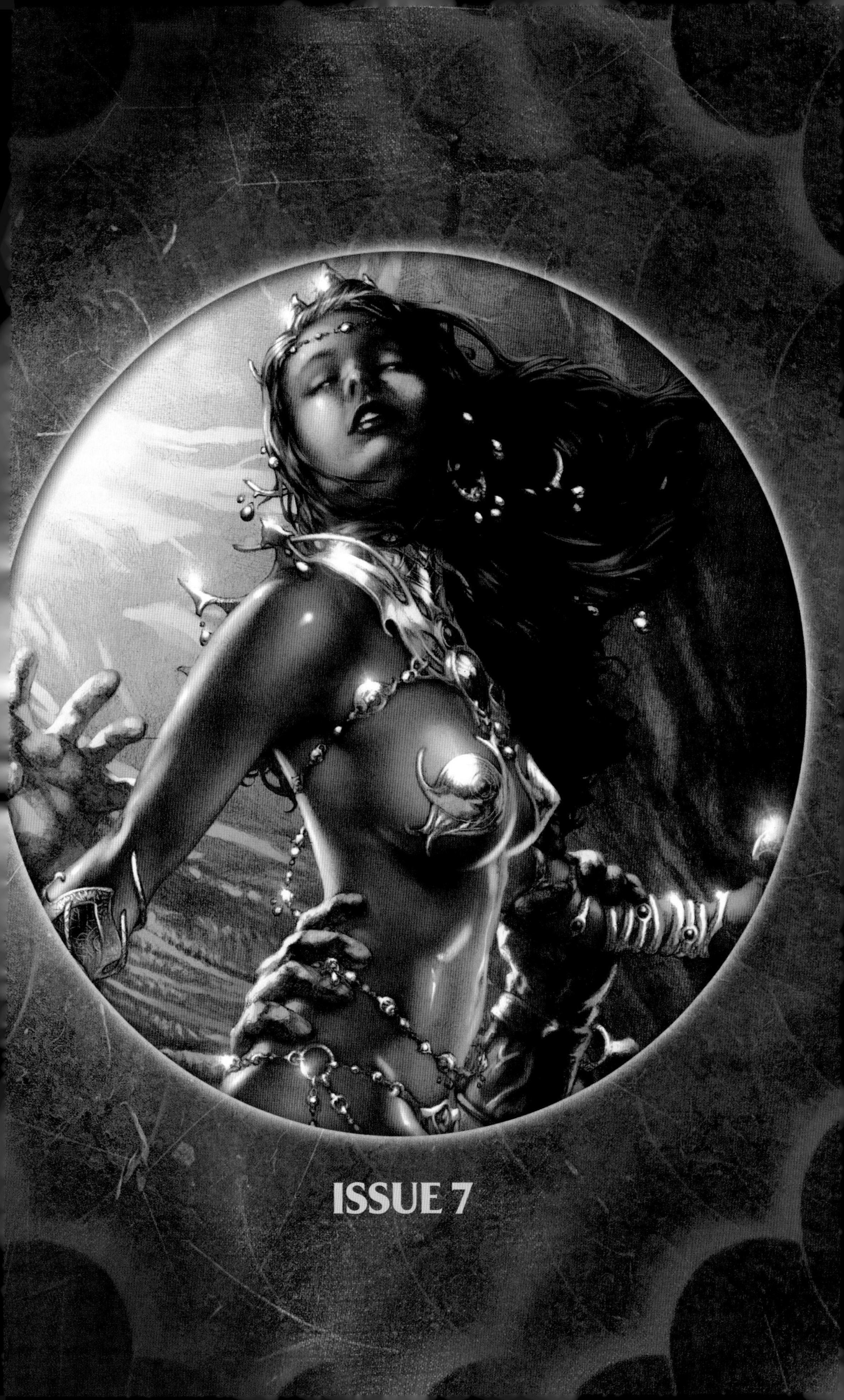
ISSUE 7

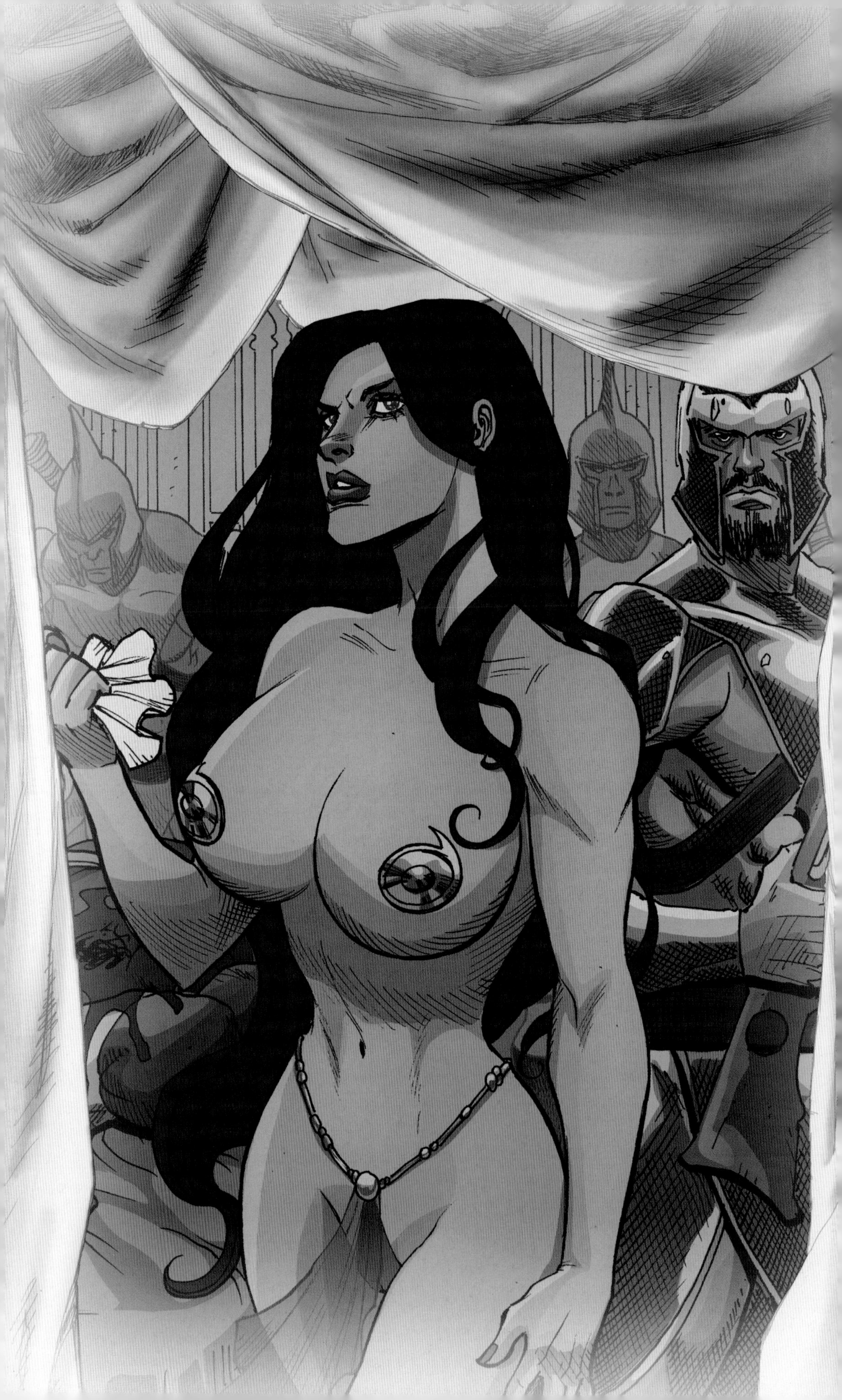

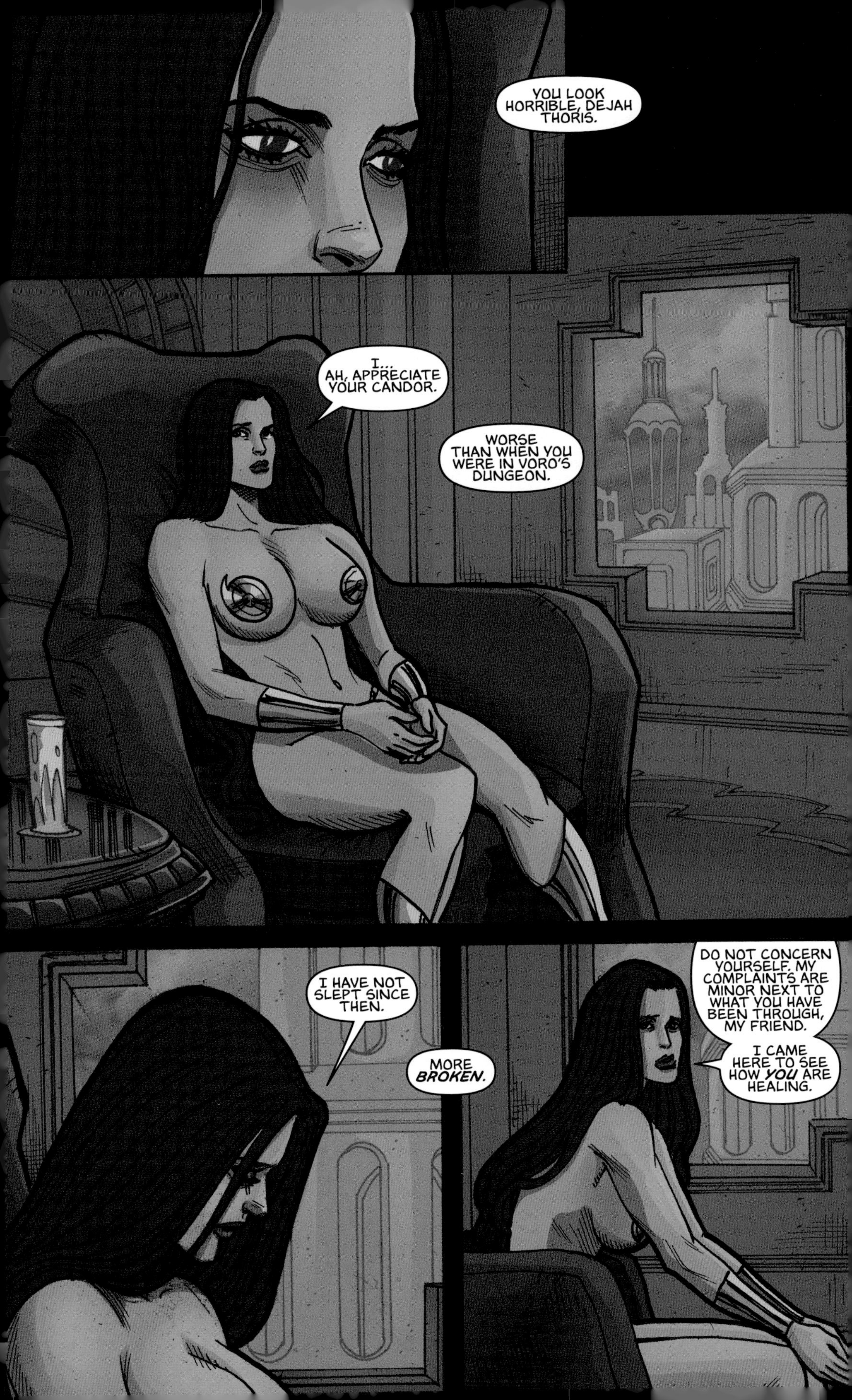
YOU LOOK HORRIBLE, DEJAH THORIS.
I... AH, APPRECIATE YOUR CANDOR.
WORSE THAN WHEN YOU WERE IN VORO'S DUNGEON.
I HAVE NOT SLEPT SINCE THEN.
MORE *BROKEN*.
DO NOT CONCERN YOURSELF. MY COMPLAINTS ARE MINOR NEXT TO WHAT YOU HAVE BEEN THROUGH, MY FRIEND.
I CAME HERE TO SEE HOW *YOU* ARE HEALING.

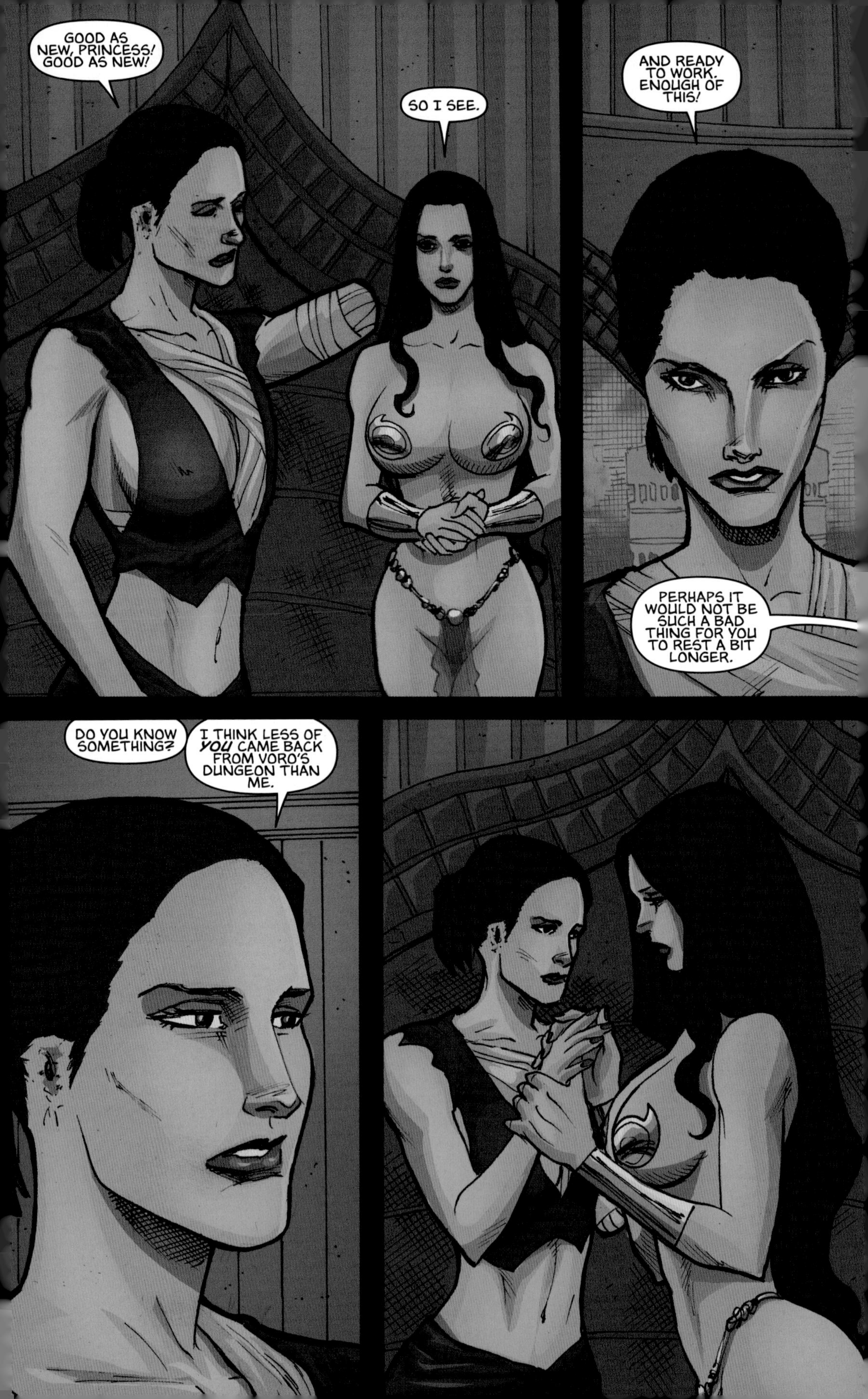
GOOD AS NEW, PRINCESS! GOOD AS NEW!
SO I SEE.
AND READY TO WORK. ENOUGH OF THIS!
PERHAPS IT WOULD NOT BE SUCH A BAD THING FOR YOU TO REST A BIT LONGER.
DO YOU KNOW SOMETHING?
I THINK LESS OF *YOU* CAME BACK FROM VORO'S DUNGEON THAN ME.

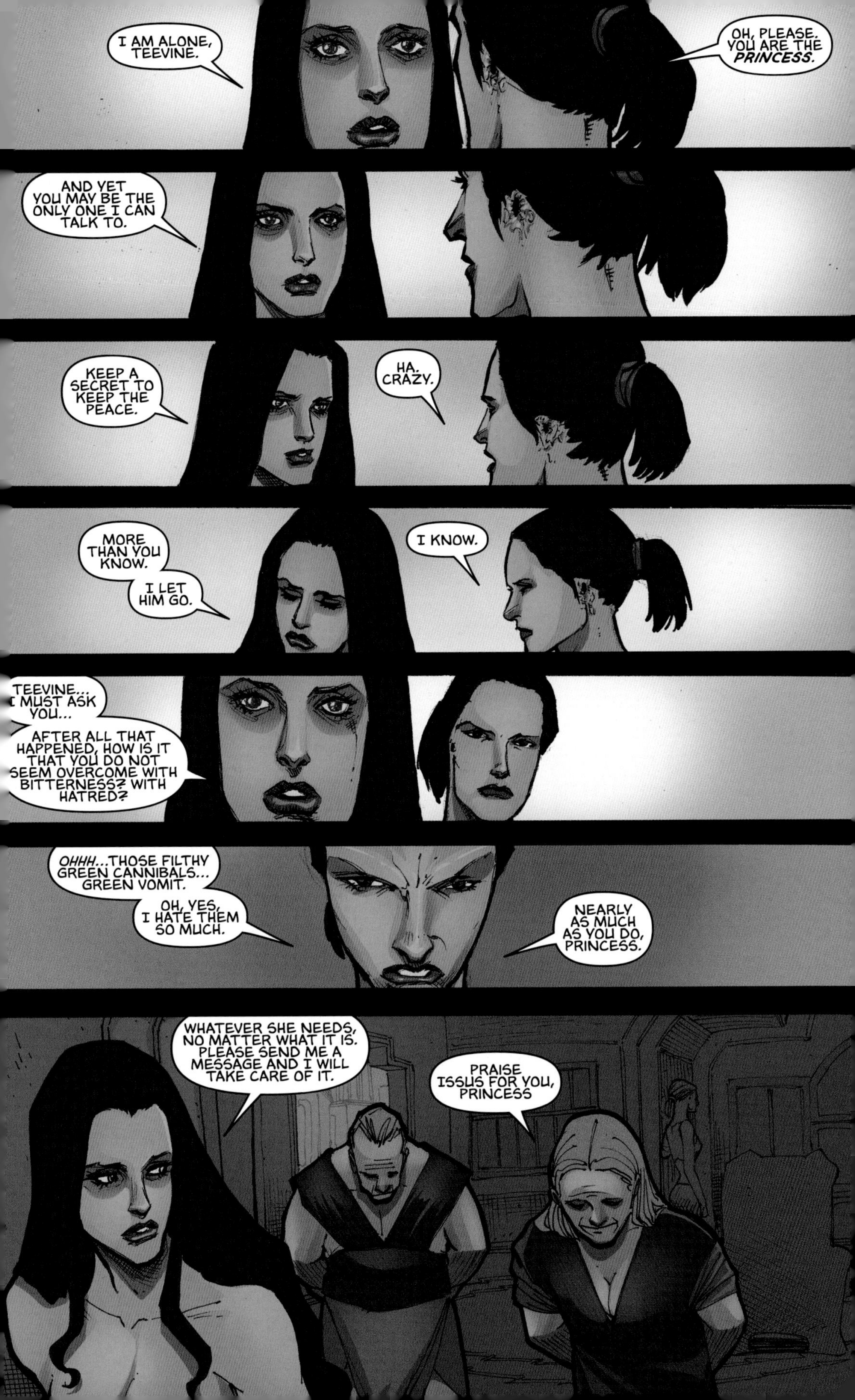

I AM ALONE, TEEVINE.
OH, PLEASE. YOU ARE THE *PRINCESS.*
AND YET YOU MAY BE THE ONLY ONE I CAN TALK TO.
KEEP A SECRET TO KEEP THE PEACE.
HA. CRAZY.
MORE THAN YOU KNOW.
I LET HIM GO.
I KNOW.
TEEVINE... I MUST ASK YOU...
AFTER ALL THAT HAPPENED, HOW IS IT THAT YOU DO NOT SEEM OVERCOME WITH BITTERNESS? WITH HATRED?
OHHH...THOSE FILTHY GREEN CANNIBALS... GREEN VOMIT.
OH, YES, I HATE THEM SO MUCH.
NEARLY AS MUCH AS YOU DO, PRINCESS.
WHATEVER SHE NEEDS, NO MATTER WHAT IT IS. PLEASE SEND ME A MESSAGE AND I WILL TAKE CARE OF IT.
PRAISE ISSUS FOR YOU, PRINCESS

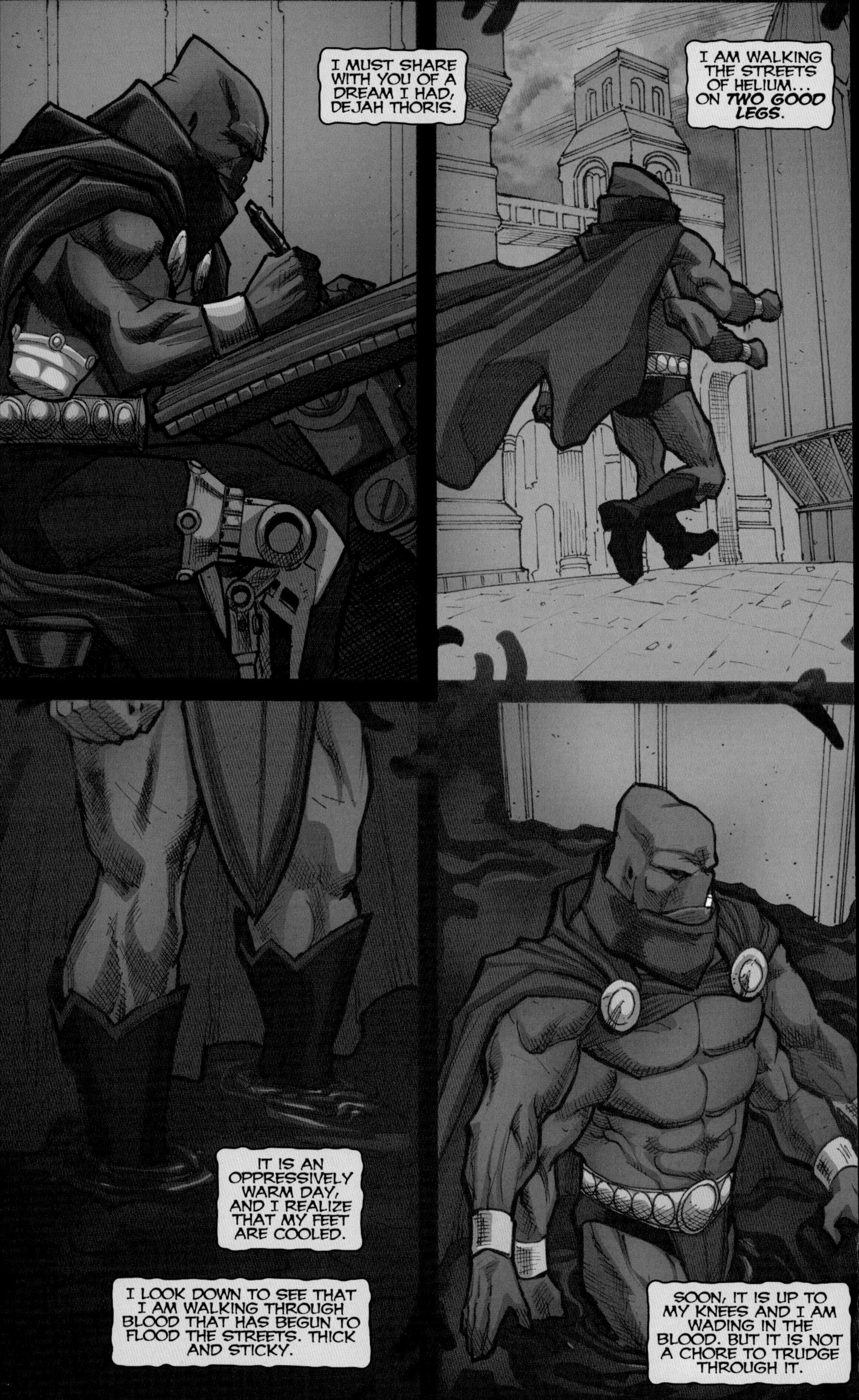
I MUST SHARE WITH YOU OF A DREAM I HAD, DEJAH THORIS.
I AM WALKING THE STREETS OF HELIUM... ON TWO GOOD LEGS.
IT IS AN OPPRESSIVELY WARM DAY, AND I REALIZE THAT MY FEET ARE COOLED.
I LOOK DOWN TO SEE THAT I AM WALKING THROUGH BLOOD THAT HAS BEGUN TO FLOOD THE STREETS. THICK AND STICKY.
SOON, IT IS UP TO MY KNEES AND I AM WADING IN THE BLOOD. BUT IT IS NOT A CHORE TO TRUDGE THROUGH IT.

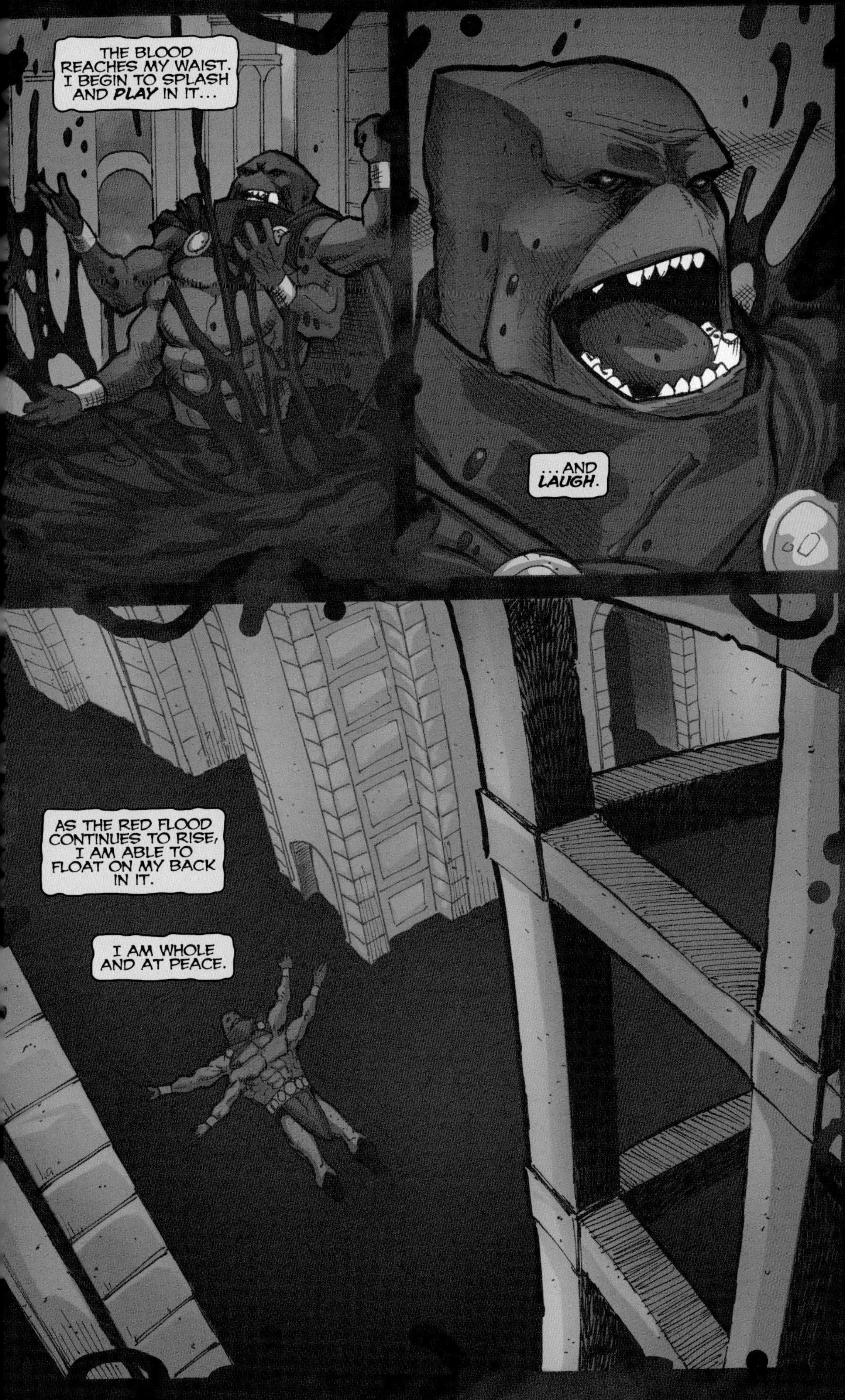
THE BLOOD REACHES MY WAIST. I BEGIN TO SPLASH AND PLAY IN IT...
...AND LAUGH.
AS THE RED FLOOD CONTINUES TO RISE, I AM ABLE TO FLOAT ON MY BACK IN IT.
I AM WHOLE AND AT PEACE.

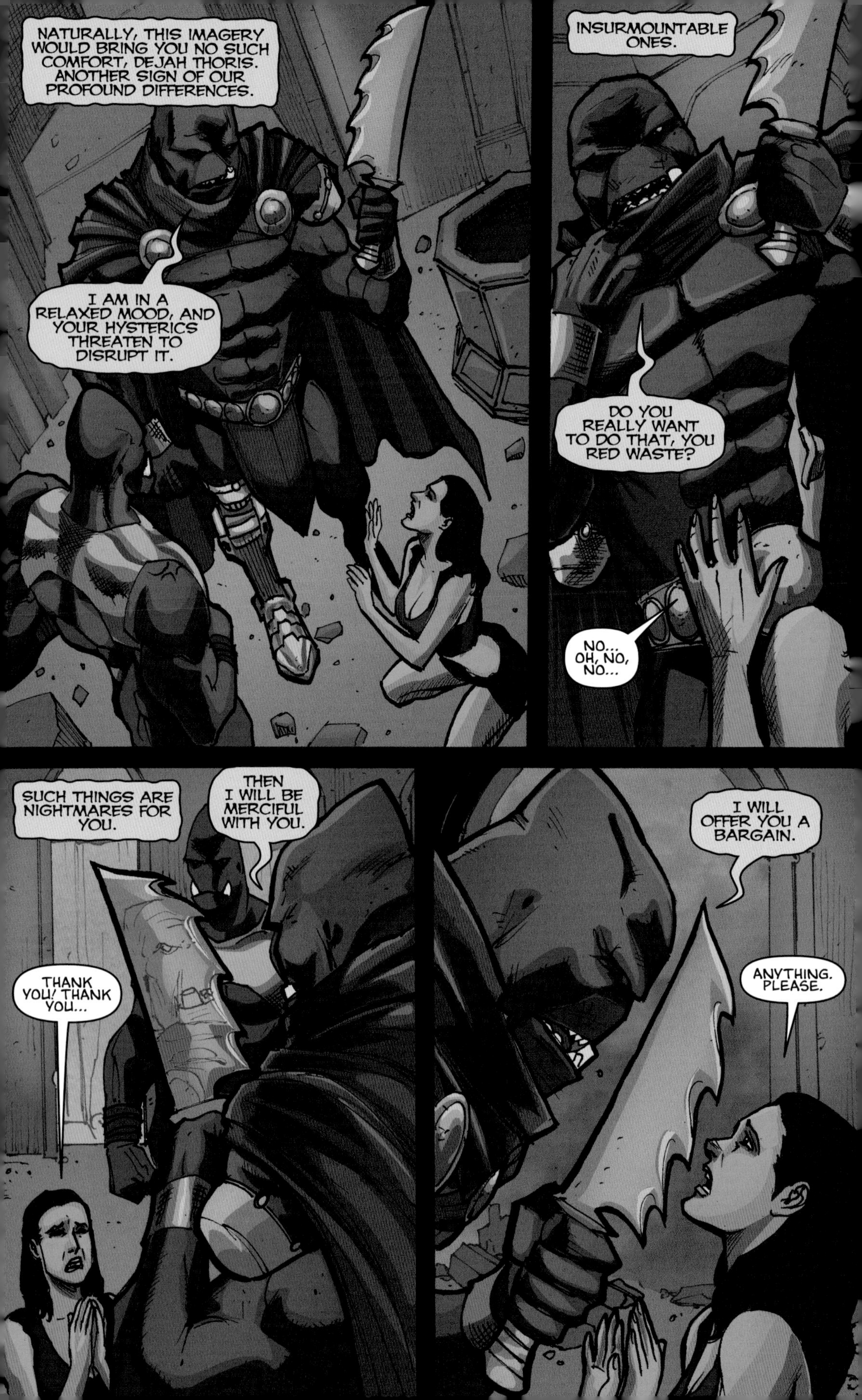
NATURALLY, THIS IMAGERY WOULD BRING YOU NO SUCH COMFORT, DEJAH THORIS. ANOTHER SIGN OF OUR PROFOUND DIFFERENCES.
I AM IN A RELAXED MOOD, AND YOUR HYSTERICS THREATEN TO DISRUPT IT.
INSURMOUNTABLE ONES.
DO YOU REALLY WANT TO DO THAT, YOU RED WASTE?
NO... OH, NO, NO...
SUCH THINGS ARE NIGHTMARES FOR YOU.
THEN I WILL BE MERCIFUL WITH YOU.
THANK YOU! THANK YOU...
I WILL OFFER YOU A BARGAIN.
ANYTHING. PLEASE.

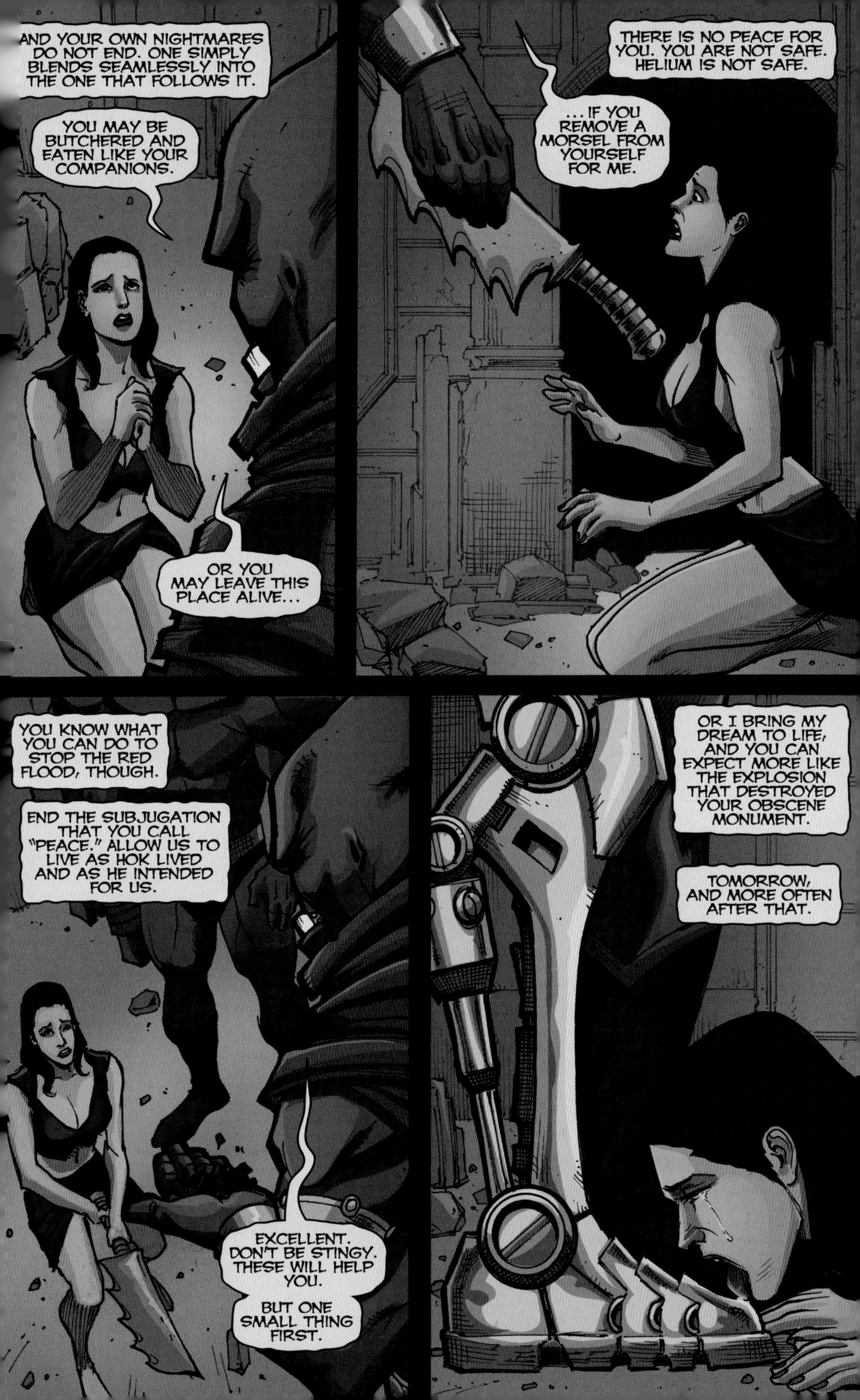
AND YOUR OWN NIGHTMARES DO NOT END. ONE SIMPLY BLENDS SEAMLESSLY INTO THE ONE THAT FOLLOWS IT.
YOU MAY BE BUTCHERED AND EATEN LIKE YOUR COMPANIONS.
OR YOU MAY LEAVE THIS PLACE ALIVE...
...IF YOU REMOVE A MORSEL FROM YOURSELF FOR ME.
THERE IS NO PEACE FOR YOU. YOU ARE NOT SAFE. HELIUM IS NOT SAFE.
YOU KNOW WHAT YOU CAN DO TO STOP THE RED FLOOD, THOUGH.
END THE SUBJUGATION THAT YOU CALL "PEACE." ALLOW US TO LIVE AS HOK LIVED AND AS HE INTENDED FOR US.
EXCELLENT. DON'T BE STINGY. THESE WILL HELP YOU.
BUT ONE SMALL THING FIRST.
OR I BRING MY DREAM TO LIFE, AND YOU CAN EXPECT MORE LIKE THE EXPLOSION THAT DESTROYED YOUR OBSCENE MONUMENT.
TOMORROW, AND MORE OFTEN AFTER THAT.

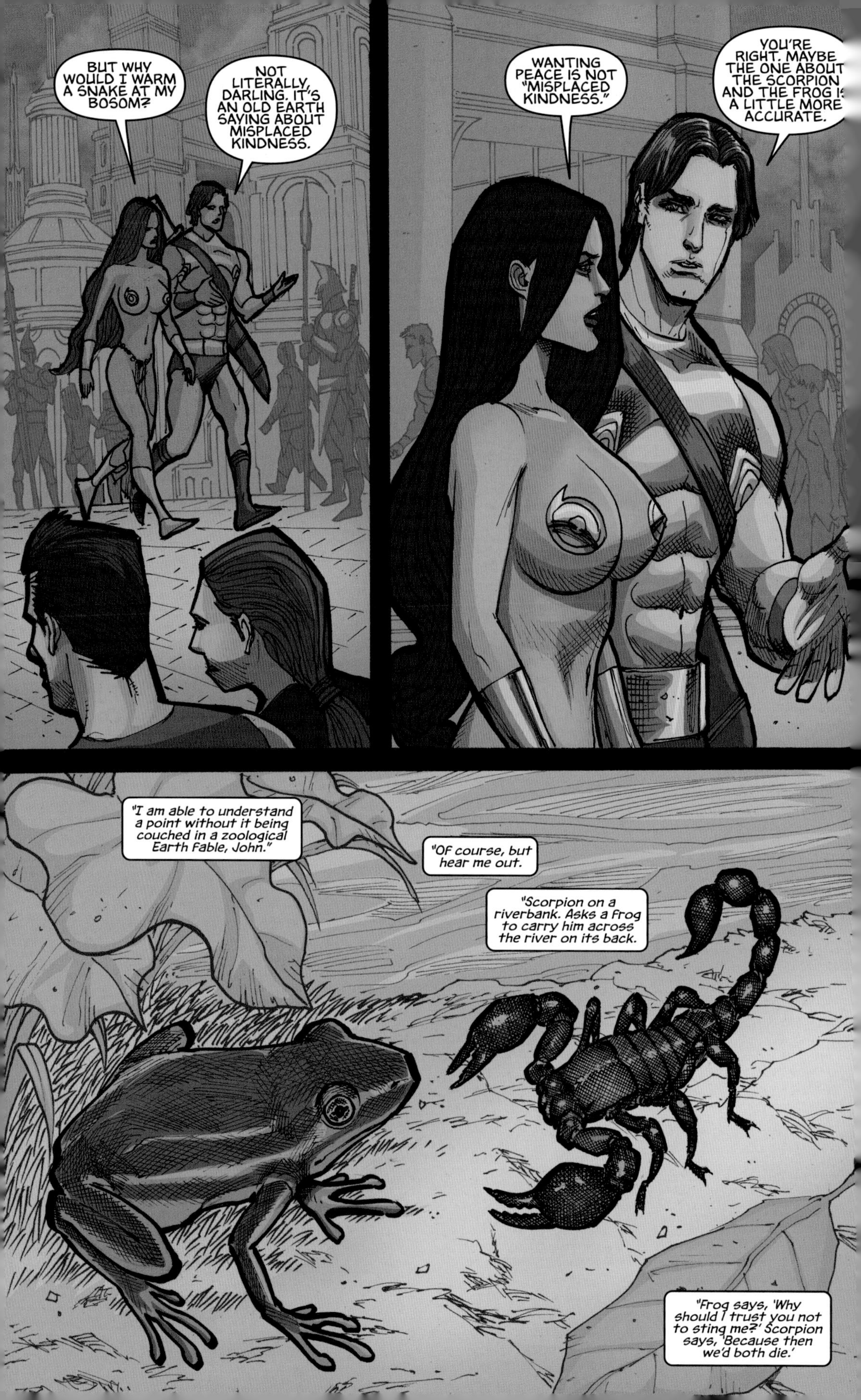
BUT WHY WOULD I WARM A SNAKE AT MY BOSOM?
NOT LITERALLY, DARLING. IT'S AN OLD EARTH SAYING ABOUT MISPLACED KINDNESS.
WANTING PEACE IS NOT "MISPLACED KINDNESS."
YOU'RE RIGHT. MAYBE THE ONE ABOUT THE SCORPION AND THE FROG IS A LITTLE MORE ACCURATE.
"I am able to understand a point without it being couched in a zoological Earth Fable, John."
"Of course, but hear me out.
"Scorpion on a riverbank. Asks a frog to carry him across the river on its back.
"Frog says, 'Why should I trust you not to sting me?' Scorpion says, 'Because then we'd both die.'

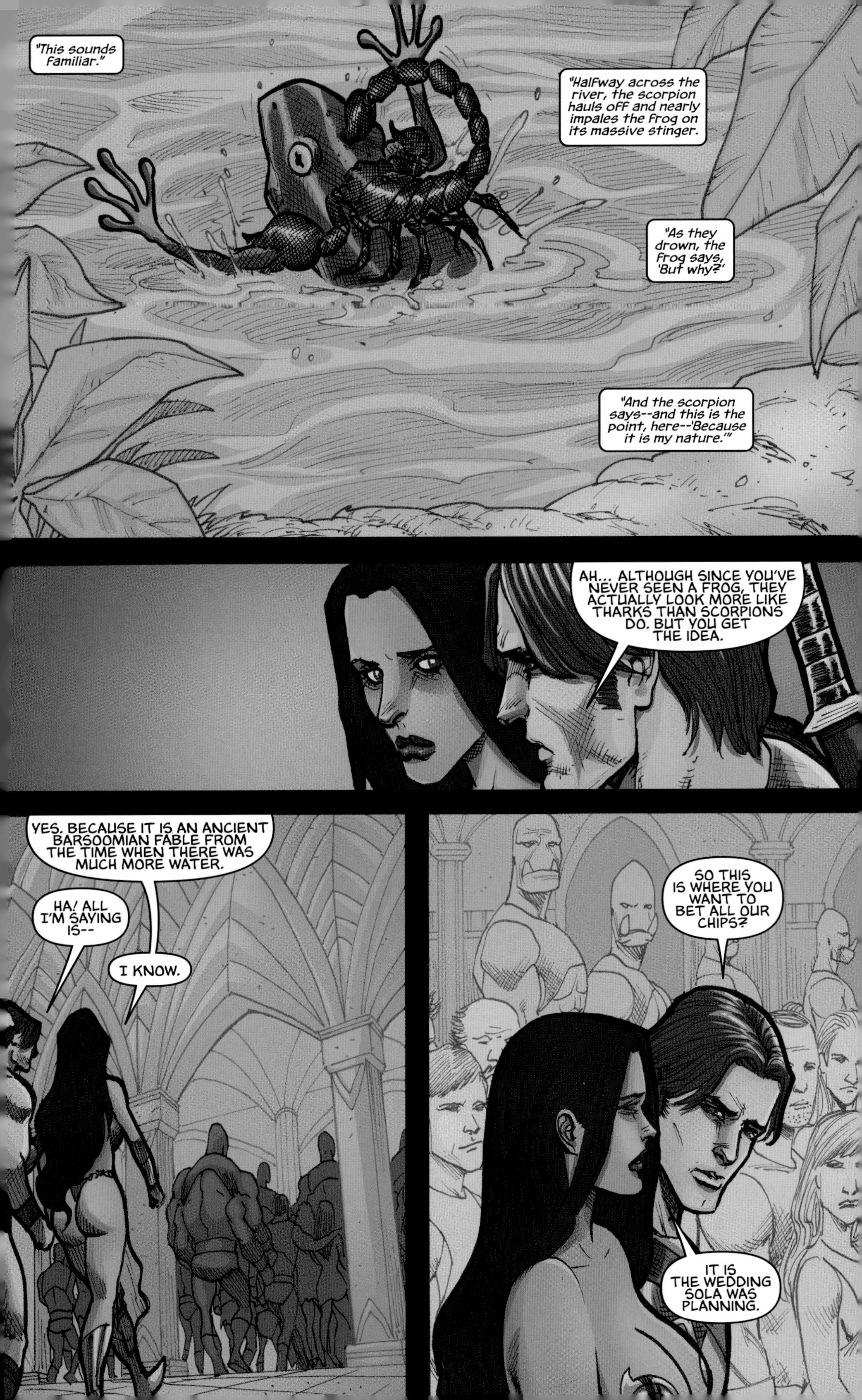
"This sounds familiar."
"Halfway across the river, the scorpion hauls off and nearly impales the frog on its massive stinger.
"As they drown, the frog says, 'But why?'
"And the scorpion says--and this is the point, here--'Because it is my nature.'"
AH... ALTHOUGH SINCE YOU'VE NEVER SEEN A FROG, THEY ACTUALLY LOOK MORE LIKE THARKS THAN SCORPIONS DO. BUT YOU GET THE IDEA.
YES. BECAUSE IT IS AN ANCIENT BARSOOMIAN FABLE FROM THE TIME WHEN THERE WAS MUCH MORE WATER.
HA! ALL I'M SAYING IS--
I KNOW.
SO THIS IS WHERE YOU WANT TO BET ALL OUR CHIPS?
IT IS THE WEDDING SOLA WAS PLANNING.

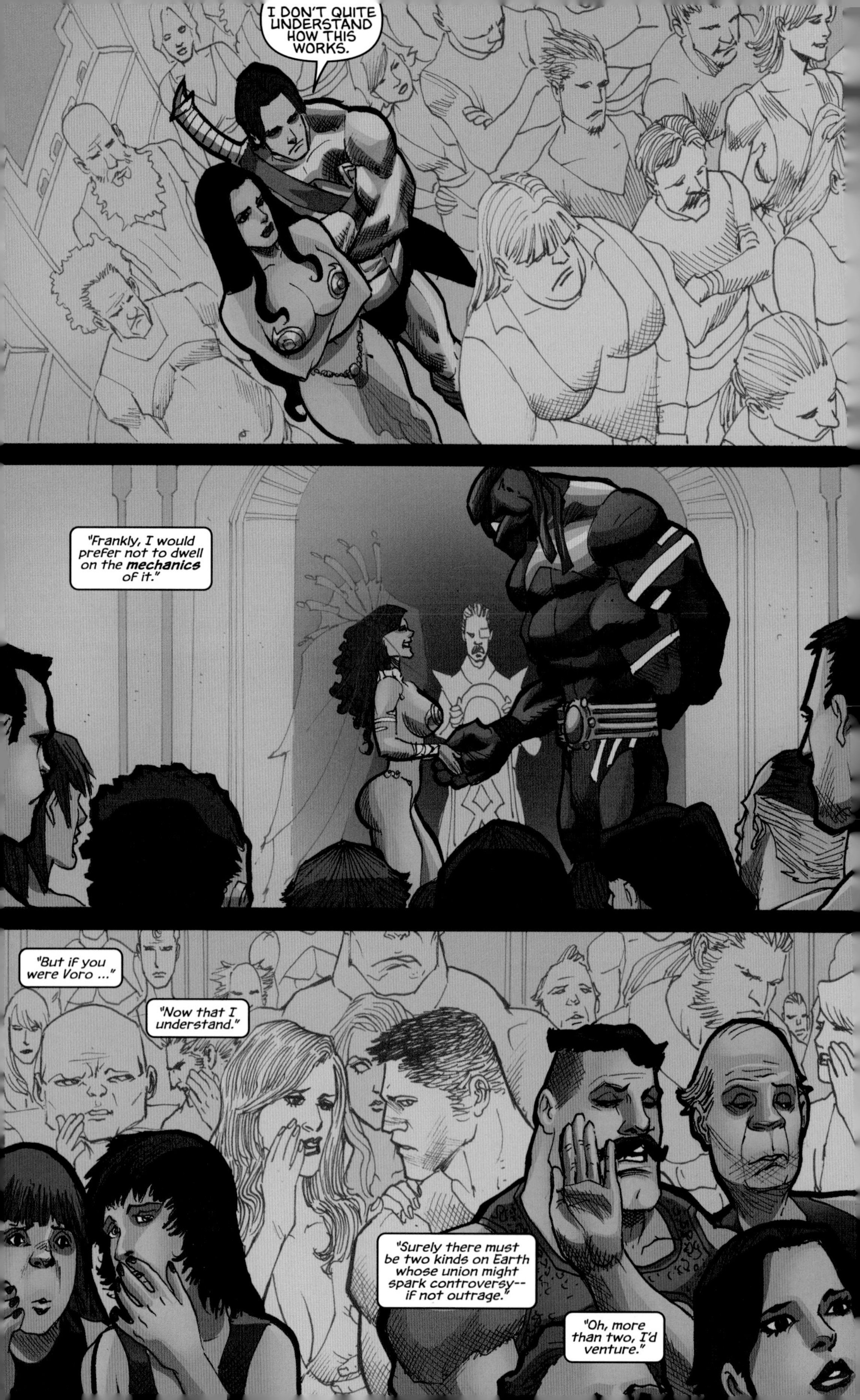
I DON'T QUITE UNDERSTAND HOW THIS WORKS.
"Frankly, I would prefer not to dwell on the **mechanics** of it."
"But if you were Voro ..."
"Now that I understand."
"Surely there must be two kinds on Earth whose union might spark controversy-- if not outrage."
"Oh, more than two, I'd venture."

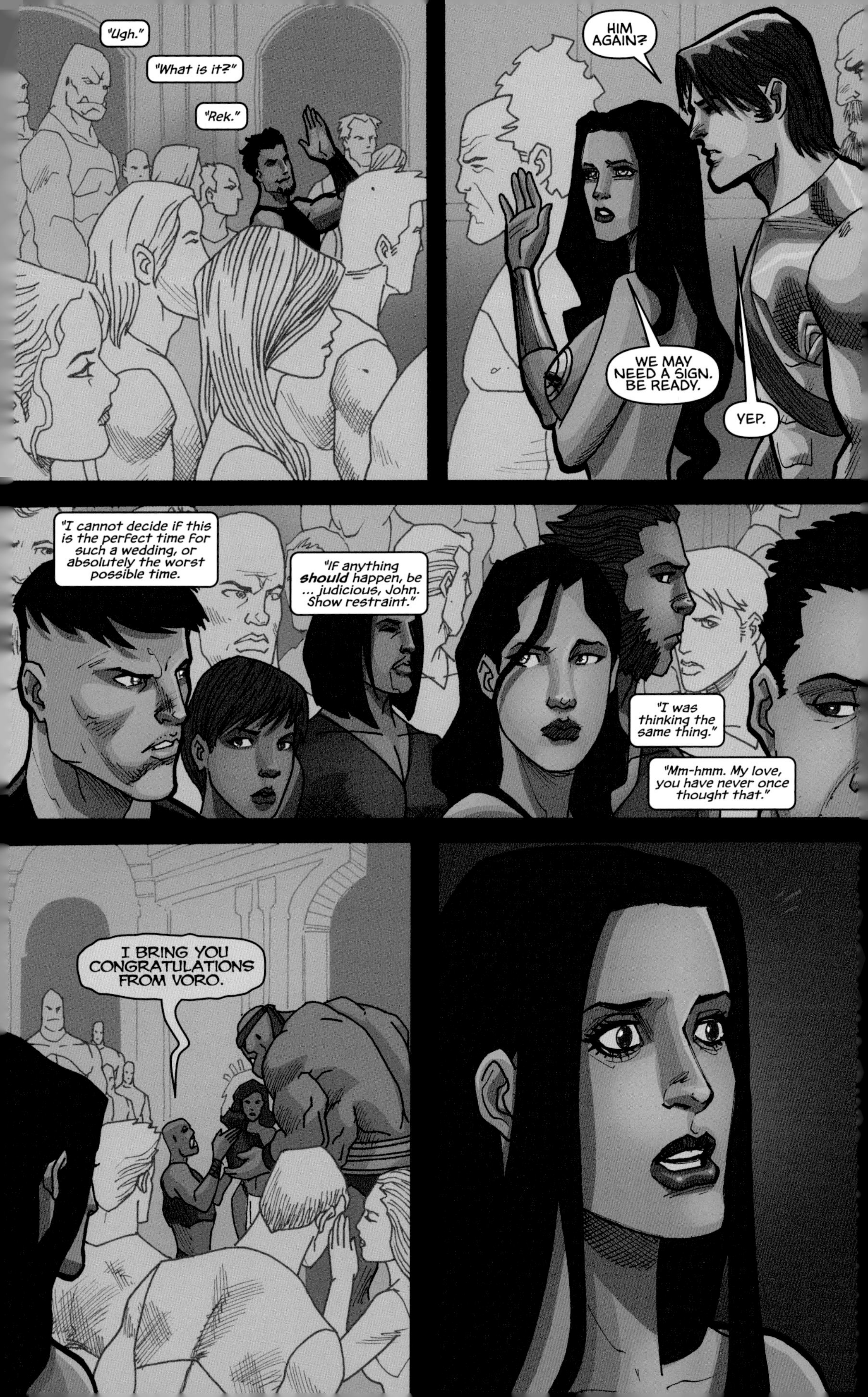
"Ugh."
"What is it?"
"Rek."
HIM AGAIN?
WE MAY NEED A SIGN. BE READY.
YEP.
"I cannot decide if this is the perfect time for such a wedding, or absolutely the worst possible time.
"If anything **should** happen, be ... judicious, John. Show restraint."
"I was thinking the same thing."
"Mm-hmm. My love, you have never once thought that."
I BRING YOU CONGRATULATIONS FROM VORO.

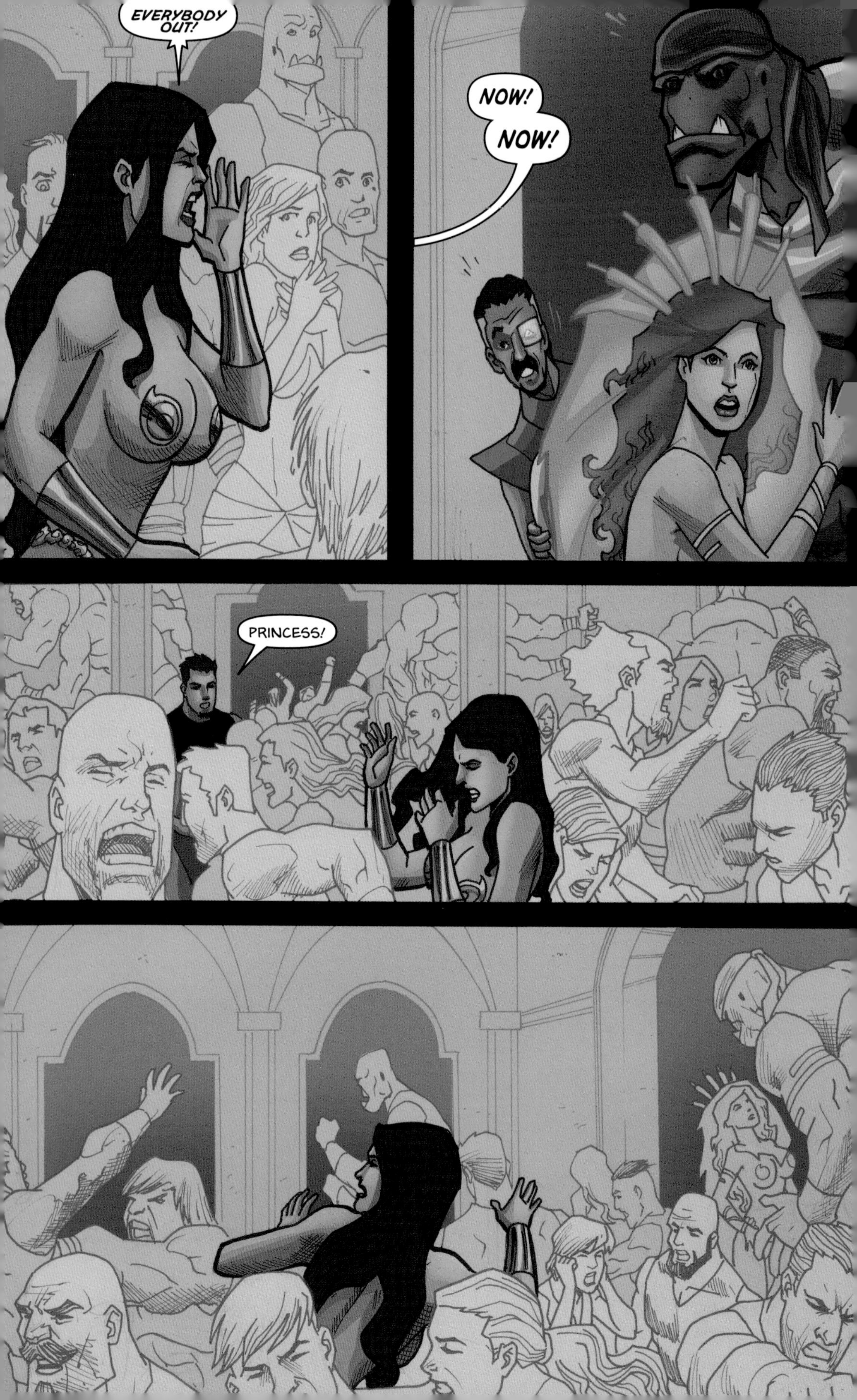
EVERYBODY OUT!
NOW!
NOW!
PRINCESS!

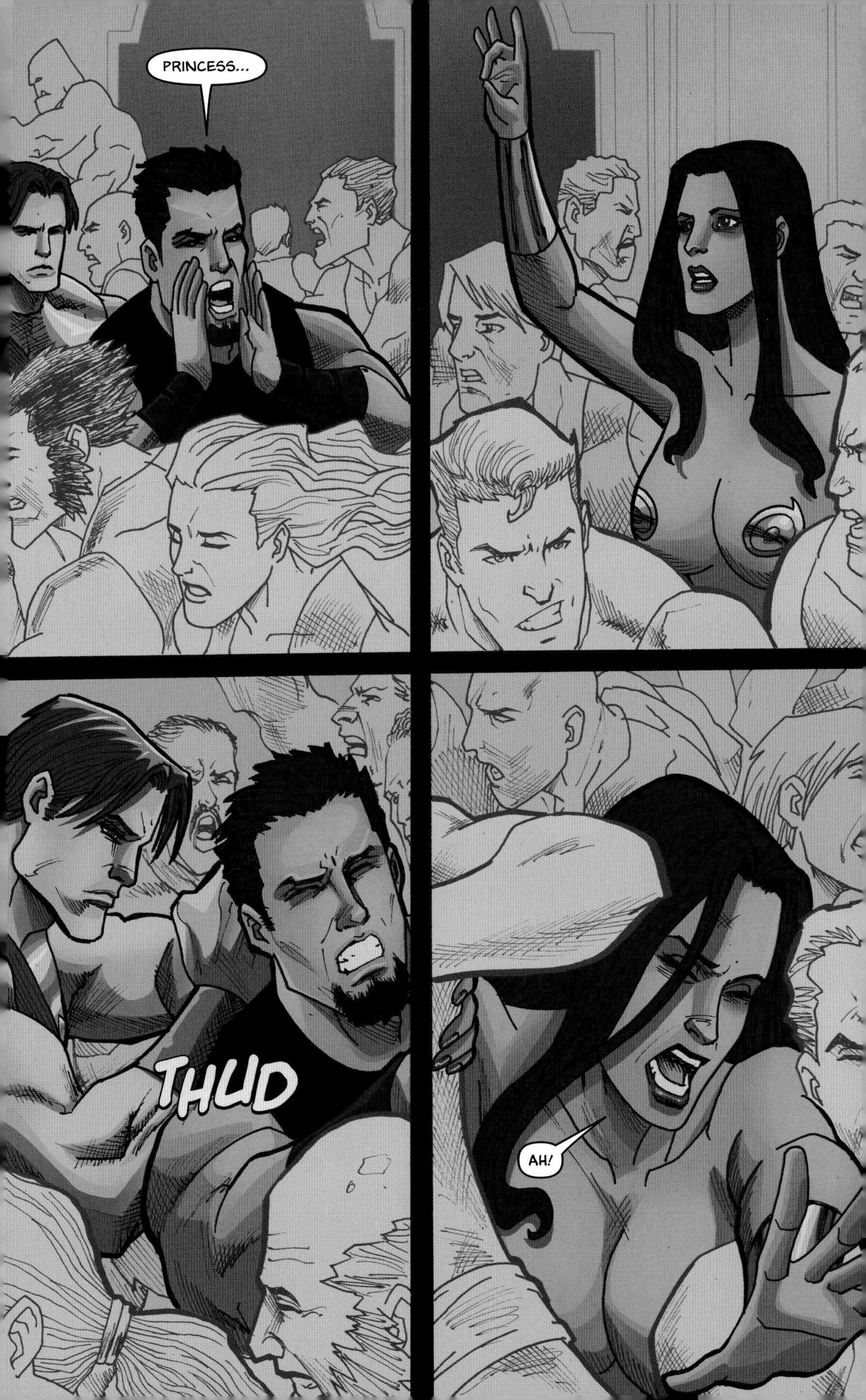
PRINCESS...
THUD
AH!

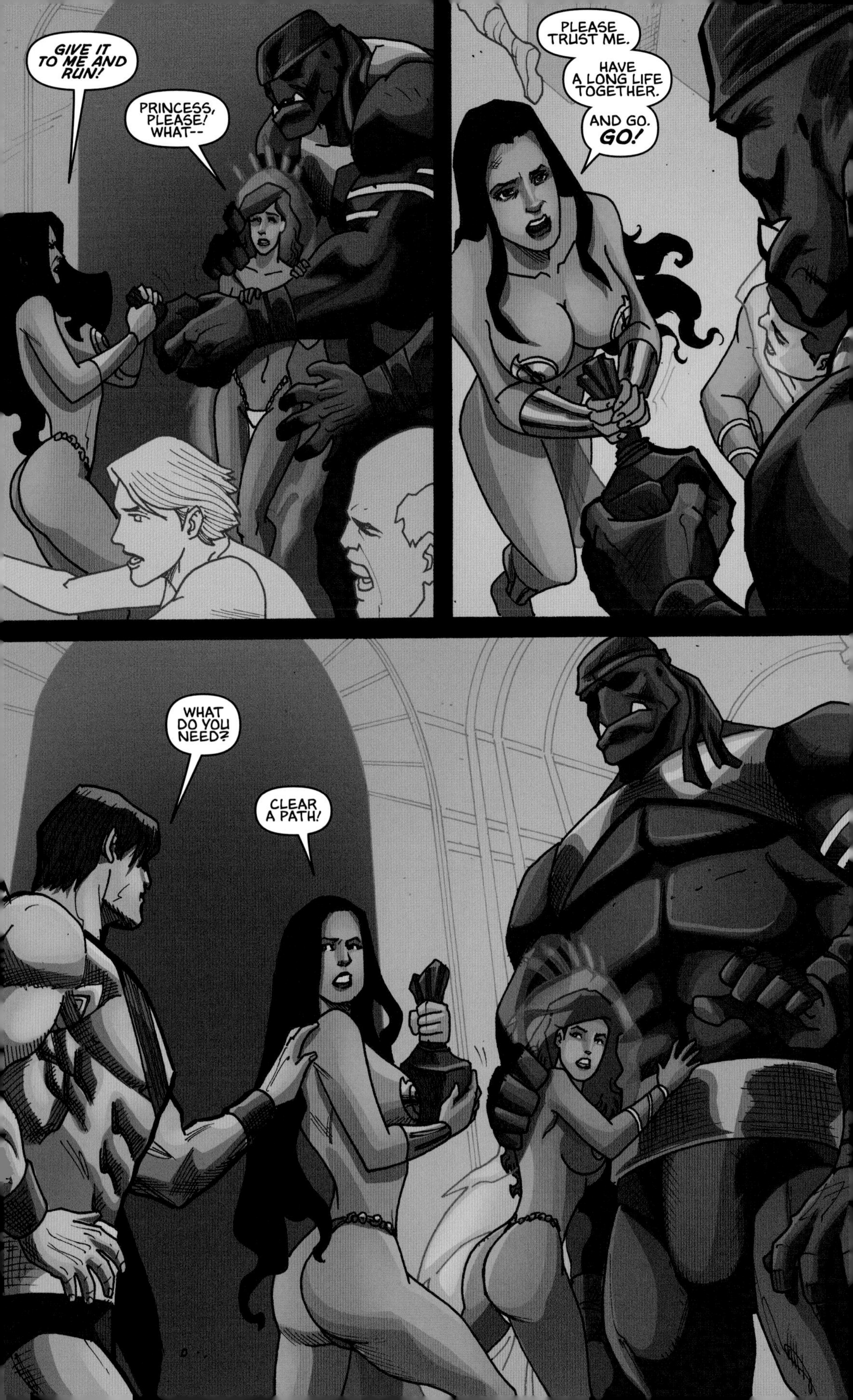
GIVE IT TO ME AND RUN!
PRINCESS, PLEASE! WHAT--
PLEASE TRUST ME.
HAVE A LONG LIFE TOGETHER.
AND GO. GO!
WHAT DO YOU NEED?
CLEAR A PATH!

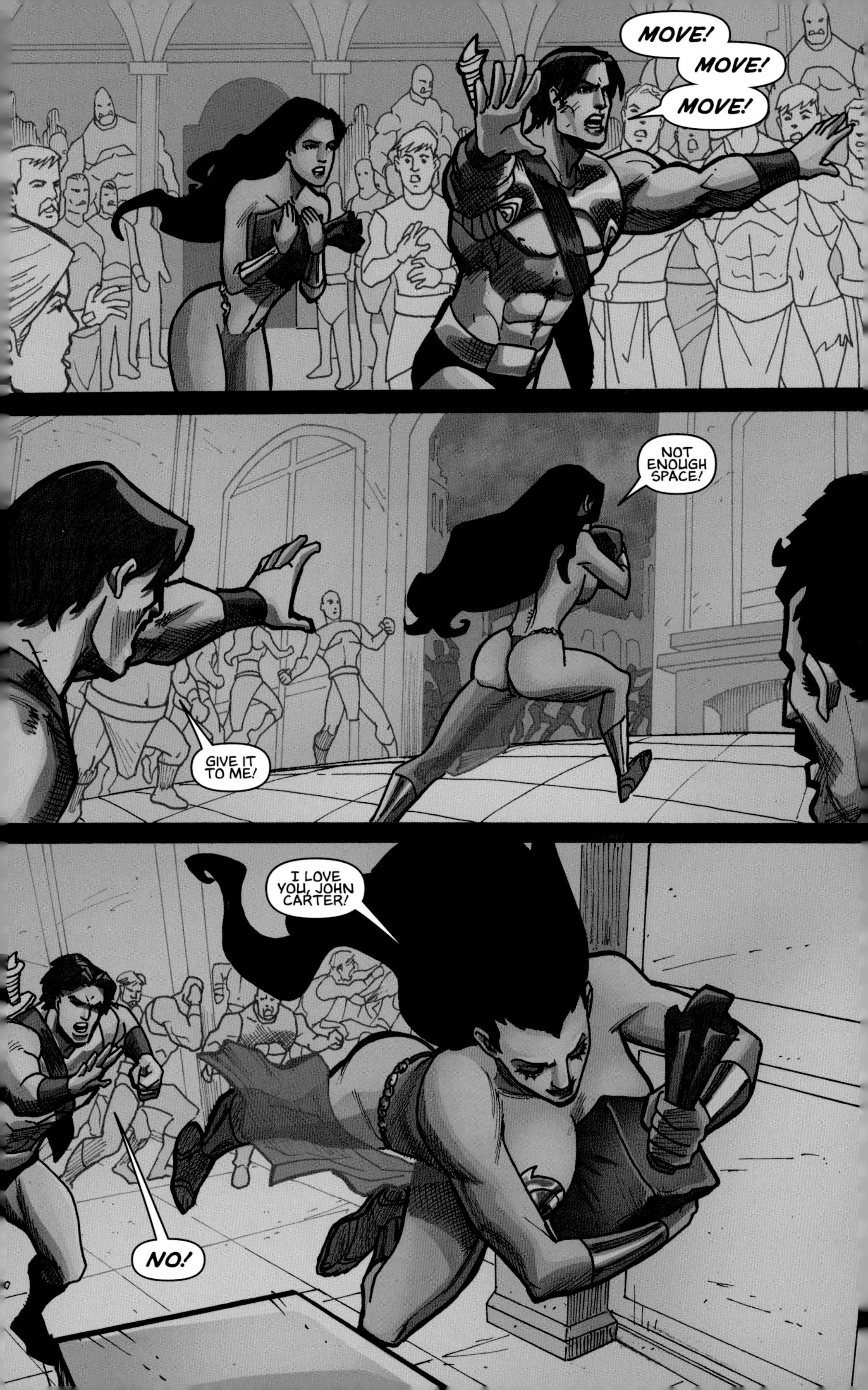
MOVE!
MOVE!
MOVE!
NOT ENOUGH SPACE!
GIVE IT TO ME!
I LOVE YOU, JOHN CARTER!
NO!

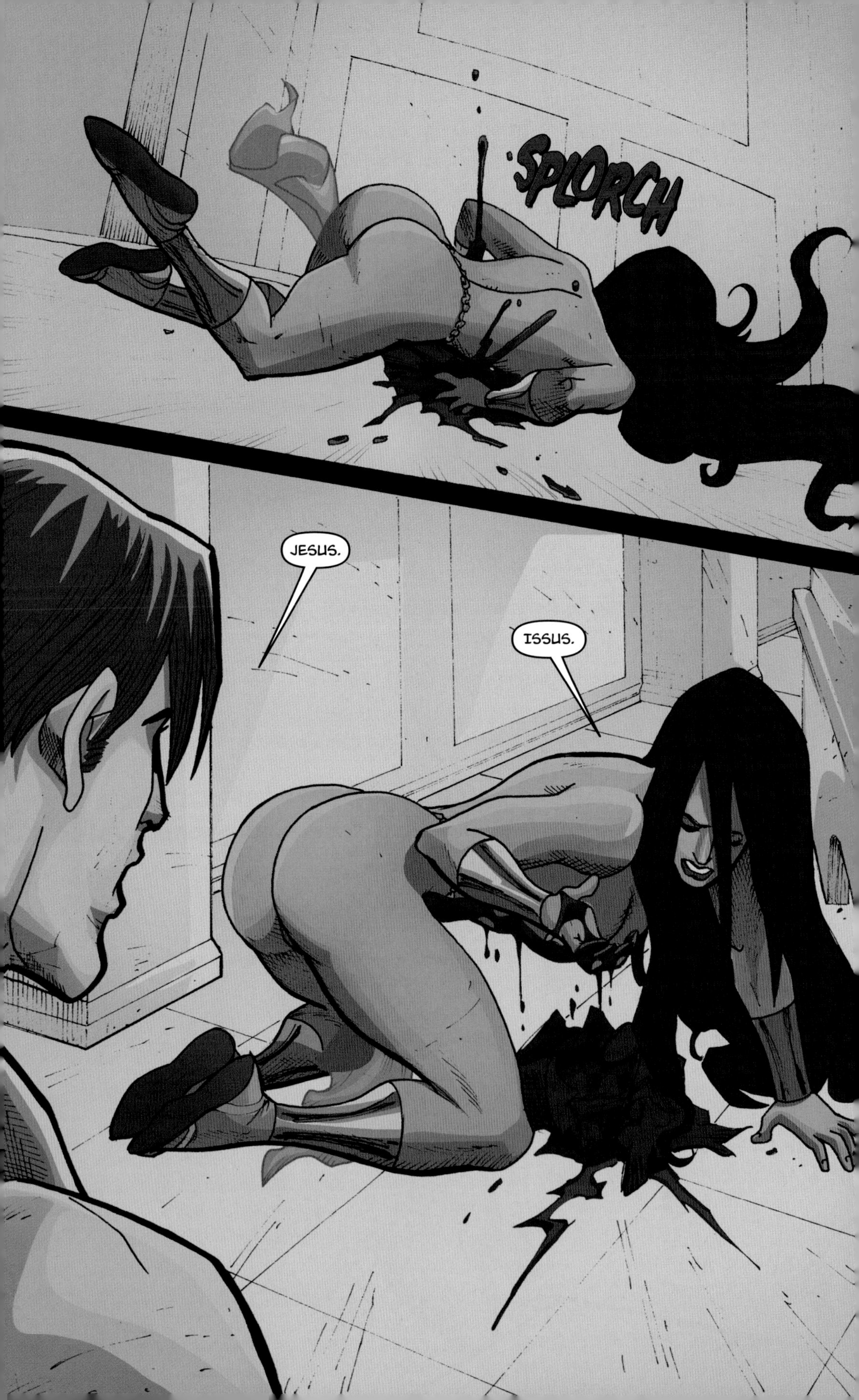
SPLORCH
JESUS.
ISSUS.

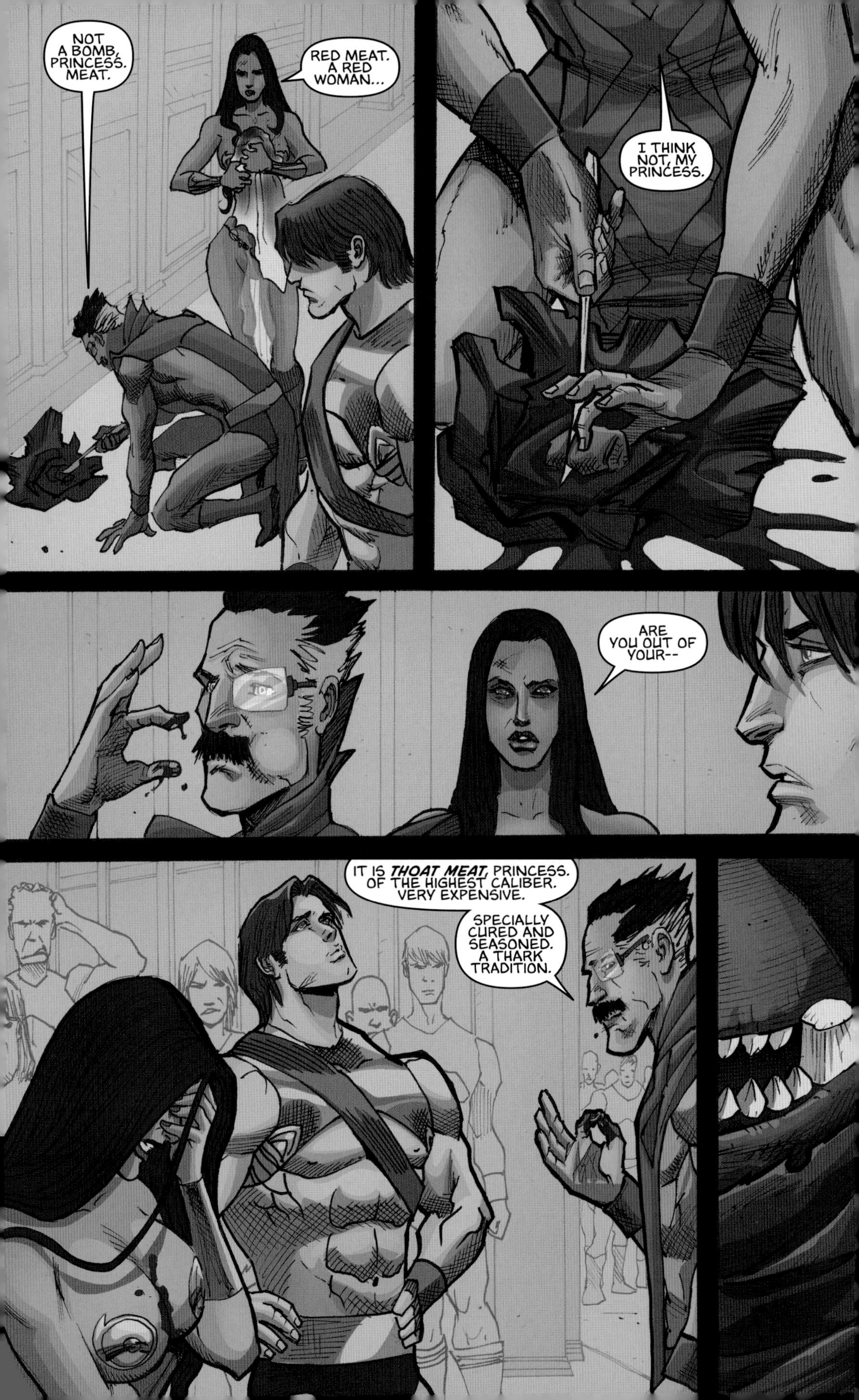
NOT A BOMB, PRINCESS. MEAT.
RED MEAT. A RED WOMAN...
I THINK NOT, MY PRINCESS.
ARE YOU OUT OF YOUR--
IT IS THOAT MEAT, PRINCESS. OF THE HIGHEST CALIBER. VERY EXPENSIVE.
SPECIALLY CURED AND SEASONED. A THARK TRADITION.

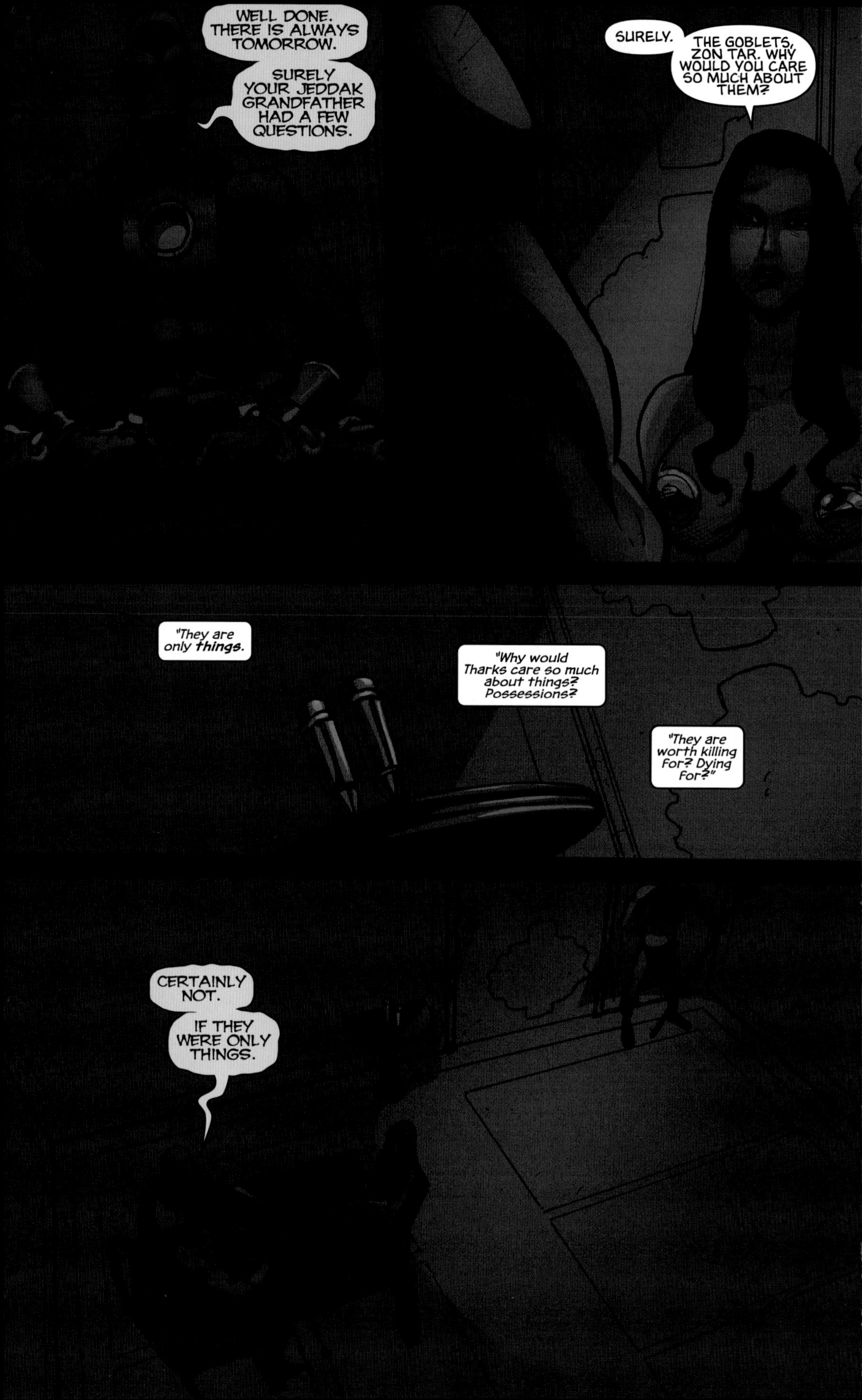

WELL DONE. THERE IS ALWAYS TOMORROW.
SURELY YOUR JEDDAK GRANDFATHER HAD A FEW QUESTIONS.
SURELY.
THE GOBLETS, ZON TAR. WHY WOULD YOU CARE SO MUCH ABOUT THEM?
"They are only *things*.
"Why would Tharks care so much about things? Possessions?
"They are worth killing For? Dying For?"
CERTAINLY NOT.
IF THEY WERE ONLY THINGS.

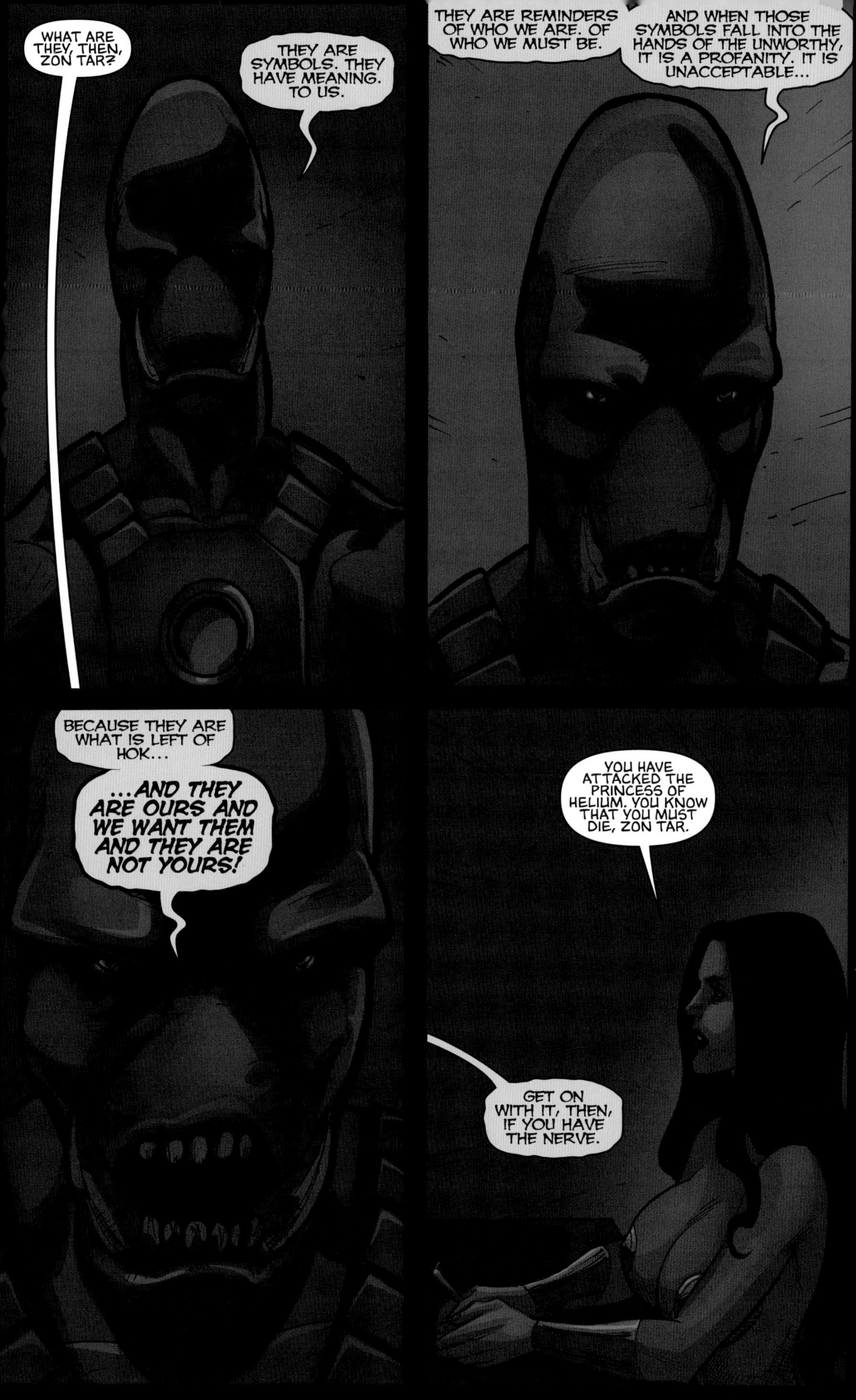
WHAT ARE THEY, THEN, ZON TAR?
THEY ARE SYMBOLS. THEY HAVE MEANING. TO US.
THEY ARE REMINDERS OF WHO WE ARE. OF WHO WE MUST BE.
AND WHEN THOSE SYMBOLS FALL INTO THE HANDS OF THE UNWORTHY, IT IS A PROFANITY. IT IS UNACCEPTABLE...
BECAUSE THEY ARE WHAT IS LEFT OF HOK...
...AND THEY ARE OURS AND WE WANT THEM AND THEY ARE NOT YOURS!
YOU HAVE ATTACKED THE PRINCESS OF HELIUM. YOU KNOW THAT YOU MUST DIE, ZON TAR.
GET ON WITH IT, THEN, IF YOU HAVE THE NERVE.

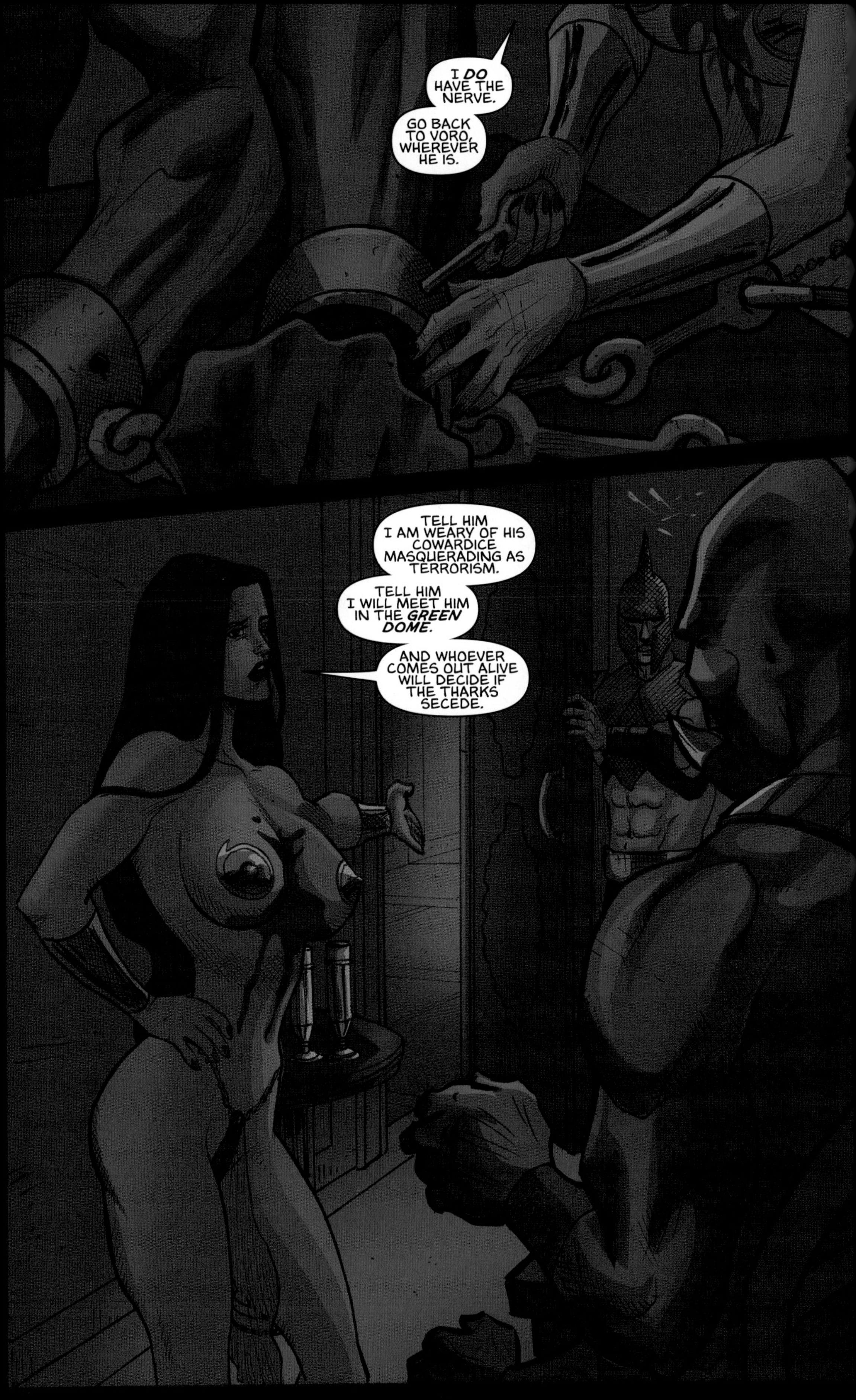
I DO HAVE THE NERVE.
GO BACK TO VORO, WHEREVER HE IS.
TELL HIM I AM WEARY OF HIS COWARDICE MASQUERADING AS TERRORISM.
TELL HIM I WILL MEET HIM IN THE GREEN DOME.
AND WHOEVER COMES OUT ALIVE WILL DECIDE IF THE THARKS SECEDE.

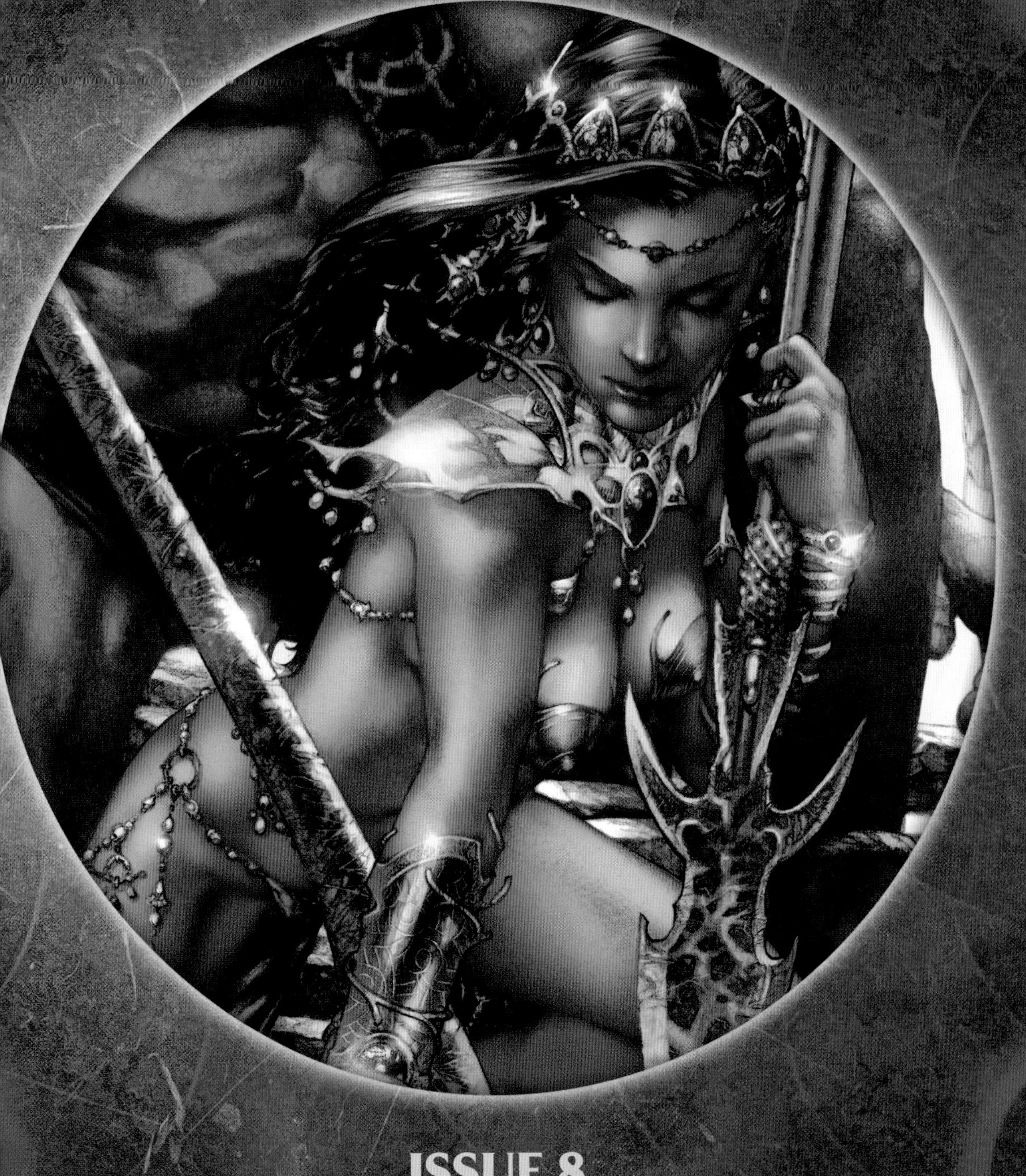

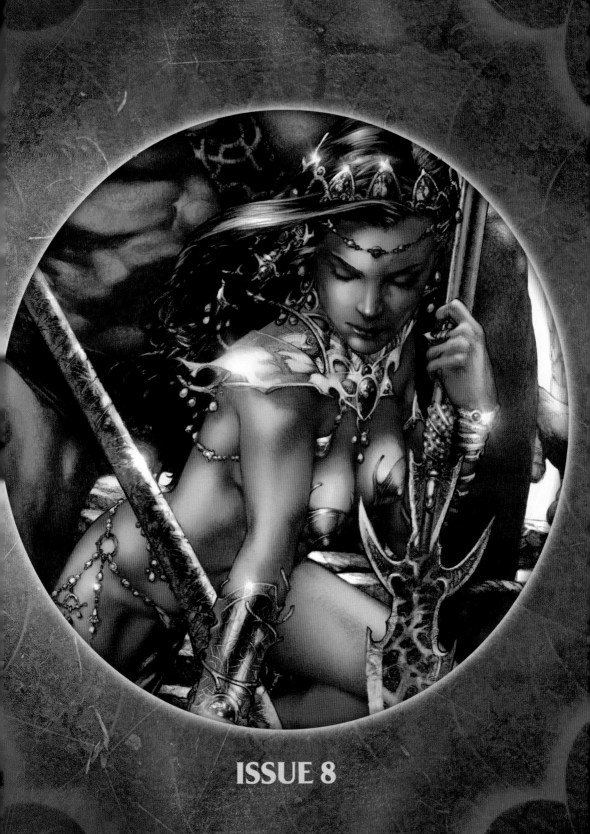

ISSUE 8

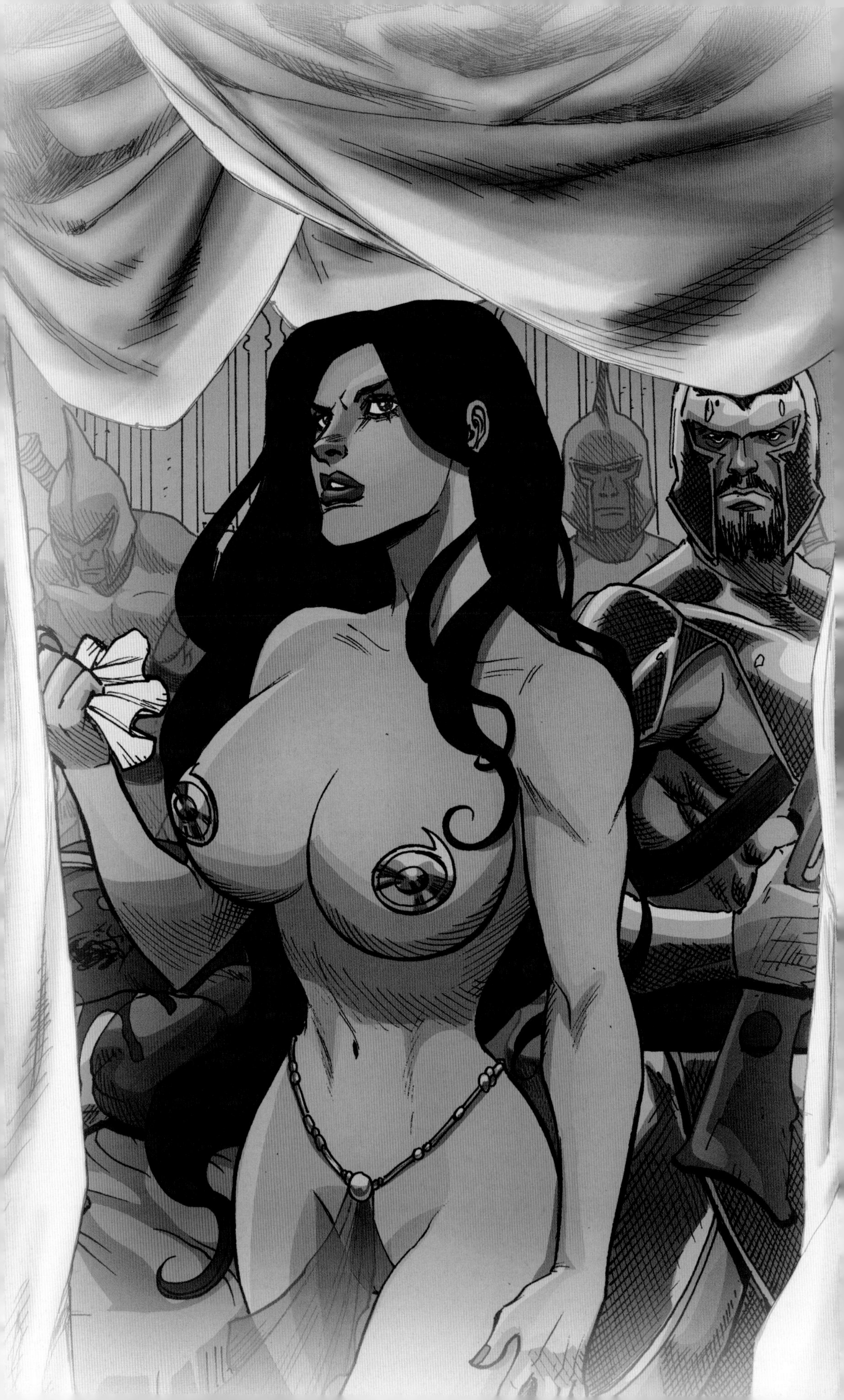

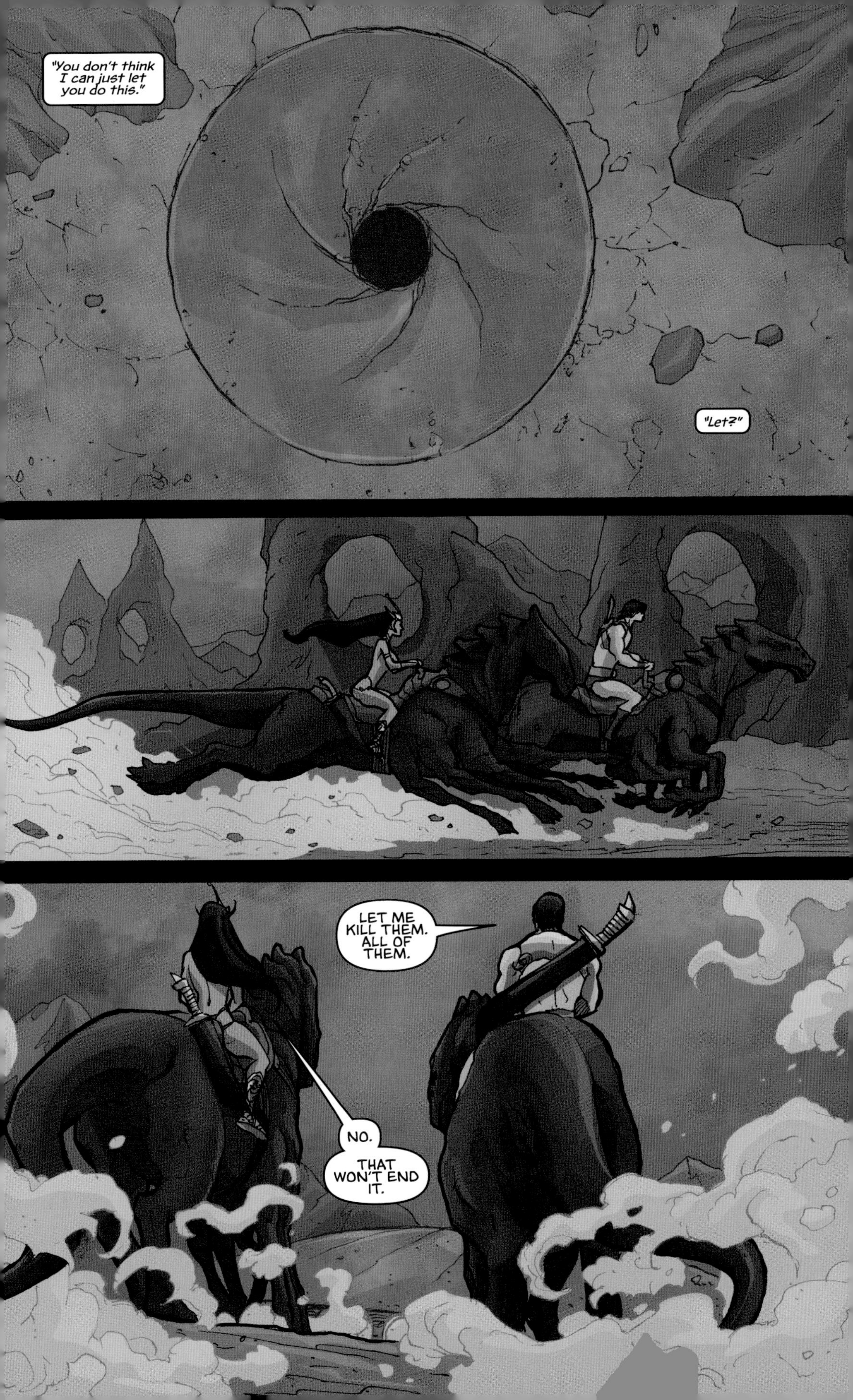
"You don't think I can just let you do this."
"Let?"
LET ME KILL THEM. ALL OF THEM.
NO.
THAT WON'T END IT.

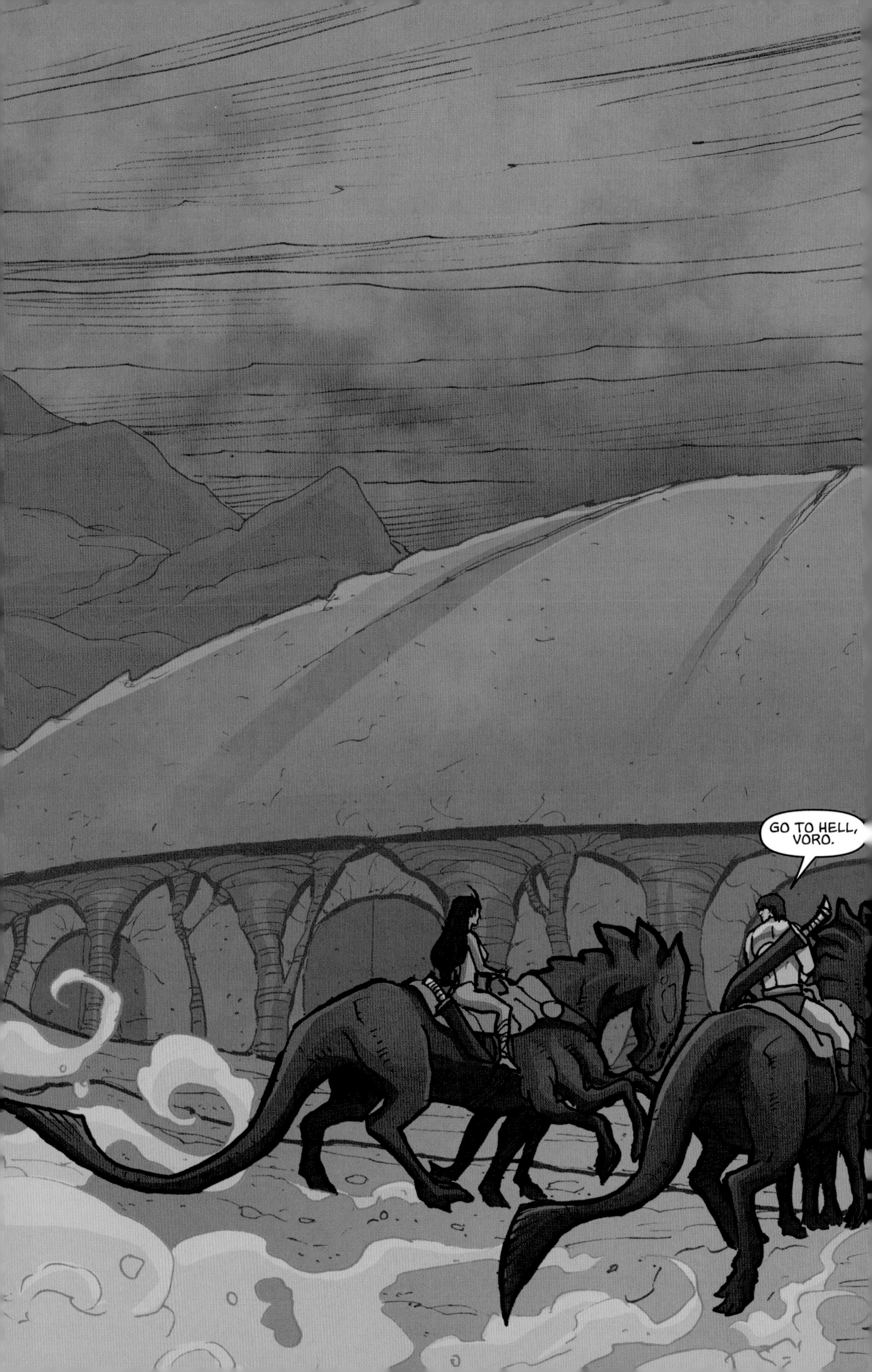
GO TO HELL, VORO.

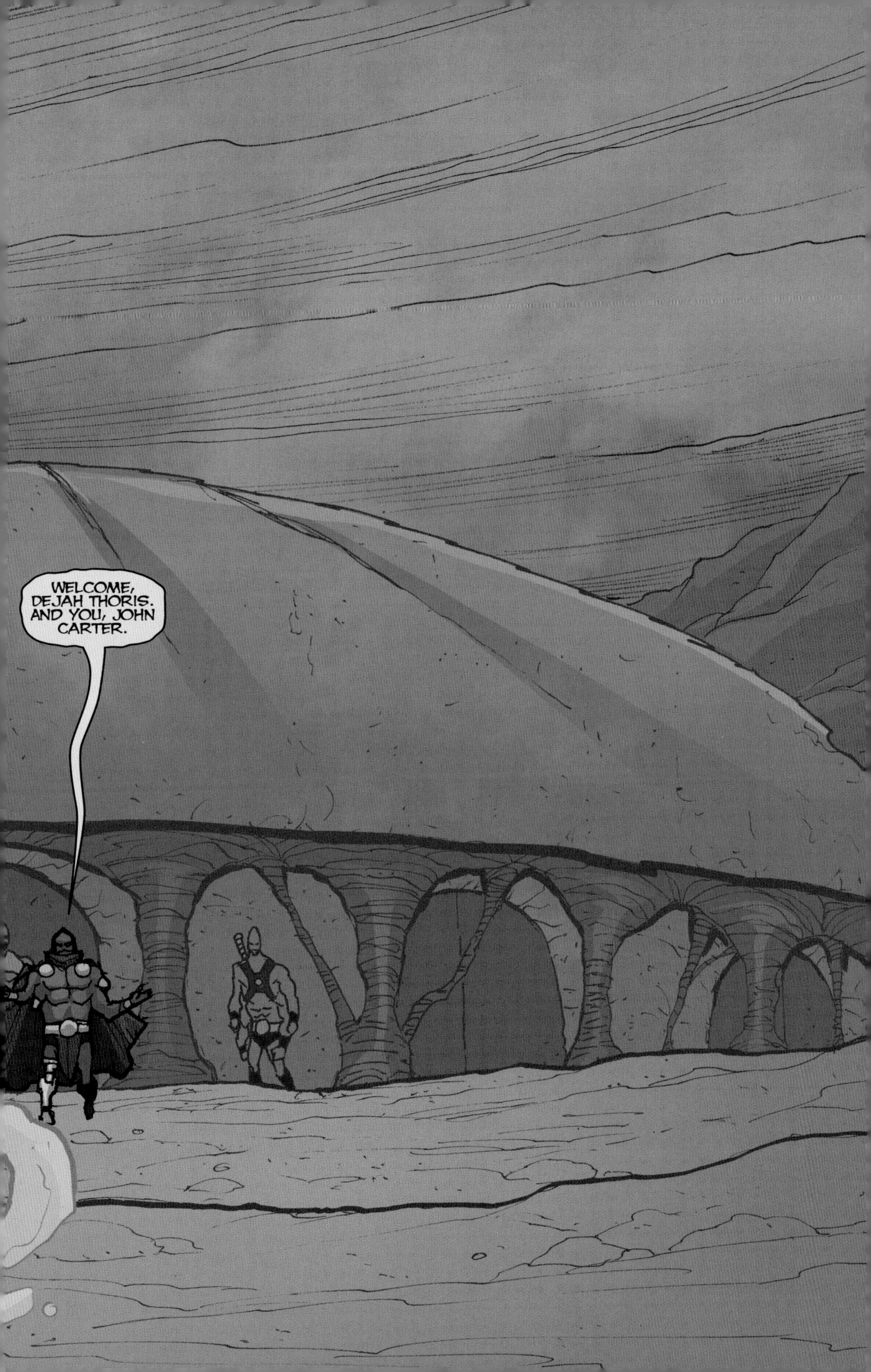
WELCOME, DEJAH THORIS. AND YOU, JOHN CARTER.

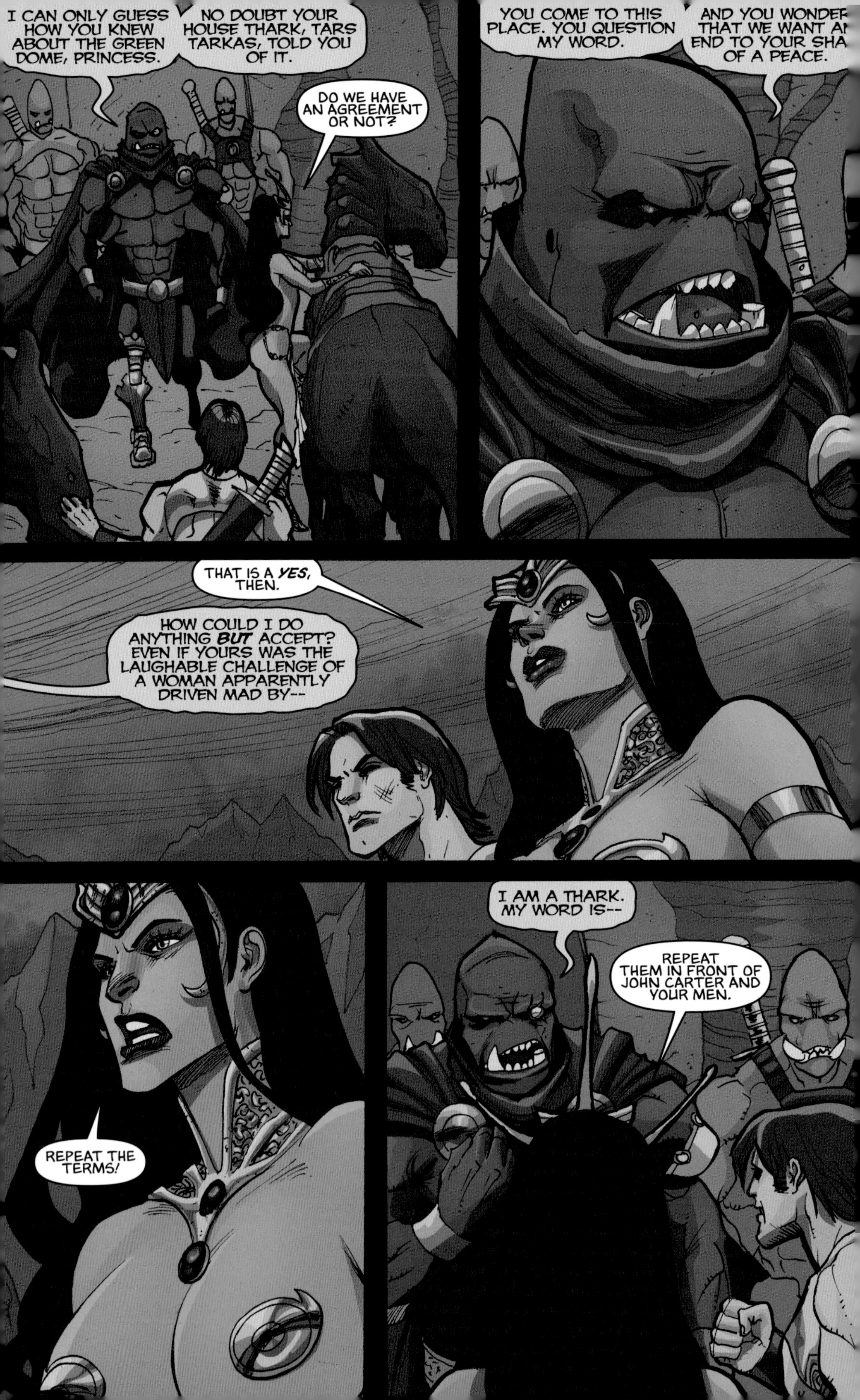
I CAN ONLY GUESS HOW YOU KNEW ABOUT THE GREEN DOME, PRINCESS.
NO DOUBT YOUR HOUSE THARK, TARS TARKAS, TOLD YOU OF IT.
DO WE HAVE AN AGREEMENT OR NOT?
YOU COME TO THIS PLACE. YOU QUESTION MY WORD.
AND YOU WONDER THAT WE WANT AN END TO YOUR SHAM OF A PEACE.
THAT IS A *YES*, THEN.
HOW COULD I DO ANYTHING *BUT* ACCEPT? EVEN IF YOURS WAS THE LAUGHABLE CHALLENGE OF A WOMAN APPARENTLY DRIVEN MAD BY--
REPEAT THE TERMS!
I AM A THARK. MY WORD IS--
REPEAT THEM IN FRONT OF JOHN CARTER AND YOUR MEN.

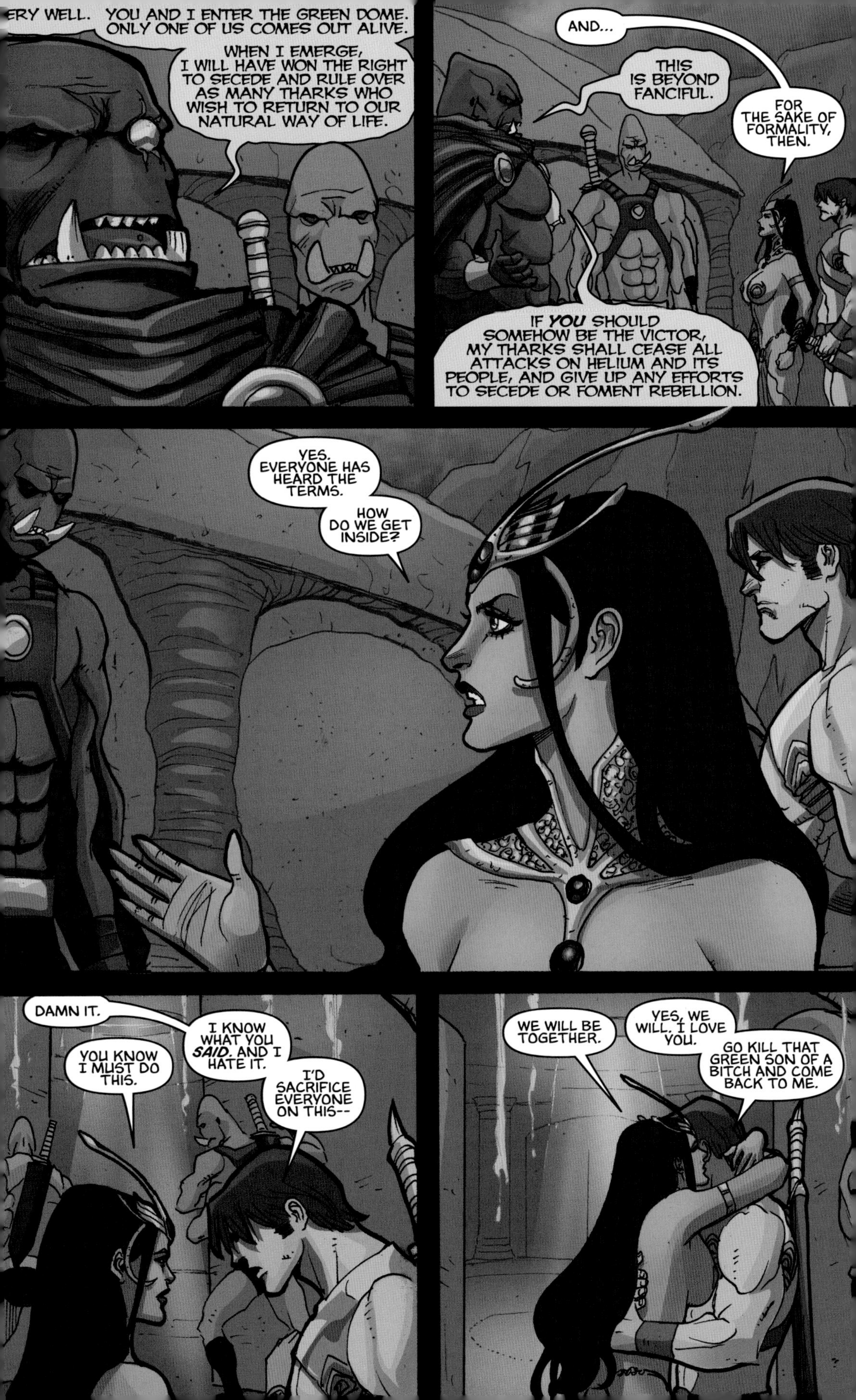
ERY WELL. YOU AND I ENTER THE GREEN DOME. ONLY ONE OF US COMES OUT ALIVE.
WHEN I EMERGE, I WILL HAVE WON THE RIGHT TO SECEDE AND RULE OVER AS MANY THARKS WHO WISH TO RETURN TO OUR NATURAL WAY OF LIFE.
AND...
THIS IS BEYOND FANCIFUL.
FOR THE SAKE OF FORMALITY, THEN.
IF *YOU* SHOULD SOMEHOW BE THE VICTOR, MY THARKS SHALL CEASE ALL ATTACKS ON HELIUM AND ITS PEOPLE, AND GIVE UP ANY EFFORTS TO SECEDE OR FOMENT REBELLION.
YES. EVERYONE HAS HEARD THE TERMS.
HOW DO WE GET INSIDE?
DAMN IT.
YOU KNOW I MUST DO THIS.
I KNOW WHAT YOU *SAID*. AND I HATE IT.
I'D SACRIFICE EVERYONE ON THIS--
WE WILL BE TOGETHER.
YES, WE WILL. I LOVE YOU.
GO KILL THAT GREEN SON OF A BITCH AND COME BACK TO ME.

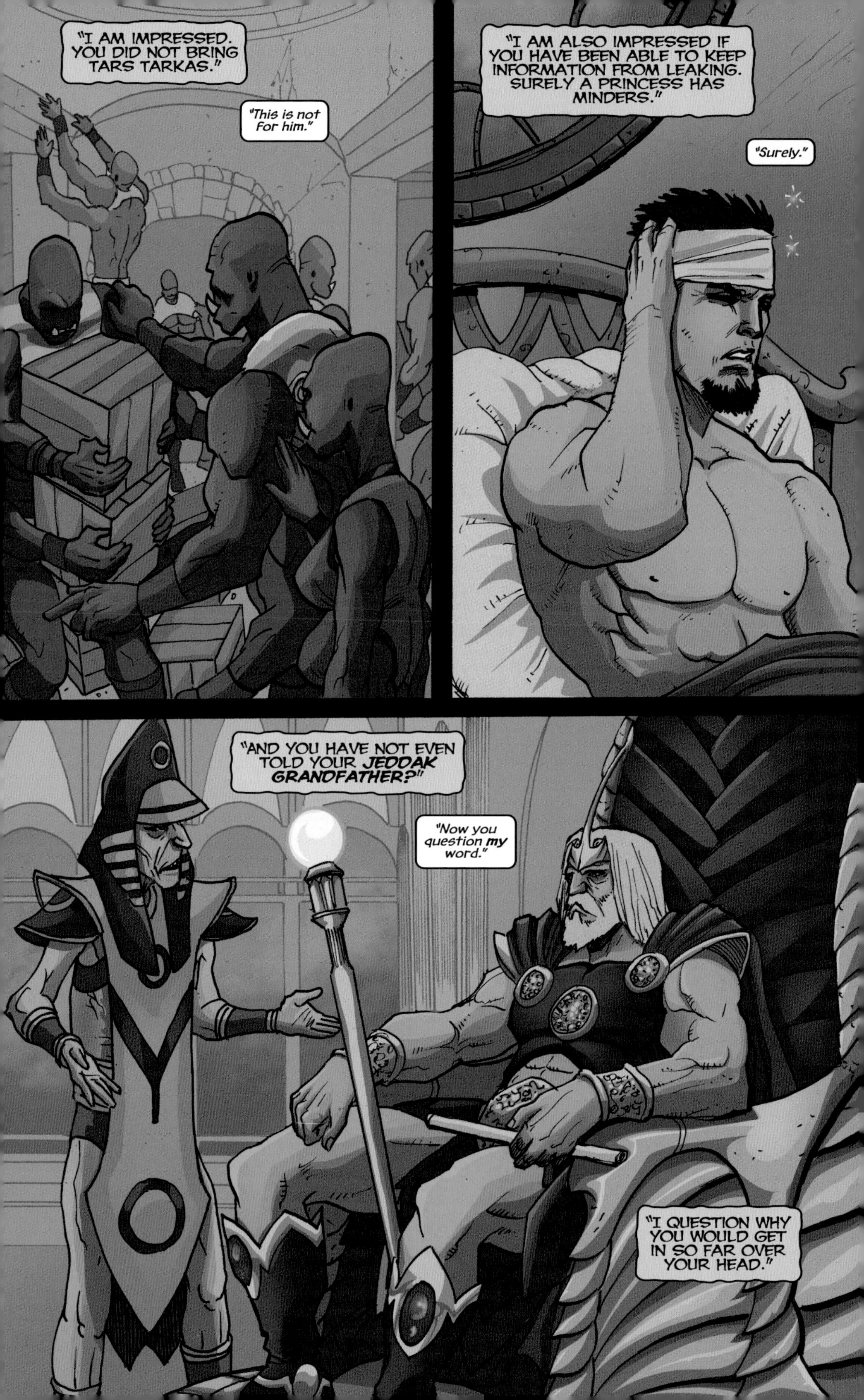
"I AM IMPRESSED. YOU DID NOT BRING TARS TARKAS."
"This is not for him."
"I AM ALSO IMPRESSED IF YOU HAVE BEEN ABLE TO KEEP INFORMATION FROM LEAKING. SURELY A PRINCESS HAS MINDERS."
"Surely."
"AND YOU HAVE NOT EVEN TOLD YOUR JEDDAK GRANDFATHER?"
"Now you question my word."
"I QUESTION WHY YOU WOULD GET IN SO FAR OVER YOUR HEAD."

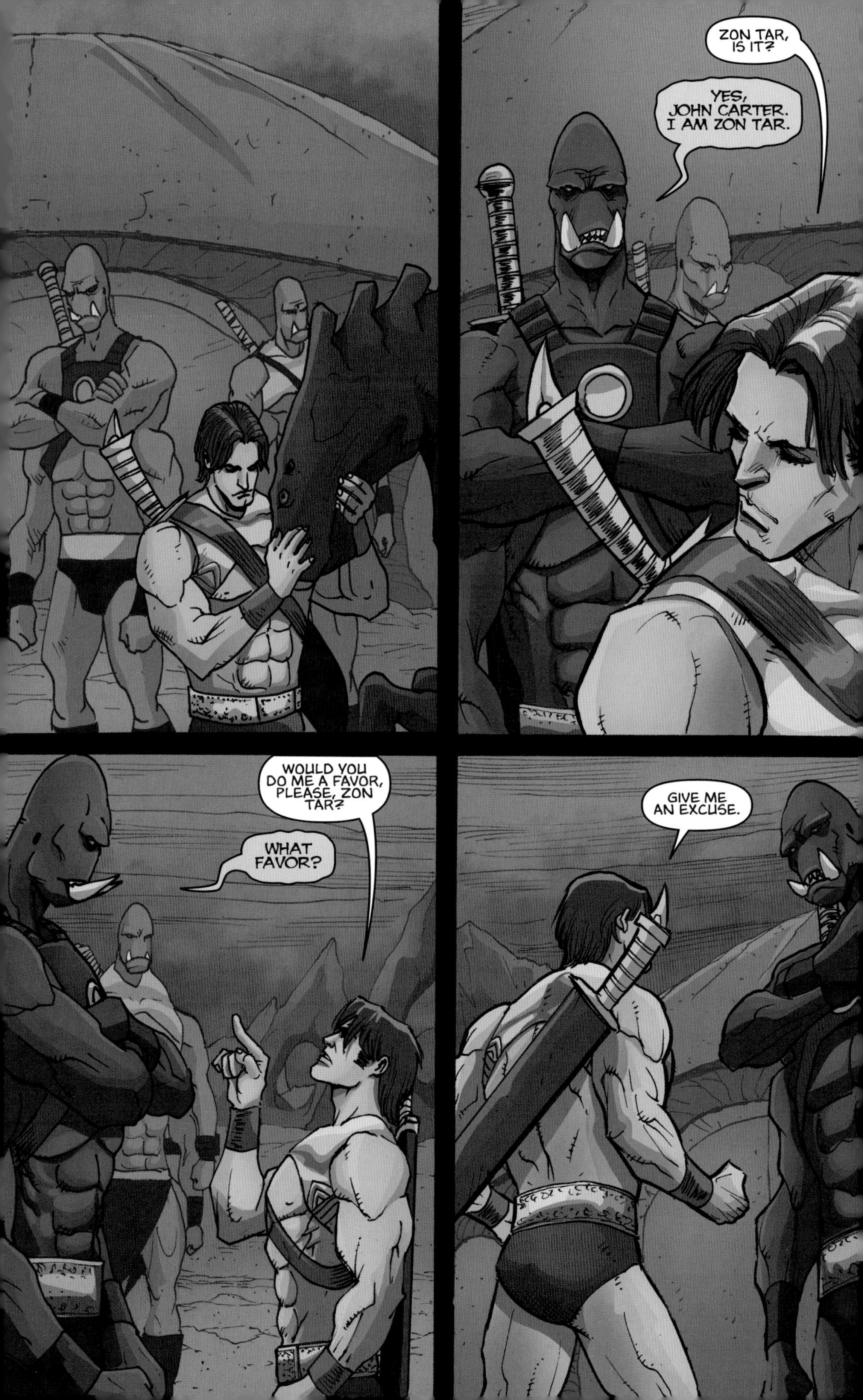
ZON TAR, IS IT?
YES, JOHN CARTER. I AM ZON TAR.
WOULD YOU DO ME A FAVOR, PLEASE, ZON TAR?
WHAT FAVOR?
GIVE ME AN EXCUSE.

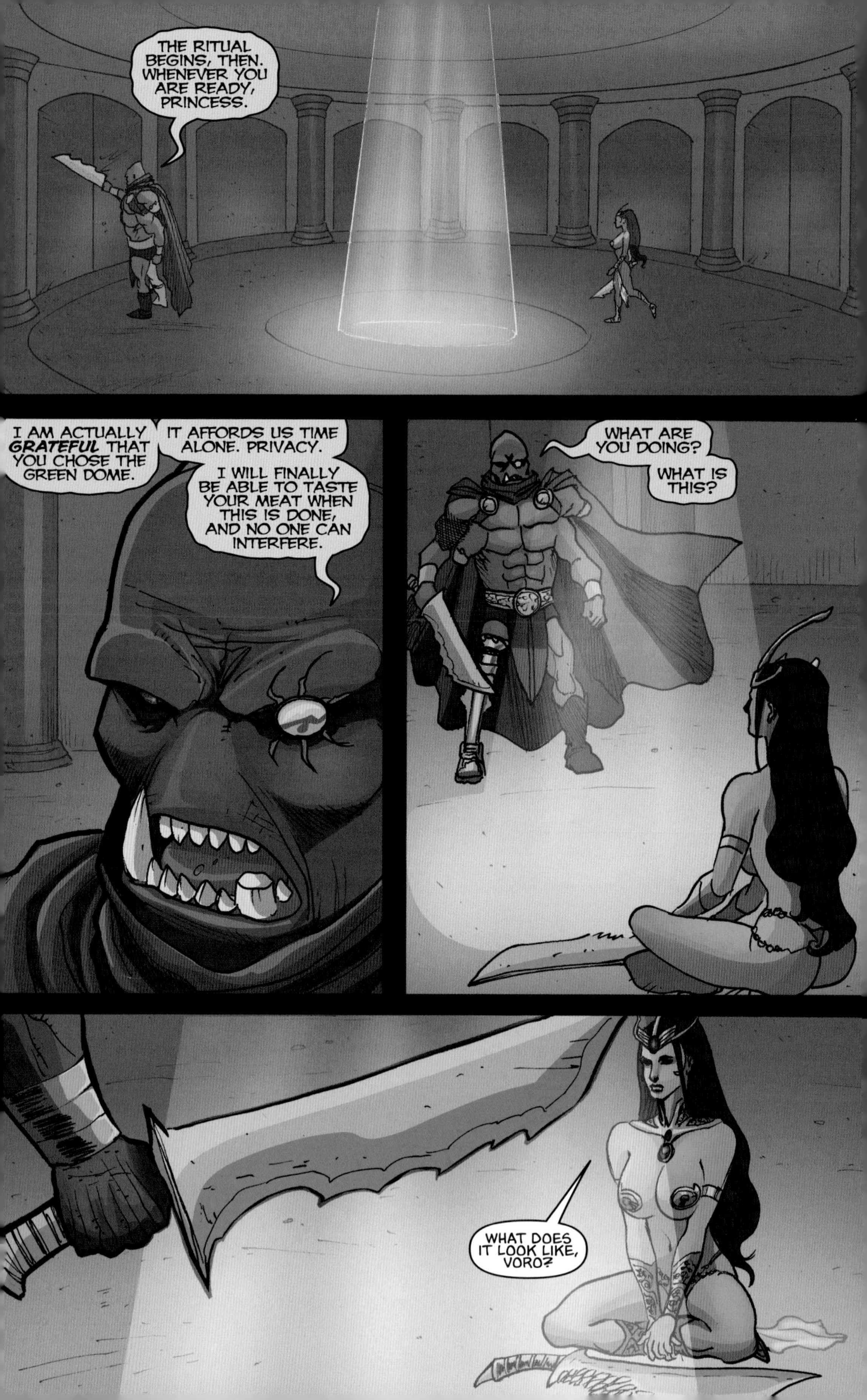

THE RITUAL BEGINS, THEN. WHENEVER YOU ARE READY, PRINCESS.
I AM ACTUALLY **GRATEFUL** THAT YOU CHOSE THE GREEN DOME.
IT AFFORDS US TIME ALONE. PRIVACY.
I WILL FINALLY BE ABLE TO TASTE YOUR MEAT WHEN THIS IS DONE, AND NO ONE CAN INTERFERE.
WHAT ARE YOU DOING?
WHAT IS THIS?
WHAT DOES IT LOOK LIKE, VORO?

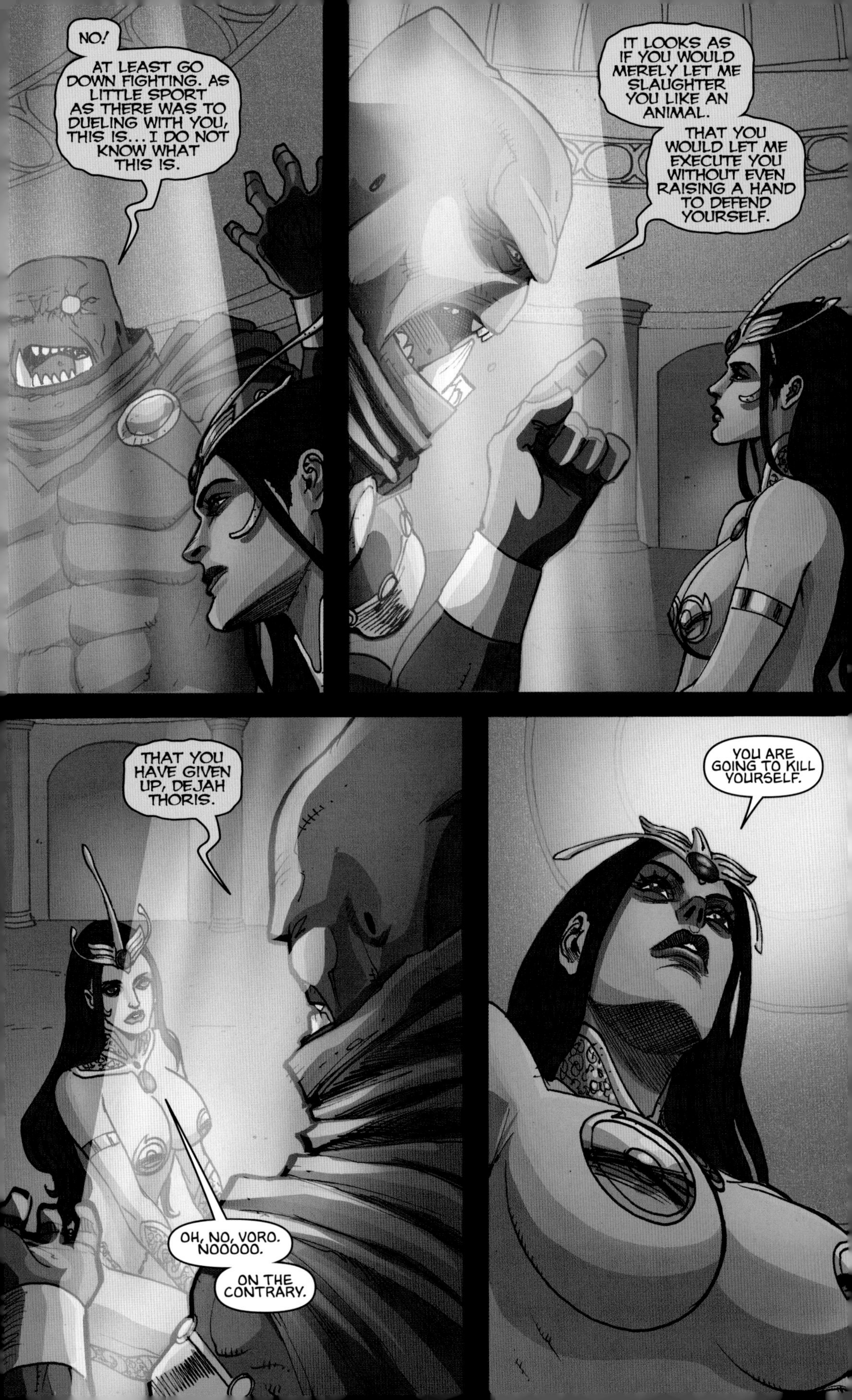
NO!
AT LEAST GO DOWN FIGHTING. AS LITTLE SPORT AS THERE WAS TO DUELING WITH YOU, THIS IS... I DO NOT KNOW WHAT THIS IS.
IT LOOKS AS IF YOU WOULD MERELY LET ME SLAUGHTER YOU LIKE AN ANIMAL.
THAT YOU WOULD LET ME EXECUTE YOU WITHOUT EVEN RAISING A HAND TO DEFEND YOURSELF.
THAT YOU HAVE GIVEN UP, DEJAH THORIS.
OH, NO, VORO. NOOOOO.
ON THE CONTRARY.
YOU ARE GOING TO KILL YOURSELF.

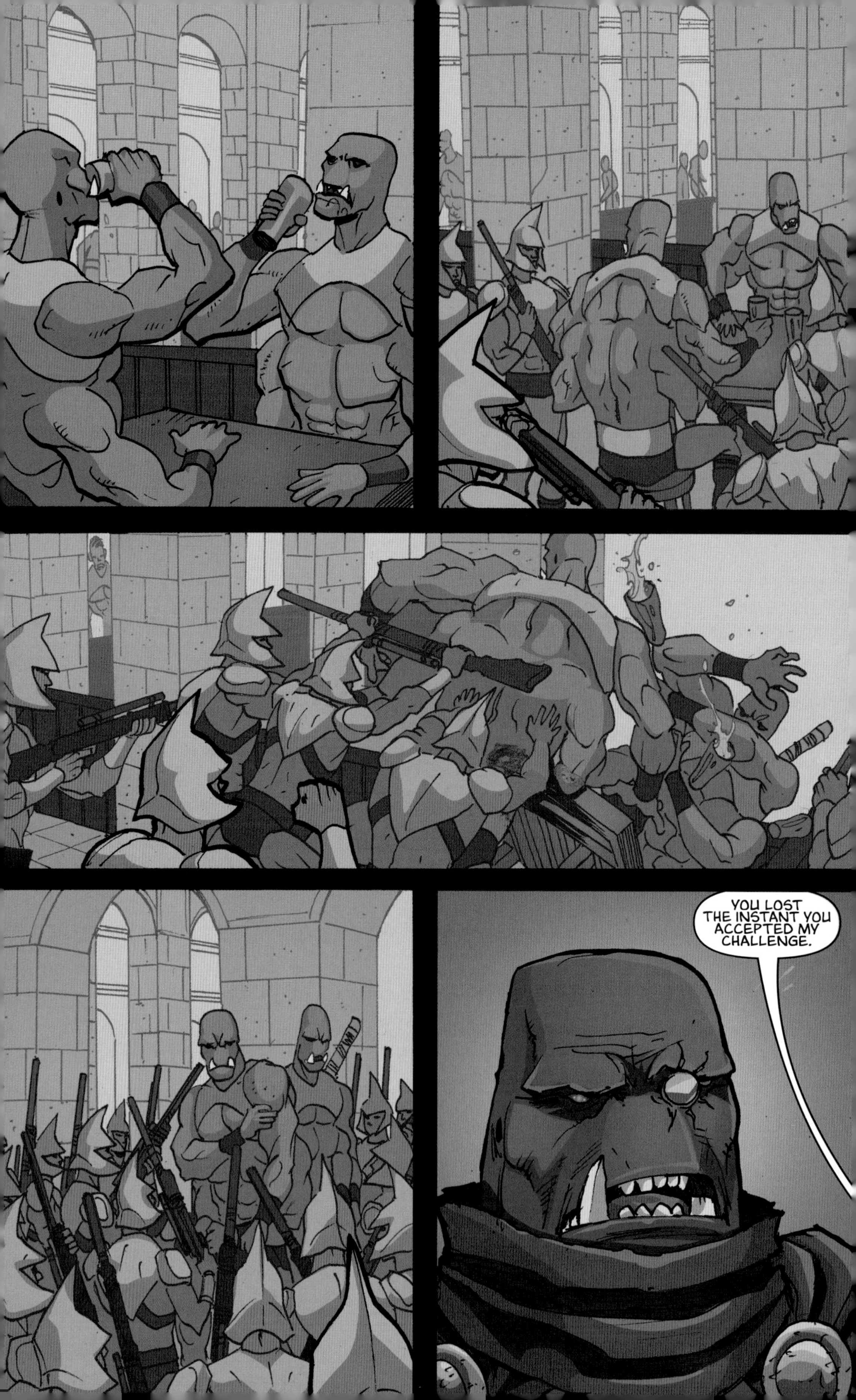
YOU LOST THE INSTANT YOU ACCEPTED MY CHALLENGE.

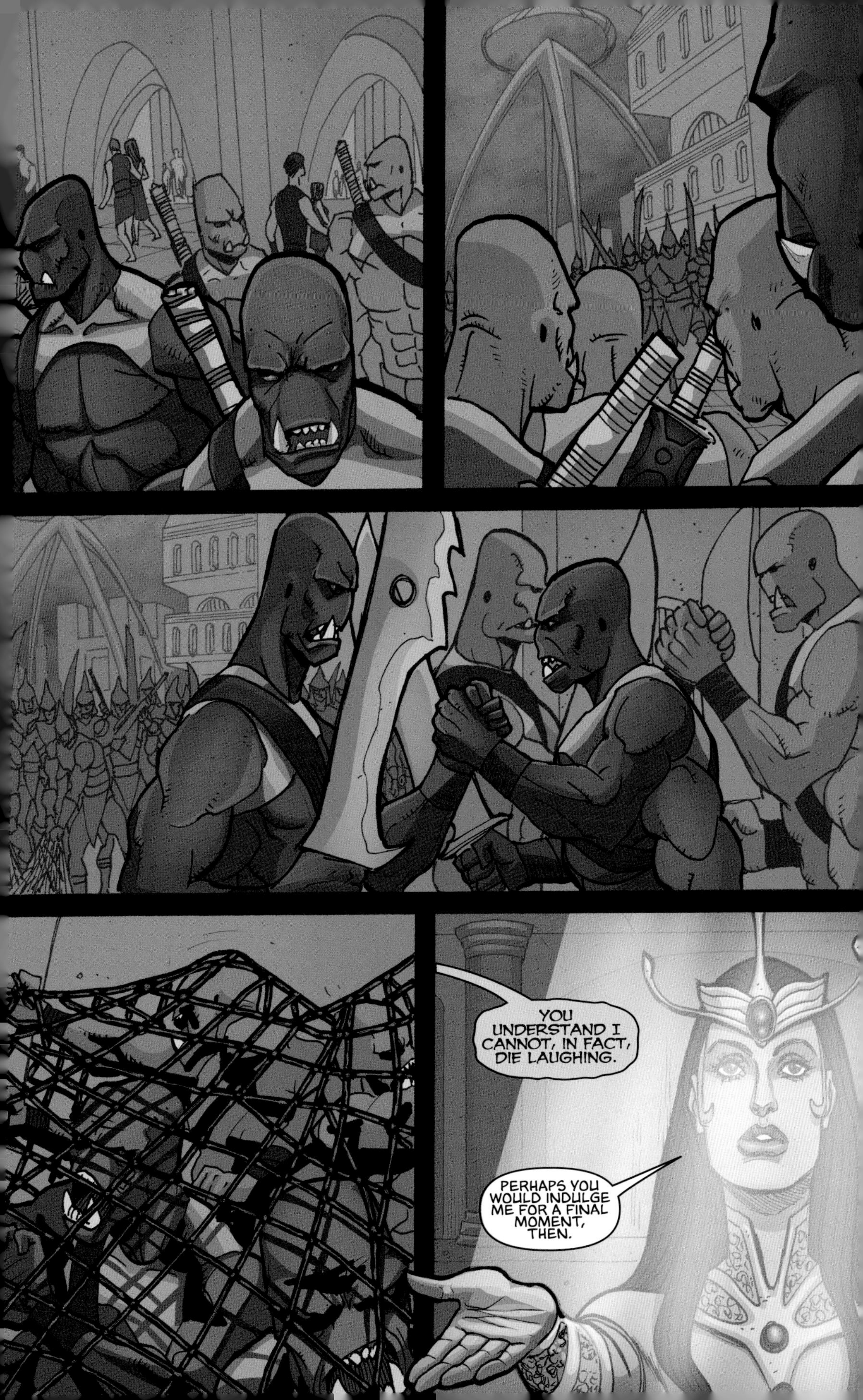
YOU UNDERSTAND I CANNOT, IN FACT, DIE LAUGHING.
PERHAPS YOU WOULD INDULGE ME FOR A FINAL MOMENT, THEN.

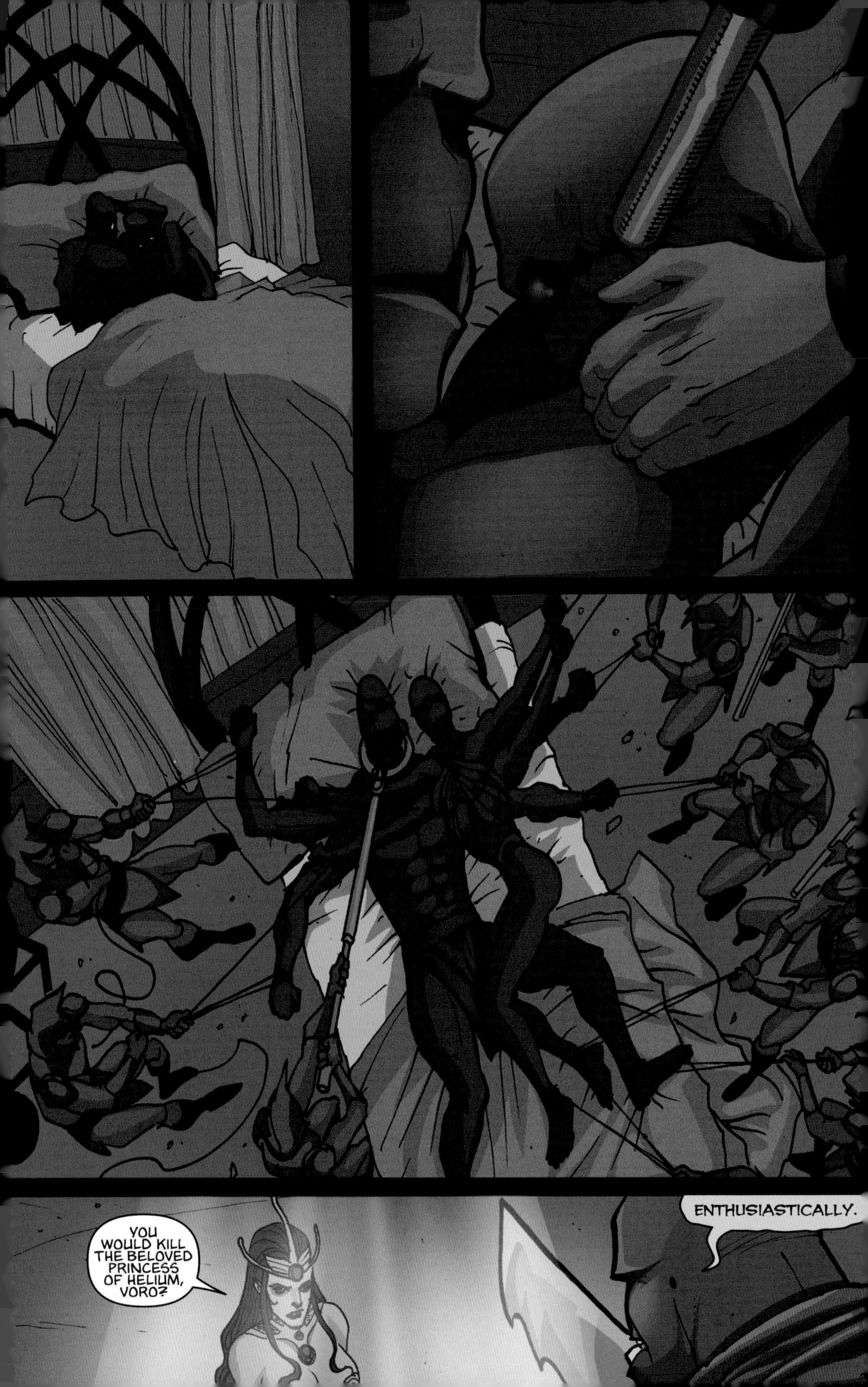
YOU WOULD KILL THE BELOVED PRINCESS OF HELIUM, VORO?
ENTHUSIASTICALLY.

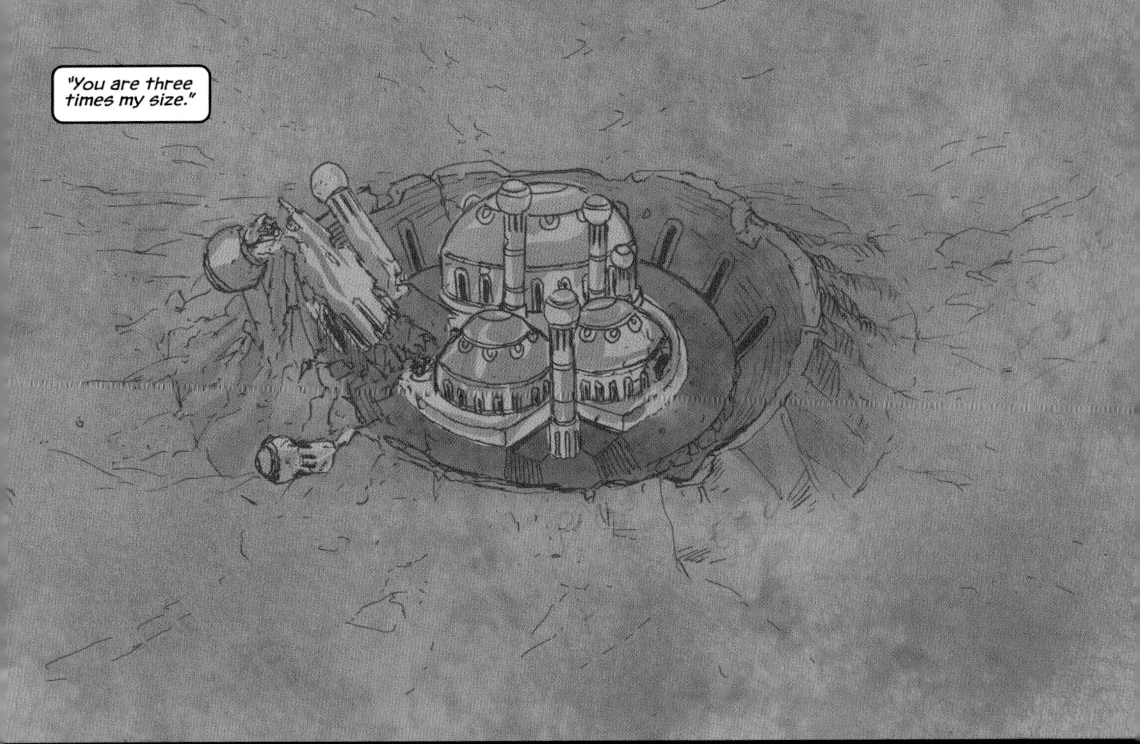
"You are three times my size."

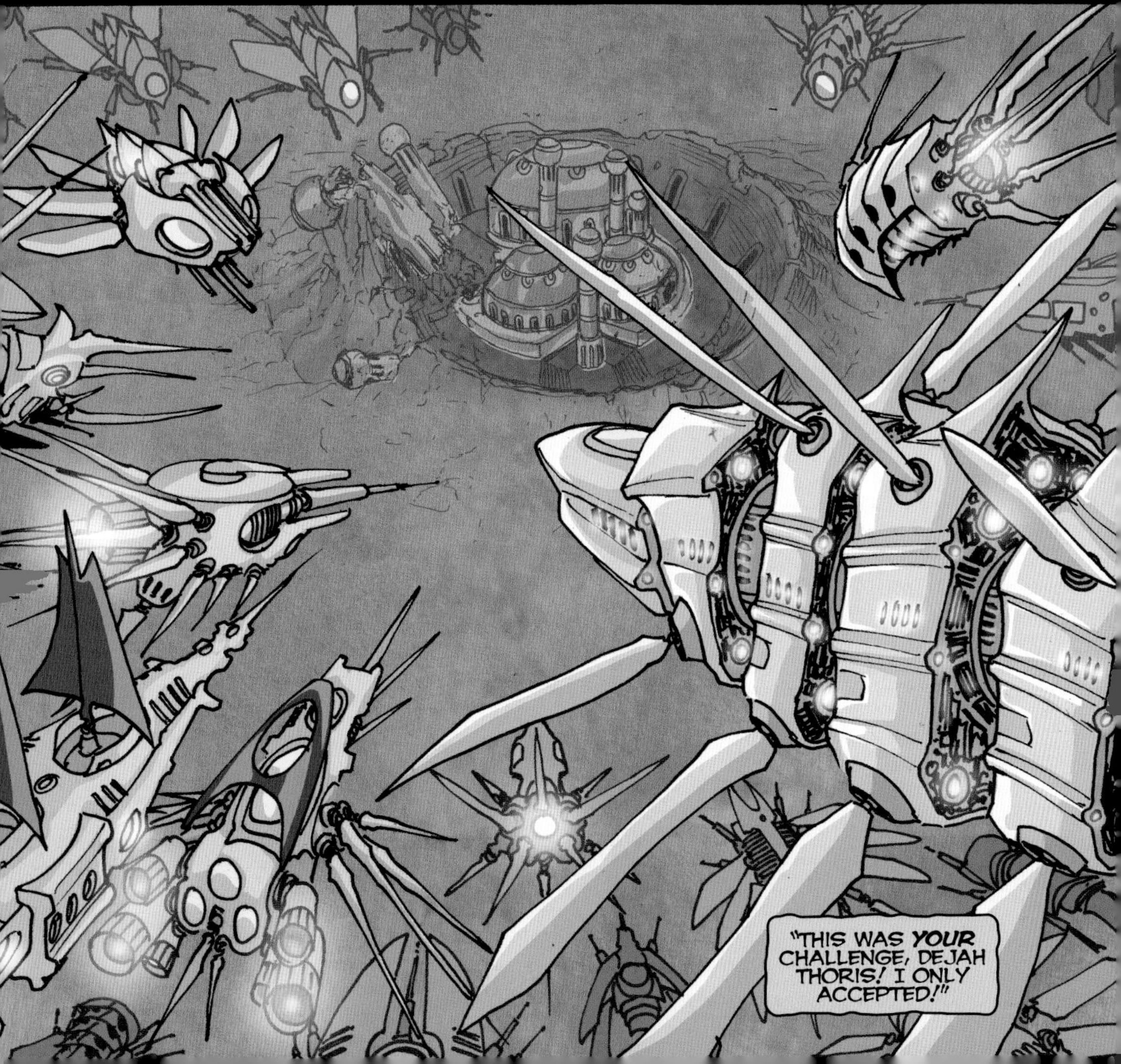
"THIS WAS ***YOUR*** CHALLENGE, DEJAH THORIS! I ONLY ACCEPTED!"

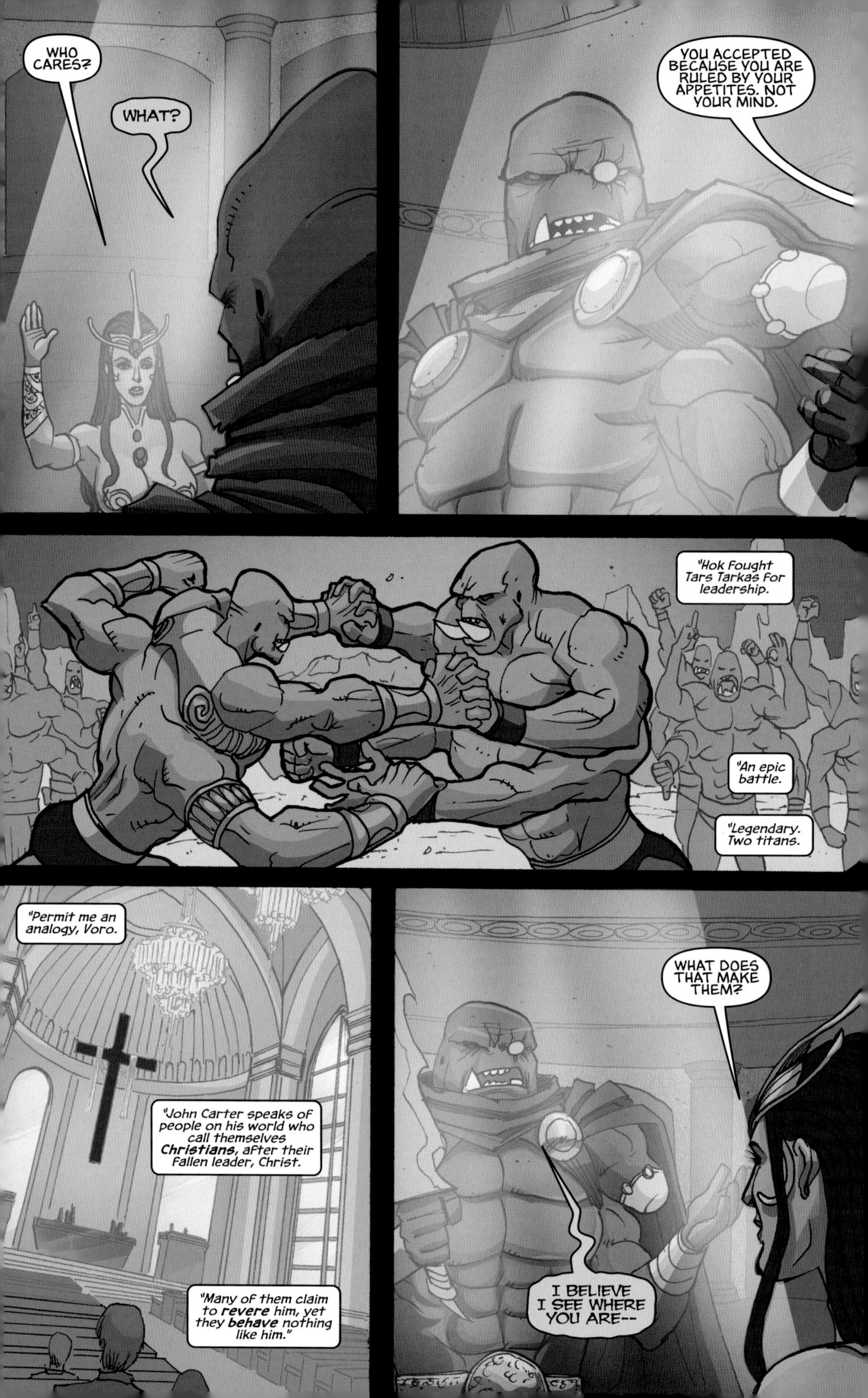
WHO CARES?
WHAT?
YOU ACCEPTED BECAUSE YOU ARE RULED BY YOUR APPETITES. NOT YOUR MIND.
"Hok fought Tars Tarkas for leadership.
"An epic battle.
"Legendary. Two titans.
"Permit me an analogy, Voro.
"John Carter speaks of people on his world who call themselves Christians, after their fallen leader, Christ.
"Many of them claim to revere him, yet they behave nothing like him."
WHAT DOES THAT MAKE THEM?
I BELIEVE I SEE WHERE YOU ARE--

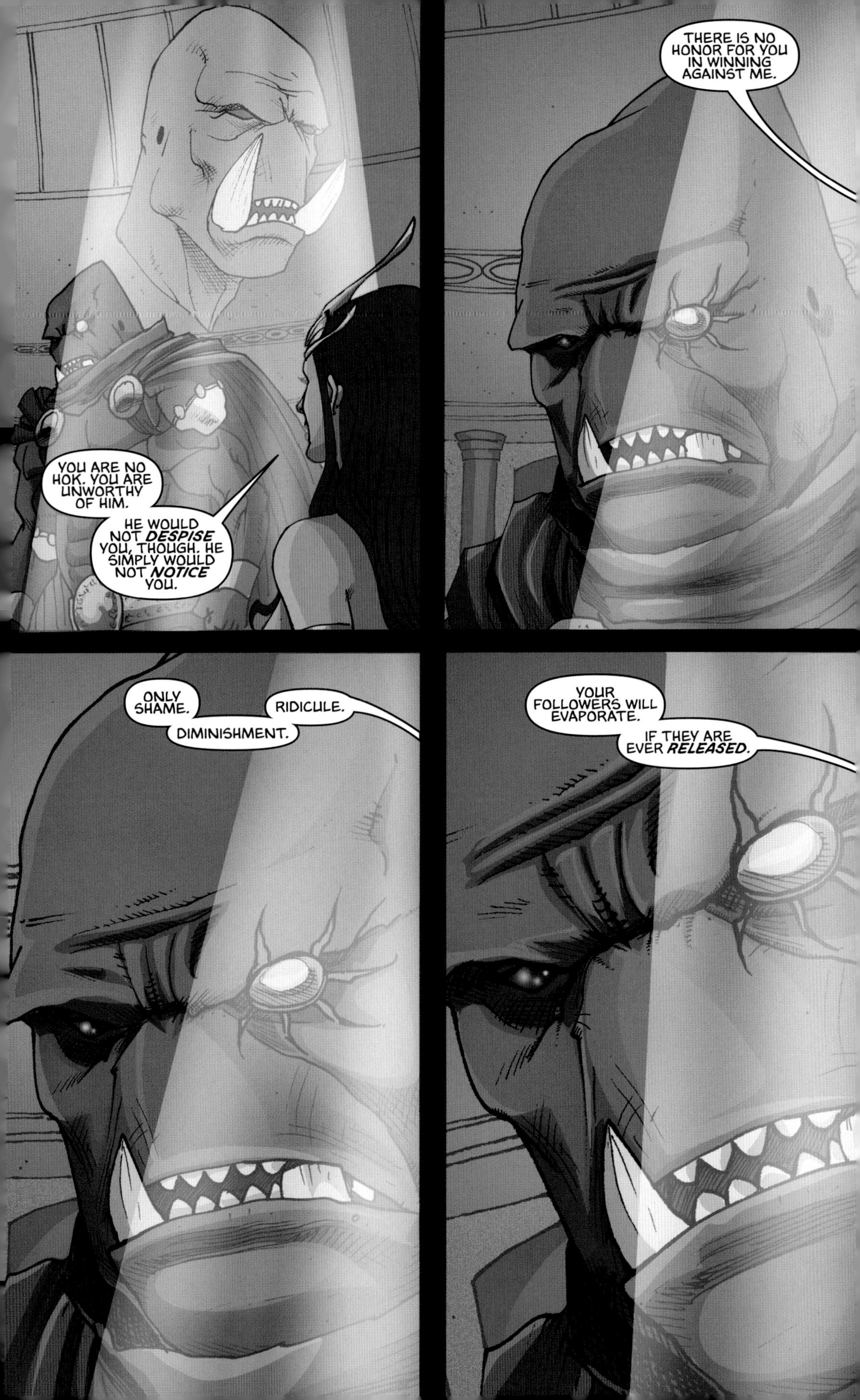
YOU ARE NO HOK. YOU ARE UNWORTHY OF HIM.
HE WOULD NOT *DESPISE* YOU, THOUGH. HE SIMPLY WOULD NOT *NOTICE* YOU.
THERE IS NO HONOR FOR YOU IN WINNING AGAINST ME.
ONLY SHAME.
DIMINISHMENT.
RIDICULE.
YOUR FOLLOWERS WILL EVAPORATE.
IF THEY ARE EVER *RELEASED*.

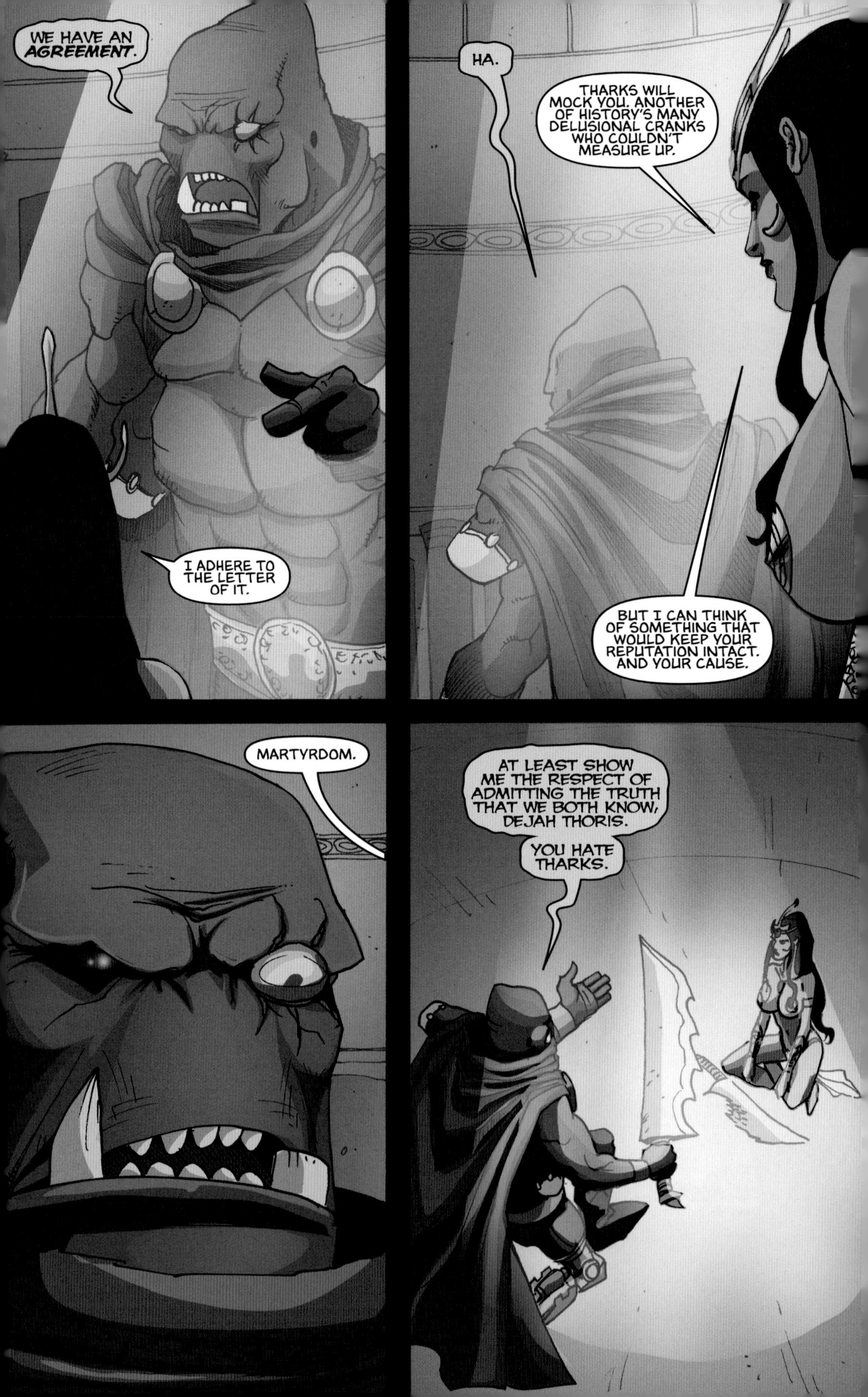
WE HAVE AN AGREEMENT.
I ADHERE TO THE LETTER OF IT.
HA.
THARKS WILL MOCK YOU. ANOTHER OF HISTORY'S MANY DELUSIONAL CRANKS WHO COULDN'T MEASURE UP.
BUT I CAN THINK OF SOMETHING THAT WOULD KEEP YOUR REPUTATION INTACT. AND YOUR CAUSE.
MARTYRDOM.
AT LEAST SHOW ME THE RESPECT OF ADMITTING THE TRUTH THAT WE BOTH KNOW, DEJAH THORIS.
YOU HATE THARKS.

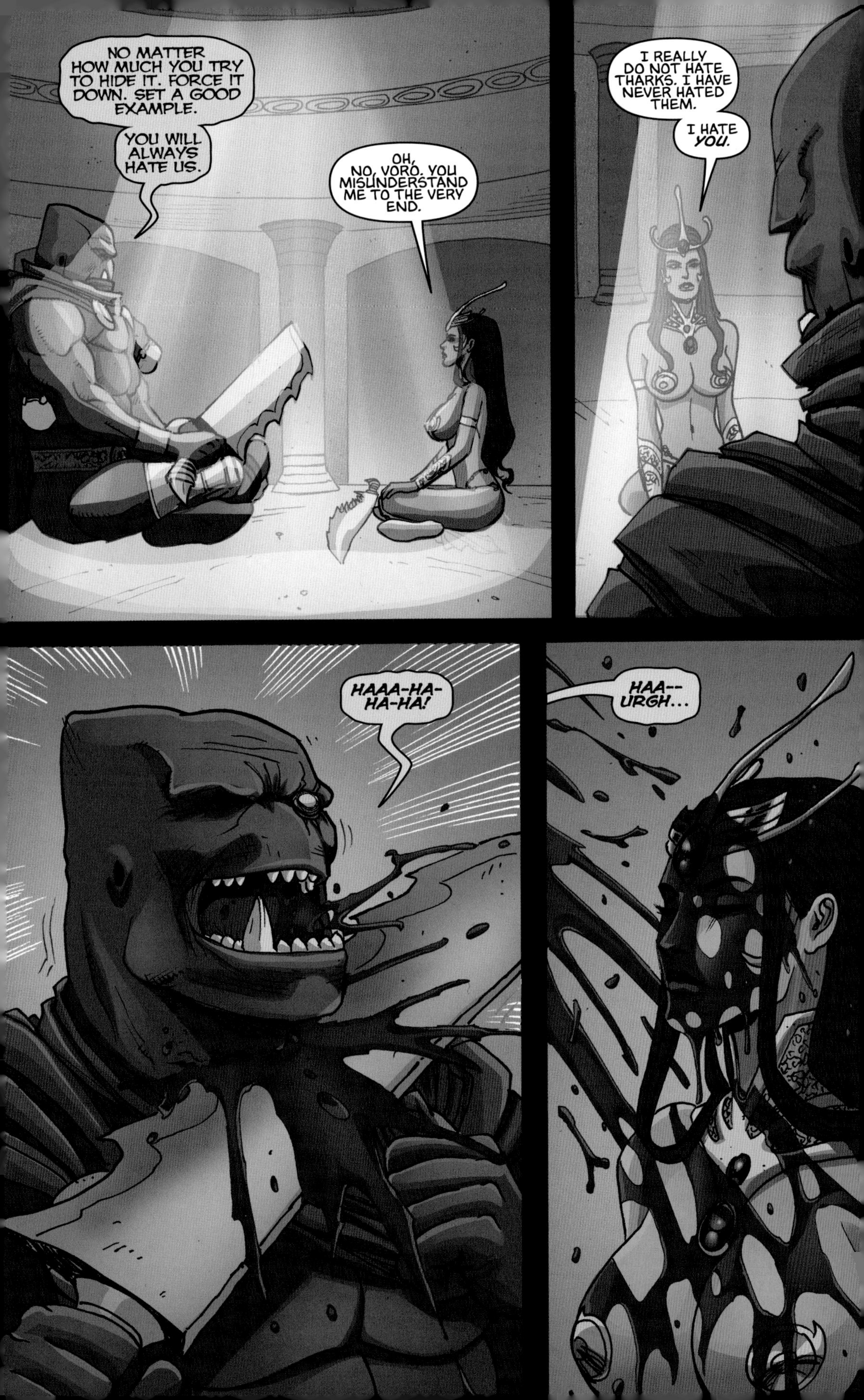
NO MATTER HOW MUCH YOU TRY TO HIDE IT. FORCE IT DOWN. SET A GOOD EXAMPLE.
YOU WILL ALWAYS HATE US.
OH, NO, VORO. YOU MISUNDERSTAND ME TO THE VERY END.
I REALLY DO NOT HATE THARKS. I HAVE NEVER HATED THEM.
I HATE *YOU*.
HAAA-HA-HA-HA!
HAA-- URGH...

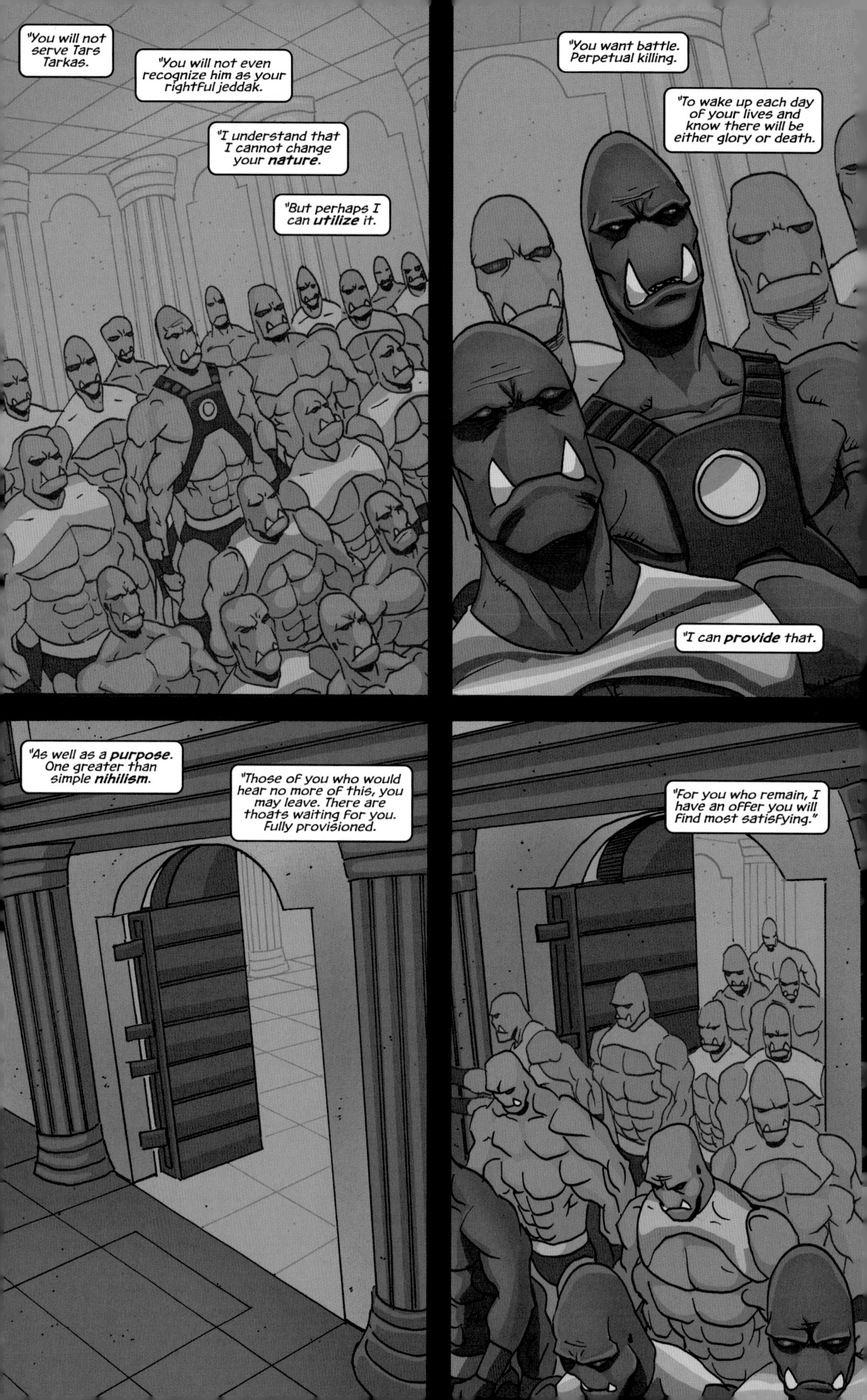
"You will not serve Tars Tarkas.
"You will not even recognize him as your rightful jeddak.
"I understand that I cannot change your **nature**.
"But perhaps I can **utilize** it.
"You want battle. Perpetual killing.
"To wake up each day of your lives and know there will be either glory or death.
"I can **provide** that.
"As well as a **purpose**. One greater than simple **nihilism**.
"Those of you who would hear no more of this, you may leave. There are thoats waiting for you. Fully provisioned.
"For you who remain, I have an offer you will find most satisfying."

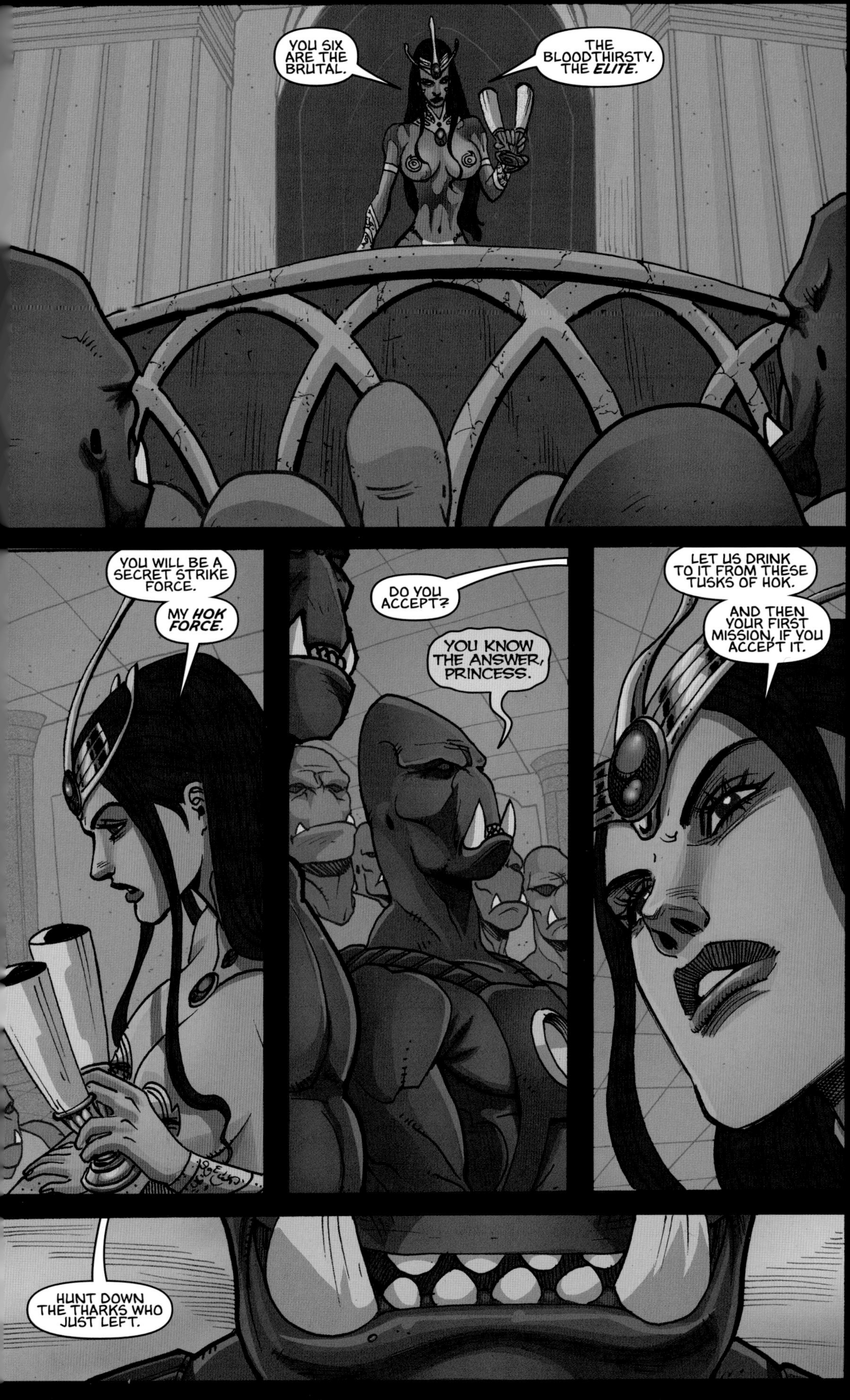
YOU SIX ARE THE BRUTAL.
THE BLOODTHIRSTY. THE *ELITE*.
YOU WILL BE A SECRET STRIKE FORCE.
MY ***HOK FORCE***.
DO YOU ACCEPT?
YOU KNOW THE ANSWER, PRINCESS.
LET US DRINK TO IT FROM THESE TUSKS OF HOK.
AND THEN YOUR FIRST MISSION, IF YOU ACCEPT IT.
HUNT DOWN THE THARKS WHO JUST LEFT.

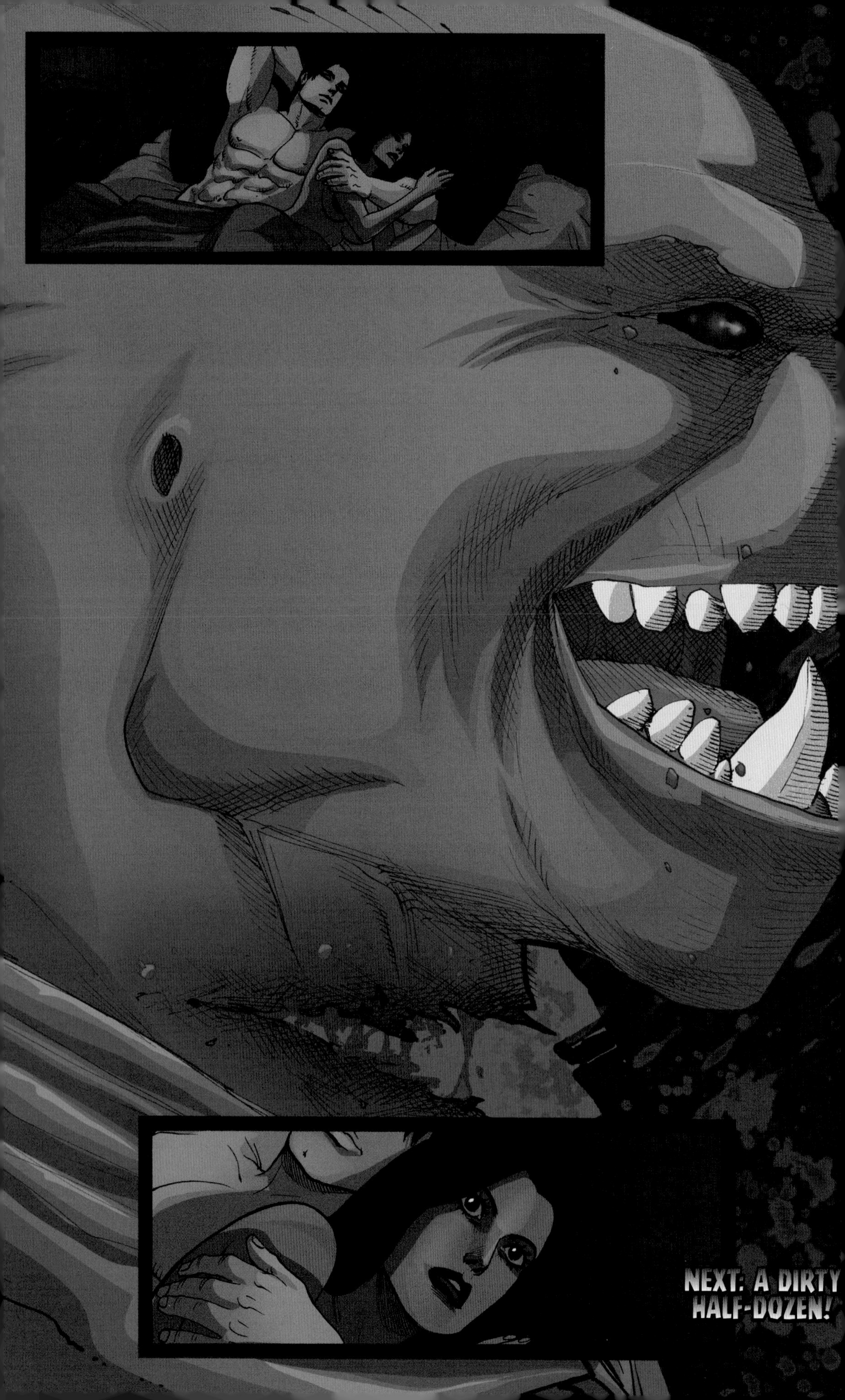
NEXT: A DIRTY HALF-DOZEN!

DEJAH THORIS AND THE GREEN MEN OF MARS
ISSUE 5

By Mark Rahner

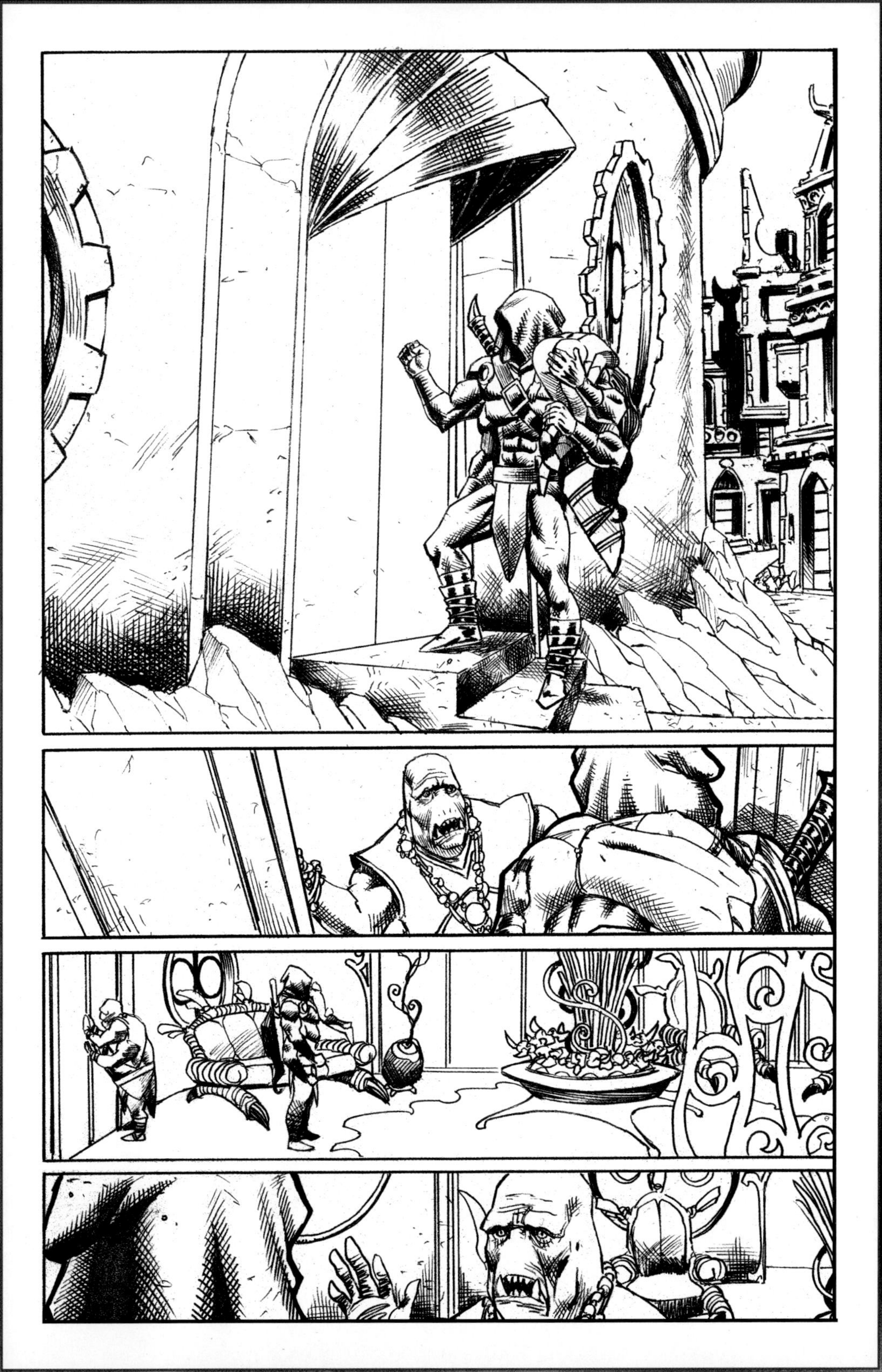

PAGE ONE

Panel 1.1: A Thark knocks at a door with an unconscious Dejah Thoris slung over his shoulder, limp, her arms hanging down. The Thark's face can't be seen. Same hooded outfit as at the conclusion of Issue 4.

Panel 1.2: An older, schlubbier – but rich – Thark opens the door, mildly surprised.

HUNGRY THARK: Are you insane?

DELIVERER: I was not seen.

HUNGRY THARK: Get in here, you fool!

Panel 1.3: Inside the Hungry Thark's opulent living quarter, he peers through the crack before he shuts the door. The Deliverer's face is still unseen.

HUNGRY THARK: The whole thing? But not even cleaned and dressed?

DELIVERER: No time. There was a problem. This is the last shipment.

Panel 1.4: On the Hungry Thark, looking like an outraged Charles Laughton.

HUNGRY THARK: What? Unacceptable.

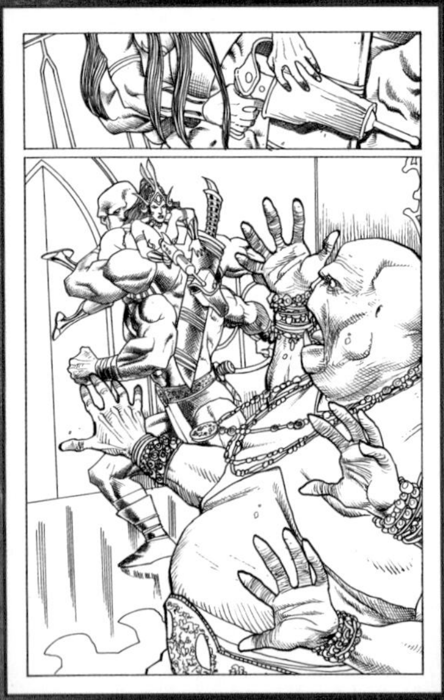

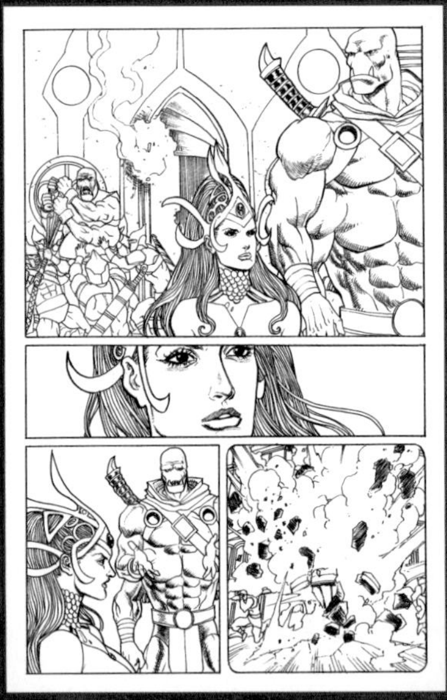

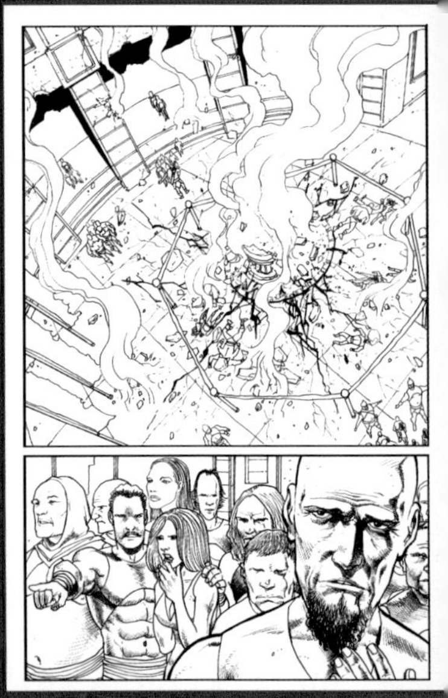

PAGE TWO

Panel 2.1: One tier. Close on DT's hand grabbing the gun out of the Deliverer's holster.

HUNGRY THARK: What problem, exactly?

Panel 2.2: The rest of the page. The Deliverer is Tars Tarkas, and now he's facing away enough from the Hungry Thark for DT to be arching up and pointing the gun at him as she's still hanging over Tars' shoulder.

DT: The meat went bad.

ARTIST NOTE: DEJAH THORIS LOOKS TIRED, CIRCLES UNDER THE EYES,
HAGGARD HERE AND GETS PROGRESSIVELY WORSE THROUGHOUT THIS AND
THE NEXT THREE ISSUES.

CREDITS:
DEJAH THORIS AND THE GREEN MEN OF MARS PART 5
WRITTEN BY MARK RAHNER, ETC. …

PAGE THREE

Panel 3.1: DT and Tars are walking outside the Hungry Thark's place in the foreground. In
the background, Heliumite guards are leading the Hungry Thark away in chains – and he
looks like he's just had the shit kicked out of him – bruised, bloody and slumped. BUT:
he's also turned his head back and is raising his cuffed fists at Tars and DT.

    Tars: Perhaps you will sleep easier now.

    Tars: Or simply **begin** sleeping again.

    DT: I wish.

Panel 3.2: Close-up on DT.

    DT: But I doubt it.

Panel 3.3: DT and Tars.

    Tars: You have been through much. Borne much. It is understandable.

    DT: Perhaps. But there is no time to dwell upon it.

Panel 3.4: The Thark-Heliumite sculpture exploding from the previous issue – in sepia to
indicate a flashback.

    DT Caption: I must find out who destroyed the peace monument. Stop them
    before they do the same damage to our peace, itself.

    DT: This was merely an indulgence.

PAGE FOUR

Panel 4.1: Establishing shot, Helium. Only a few traces of the Red & Green Celebration
remain, and the destroyed sculpture is blocked off with whatever the Barsoomian
equivalent is of yellow police tape – bright red ropes and art deco-style poles/stands?

    Tars Caption: A **worthy** indulgence, my friend. But yes.

    DT Caption: There is little to go on, and I am almost too tired to think.

    Tars Caption: Then we shall proceed from what we know. Or from what I know
    that **you** know.

Panel 4.2: Close up on the BARTENDER from the bar where DT was abducted in Issue 1. He didn't wind up getting depicted in that issue, so how he's drawn here is artist's choice. He's very nervous. He should be middle-aged or older and not physical-looking at all.

> DT (off): Remember me?

> BARTENDER: Ahh … of course I **KNOW** you, Princess … but …

PAGE FIVE

Panel 5.1: Wider shot that shows more of the bar. DT is standing at the bar, leaning in. The Bartender is behind it, sweating bullets. A few feet behing DT stand Tars and Carter, looking angry. Their arms are folded, no weapons drawn.

> BARTENDER: Can I get you a drink, your highness? All of you? Drinks?

> DT: You do not want to waste my time.

Panel 5.2: Artist's choice here. Overhead shot? NOTE: In a corner of the bar somewhere, Kil Gor and his son the Pilot from WHITE APES OF MARS are sitting quietly at a table and watching. It doesn't have to be in this panel, but somewhere in the scene.

> DT: What is your name?

> BARTENDER: Kro Zel

> DT: I was kidnapped from here, Kro Zel. My guards were taken. They have still not been found.

> BARTENDER: I was not here, Princess!

Panel 5.3: Two-shot of DT and the Bartender.

> DT: When?

BARTENDER: I do not understand.

DT: When were you not here, Kro Zel? I did not even say when this happened.

Panel 5.4: With one hand, Carter yanks the Bartender over the bar.

CARTER: Enough.

PAGE SIX

Panel 6.1: DT looks exasperated and angry, on top of fatigued. Carter holds the terrified Bartender's arms behind his back, but the man doesn't struggle. Tars looks down at him menacingly.

DT: What do you know about Voro and the Tharks who did it?

BARTENDER: Princess, please! I do not –

Panel 6.2: Close-up on DT's face. She's furious and nearly foaming at the mouth.

DT: THIS IS YOUR PLACE!

Panel 6.3: The Bartender, held tight. Carter looks hard, but he's also got an eye on DT – he's never quite seen her like this before.

BARTENDER: Please. I have children …

Panel 6.4: Carter jerks the Bartender out of frame.

CARTER: I'll bet you don't need any more of them, friend.

CARTER: Tars?

PAGE SEVEN

Panel 7.1: On Carter, calm.

CARTER: Before I came here, I fought in another little war. Not as **long** as yours, but just as **nasty**.

CARTER: If a situation was urgent enough, and a person wouldn't give us information we needed …

CARTER: We had to get even nastier.

Panel 7.2: This frame ends around the Bartender's belly. Tars is reaching below the frame with one hand and holding up an ugly-looking knife with another. The implication is obvious. The Bartender is wide-eyed with terror. DT looks on now with a little concern.

BARTENDER: NO! ISSUS, NO!

CARTER: Well, **yes**. If you don't **talk**. That's your princess that was kidnapped.

But she's also my **wife**.

TARS: He is not talking.

Panel 7.3: DT holds out a hand.

DT: Stop!

DT: Let him go!

7.4: Carter looks back casually over his shoulder at her as he begins to release the Bartender.

CARTER: Huh. I guess you heard her.

TARS: Hmph.

PAGE EIGHT

Panel 8.1: DT, Carter and Tars walk out of the bar, where a number of Heliumite guards wait.

DT (to guards): Arrest the bartender. Report anything he says to me at once.

HEAD GUARD: Yes, Princess.

Panel 8.2: DT is fuming. Carter entreats her.

CARTER: Darling, surely you know we weren't really going to torture the man. Just frighten him into talking. Right Tars?

Panel 8.3: Tars looks at Carter silently.

NO DIALOGUE

Panel 8.4: She snaps at Carter, although wearily.

DT: I do not care! We do things my way now.

Panel 8.5: KIL GOR talks furtively with his son, the PILOT in a dimly-lit corner as the guards arrest the Bartender. (Not necessary to show the bartender. Perhaps shadows?)

KIL GOR: I would not speak in front of that green dung, either, my son.

PILOT: The Princess of Helium. Letting one of them touch a red man that way.

KIL GOR: She will regret that, when word of this spreads.

PAGE NINE

Panel 9.1: Not far from the bar yet, the three stop to part ways. Carter is turning to leave and letting DT's fingers slip away. There's still a bit of tension in the air.

CARTER: I hate to let you out of my sight now, even more than before.

DT: I know. But we cannot live that way. I will be home shortly.

Panel 9.2: DT and Tars strolling away from the bar, looking at Carter in the distance.

TARS: His words did not match the speed of his departure.

DT: No.

TARS: I suspect that even with princesses and warlords, a man does not like his wife dressing him down in public.

Panel 9.3: Medium shot of the two of them, waist-up unless artist differs.

DT: Then he should not have done that. And **you** as well, Tars.

TARS (dryly): Thark jeddaks are fine with it.

Panel 9.4: Small panel or inset. DT smiles wearily up at him with the corners of her mouth.

NO DIALOGUE

Panel 9.5: DT puts a friendly hand on Tars as she turns to leave. And the Head Guard rushes back to them.

DT: Time for a rest. I will see you soon, my friend. Thank you for everything.

HEAD GUARD: Princess, a word, please!

HEAD GUARD: There is another matter you should know about.

PAGE TEN

Panel 10.1: DT and Tars are at a crime scene in a Helium alley. It's bustling with guards surrounding a dead Thark in a massive pool of blood – who can't be seen completely yet – and a few spectators. Some of the Heliumite spectators are smiling/laughing.

DT: SIGH. Issus …

DT: Well, Tars, this is likely a crime for my guards to investigate. And as it took place in Helium, I will take responsibility for it and tell you of their findings.

Panel 10.2: Two-shot. DT looks up wearily and with a bit of annoyance at Tars ...

TARS: But the victim is a Thark.

Panel 10.3: … as KENDA THAN arrives. He's an older Heliumite guard, at least 60ish-looking, with droopy eyes and a leathery face, salt-and-pepper hair that's mostly salt, the slightest pot belly – modeled on the Investigation Discovery channel's "Homicide Hunter."

KENDA THAN: Now this can NOT be what it I think it is.

DT: The corpse?

KENDA THAN: You two having a jurisdiction spat over this mess … Your Highness … Highnesses.

Panel 10.4: DT turns to him, with annoyance and mild surprise. A guard doesn't talk that way to a royal.

DT: And what concern of it is yours?

KENDA THAN: Whichever of you wins, the mess is still mine.

KENDA THAN: My name is Kenda Than, Princess. This is my job. The guards call me the Murder Master.

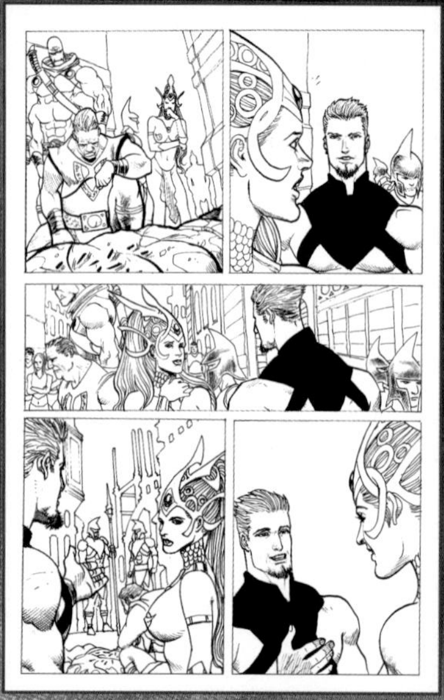

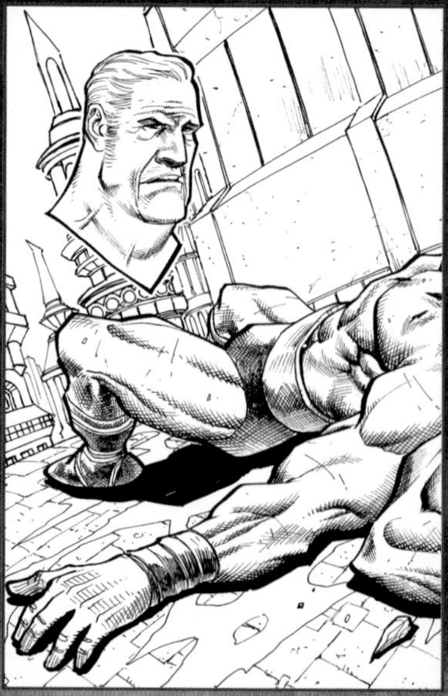

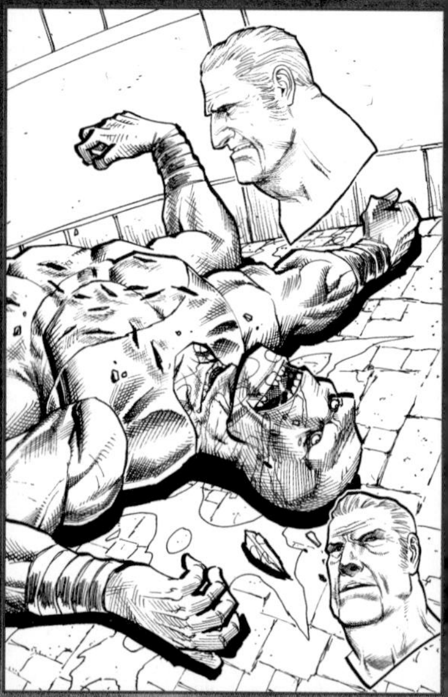

anel 11.1: Angle from the corpse's POV looking up at the three of them. Kenda couldn't ook more bland, yet slightly self-amused. DT is a bit grossed out. Tars is impossible to ead.

> KENDA: This delicate creature was surprised by someone he **knew** – who was just slightly upset with him about something.

> KENDA: Wonder what that could have been.

anel 11.2: Side view: DT in the near background and REK in the foreground. **Rek is lso a character from WHITE APES issue 1: The royal advisor who was once a uitor of DT's – and a mild, rather smarmy douchebag.** He's looking down at the ody, she's jerked her head around to look at him in surprise.

> REK: Who could ever be upset with a Thark?

> DT: Rek!

anel 11.3: On Rek and DT, now both standing up. They both look a little awkward. They have some sort of past.

> DT: It is good to see you. I hope you have been well.

> REK: I have not had a chance to congratulate you, Dejah Thoris.

> DT: That is very generous of you, Rek, considering …

anel 11.4: As DT and Rek talk, Kenda is in the background kneeling without a thought in he blood pooled around the corpse.

> REK: You may simply add me to the legions of men who envy John Carter.

> DT: Well … thank you.

> DT: But why are you here, Rek?

anel 11.5: The vibe has changed to somewhere between cold and slightly tense.

> REK: Why is a royal advisor here? One might also ask why a **royal** is here, my princess.

> REK: It is no more beneath my station than yours. Unless the matter is of greater interest than a mere Thark killing.

> DT: I do not like "mere." All the people in Helium are of interest to me.

PAGES TWELVE AND THIRTEEN

DOUBLE-PAGE SPLASH: The mutilated body of the Thark. It was a warrior, and he's been stabbed nearly to hamburger, throat cut, both tusks broken off. This should look disgusting.

There'll be a small inset of KENDA's face, with the first caption, then a few other captions from him around the page.

KENDA CAPTION: Not a lot of Thark cases in my experience, but that is quite an **abundance** of experience …

KENDA CAPTION: … And from this angle, we do not look so different.

KENDA CAPTION: So … no weapon drawn.

KENDA CAPTION: No defensive wounds on any of his arms. Slashes or the like.

KENDA CAPTION: And I take it you noticed the viciousness of these wounds. Why stab someone just once when … oh … **fifty** times will do, right?

KENDA CAPTION: This brute was not just killed. He was **destroyed**.

KENDA CAPTION: Throat cut for the sake of thoroughness. All of Barsoom appreciates a perfectionist.

KENDA CAPTION: Roll him over and I'll wager there are no wounds in his back.

KENDA CAPTION: And those tusks …

PAGE FOURTEEN

Panel 14.1: Tars' brow is knitted as he stares down at the corpse.

TARS: Hmm.

Panel 14.2: Kenda raises an eyebrow.

KENDA: Do you know this Thark, Jeddak?

Panel 14.3: Now everyone's looking at Tars.

TARS: Yes.

KENDA: I was hoping to elicit a bit more information from the question, Jeddak.

Panel 14.4: DT, with Rek looking on impatiently.

DT: What is it, Tars? Why do you hesitate?

Panel 14.5: Close on Tars, mouth curling in disgust.

TARS: I believe we have a larger problem on our hands.

PAGE FIFTEEN

Panel 15.1: Flashback: Tars in the foreground of Thark warriors riding thoats in the desert. The dead Thark is alive in this panel on a thoat behind Tars.

TARS CAPTION: He rode with me. He fought with me.

Panel 15.2: That iconic image of Tars approaching Carter with the spear from A PRINCESS OF MARS, his Thark troops behind him.

TARS CAPTION: His name is **Grost**. He was with me the day I first encountered John Carter at the hatchery.

Panel 15.3: **FROM WOM ANNUAL 1**: Tars and Hok squaring off, warriors standing in a loose semi-circle around them.

TARS CAPTION: And he was with me before that.

TARS CAPTION: When Hok challenged me.

Panel 15.4: Angle from behind several Thark Warriors – so that none of them can be identified – as Tars and Hok lock up in unarmed battle.

TARS CAPTION: Some warriors chose sides. Some simply stood aside.

TARS CAPTION: And then I killed Hok. There was only one side after that.

Panel 15.5: Close-up on the dead Hok, his own tusks sticking out of his bleeding eye sockets.

TARS CAPTION: Or so I thought.

TARS CAPTION: I believe I can explain the broken tusks.

PAGE SIXTEEN

Panel 16.1: DT abruptly turns to Rek.

DT: Kenda Than and the guards will handle the rest, Rek. You may take your leave of us.

REK: But princess –

DT: That is all. I will see you around the palace, no doubt, and introduce you to John Carter. All is under control here.

Panel 16.2: DT's back is to Rek and he eyes open wide as he mentions …

REK: A thrill, of course.

REK: Ah … does any of this have to do with your absence before and at the star of the festival?

Panel 16.3: She turns around, having gathered herself enough to look annoyed.

DT: Rek. I need not explain my comings and goings. I am princess of Helium, no prisoner of it.

REK: Of course not.

Panel 16.4: DT and Rek, others looking on.

REK: I merely ask such questions so that if anything that may pose a threat to yo or to Helium, I may advise our jeddak – your grandfather.

DT: Yes, Rek.

Panel 16.5: As Rek leaves, he looks back over his shoulder and points at Kenda.

REK: Kenda Than, you will also keep me abreast of your investigation.

KENDA: As you order.

PAGE SEVENTEEN

Panel 17.1: Kenda exchanges a silent look with DT that says, "What a piece of work." Or "What a douchebag." You get the idea.

NO DIALOGUE

anel 17.2: DT turns to Tars.

DT: Hok?

DT: HOK?!!

TARS: Yes. I had known him since we were hatchlings.

Panel 17.3: Flashback panel to ISSUE 1 with Carter holding the tusk goblets.

DT CAPTION: Issus, I know that name! John Carter began telling me about him, but I did not listen.

Panel 17.4: Flashback to ISSUE 2 with Voro standing in the door of the dungeon.

DT CAPTION: And then when I was captive in the caves, Voro spoke of him!

TARS CAPTION: Voro spoke of **Hok?**

DT CAPTION: Voro said Hok was a great warrior, that it was he who should be jeddak of the Tharks now.

DT CAPTION: And that he had great loyalty to Hok.

Panel 17.5: DT, Tars and Kenda have expressions somewhere between "Eureka" and Oh, shit."

TARS: "Had." Perhaps the loyalty was not in the past tense.

DT: And I let him go.

KENDA: If I may preempt what sounds like a guilt excursion here … we need to move.

PAGE EIGHTEEN

Panel 18.1: DT, Tars and Kenda are walking at a brisk clip – and Kenda's huffing. Behind them, a few Heliumite guards and a Thark warrior follow.

KENDA: Just to be clear, Princess, is Rek a royal advisor or royal **informant**?

DT: Good question. He is also a suitor from long ago.

Panel 18.2: Medium-close profile on DT as Kenda looks over at her. She smiles faintly at him

KENDA: Indeed.

KENDA: Just to be clear for **you**, then, you can trust me. Answering to more than one superior always made me … short of breath, anyway.

Panel 18.3: They're walking up a long stairwell in an old residential building.

DT: I was kidnapped by Voro. He was … performing **atrocities** on red women, and he nearly did to me. I let him go in exchange for names of his accomplices.

DT: If Rek discovered that and informed Tardos Mors …

KENDA: The jeddak of Helium develops an adverse reaction to the color green. So much for peace and harmony. Got it.

Panel 18.4: They approach the door of a modest dwelling/apartment.

KENDA: Then keep thinking of the names of the other Tharks who were there when you killed Hok, Tars Tarkas. We must go to all of them at once.

KENDA: Now you know my secret, by the way.

Panel 18.5: Kenda raises a hand to knock on the door. DT is on one side of him and Tars is on the other.

TARS: For solving murders?

KENDA: For maintaining this physique.

PAGE NINETEEN

Panel 19.1: Kenda knocks with the bottom of his fist on the door.

SFX: BAM! BAM! BAM!

KENDA: This is Kenda Than of the royal guard! Open the door!

KENDA: I am here with Tars –

Panel 19.2: Big panel. Gunfire splinters the door and kills Kenda in a revolting splatter of blood. DT and Tars jump aside in surprise/shock.

SFX: THWOOM!

DT: KENDA!

PAGE TWENTY

Panel 20.1: Moments later. A Heliumite guard and the Thark warrior come out of the apartment through the door – which has been kicked in and hangs askew in pieces.

GUARD: Gone.

THARK WARRIOR: Nobody.

Panel 20.2: DT looks down at Kenda's body. Smoke comes from his wounds.

DT: Prepare a cell, anyway.

GUARD: Yes, Princess. For whom?

anel 20.3: Larger panel, 3/5ths of page. DT points at Tars – who is shocked along with veryone else.

DT: For Tars Tarkas.

DT: Lock him up.

EXT: IT'S NOT EASY BEING GREEN!

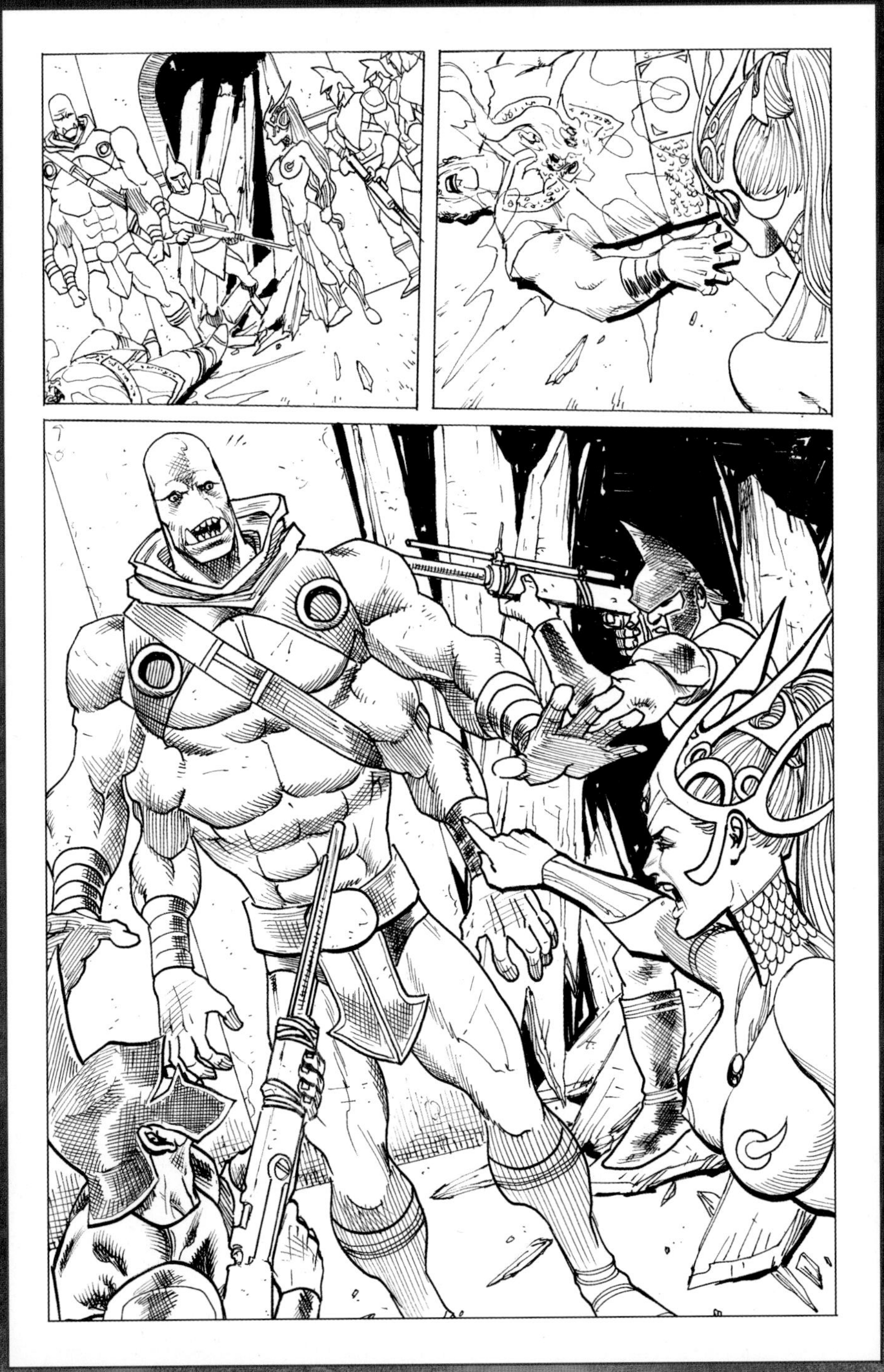

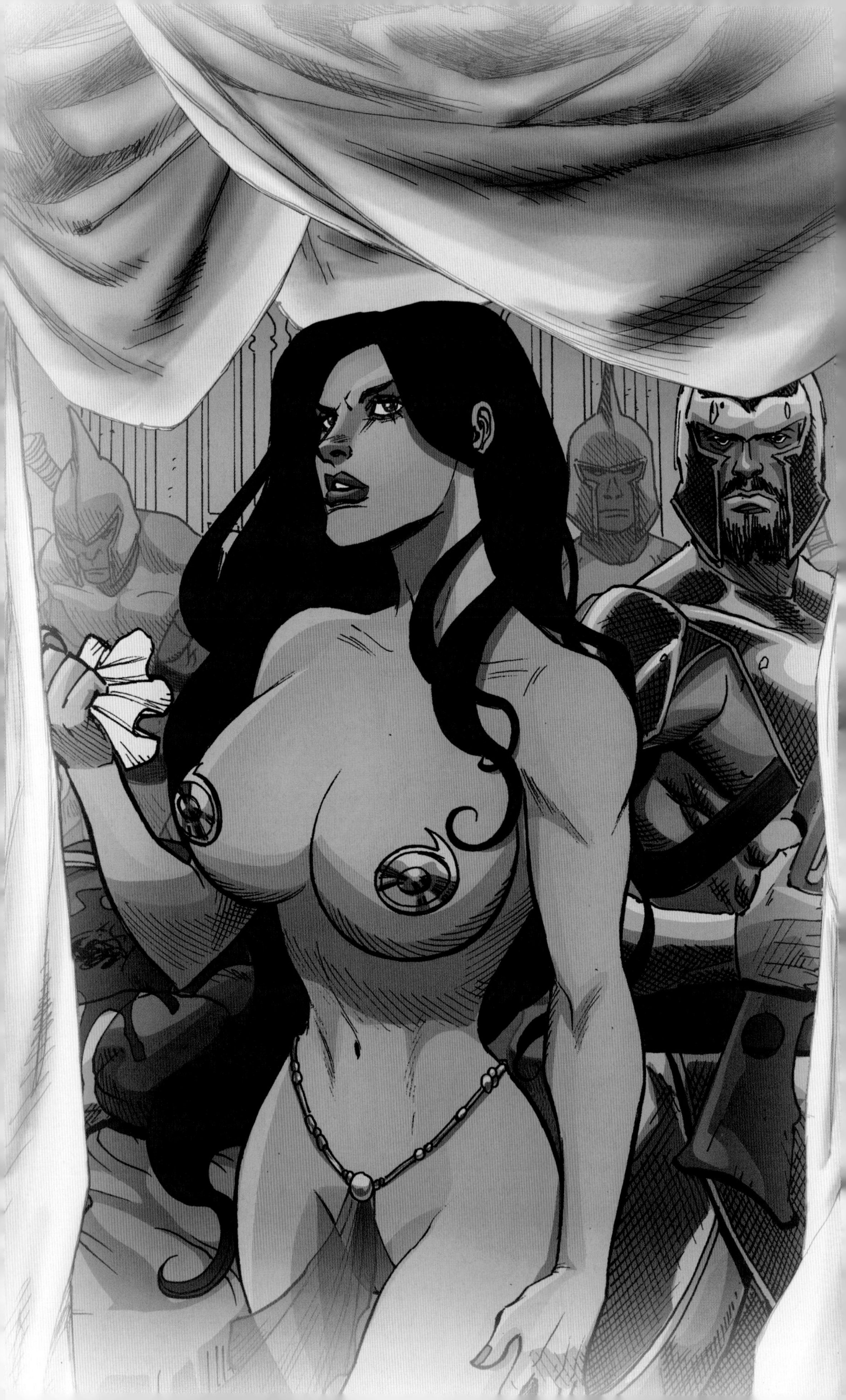

RISQUÉ COVER GALLERY

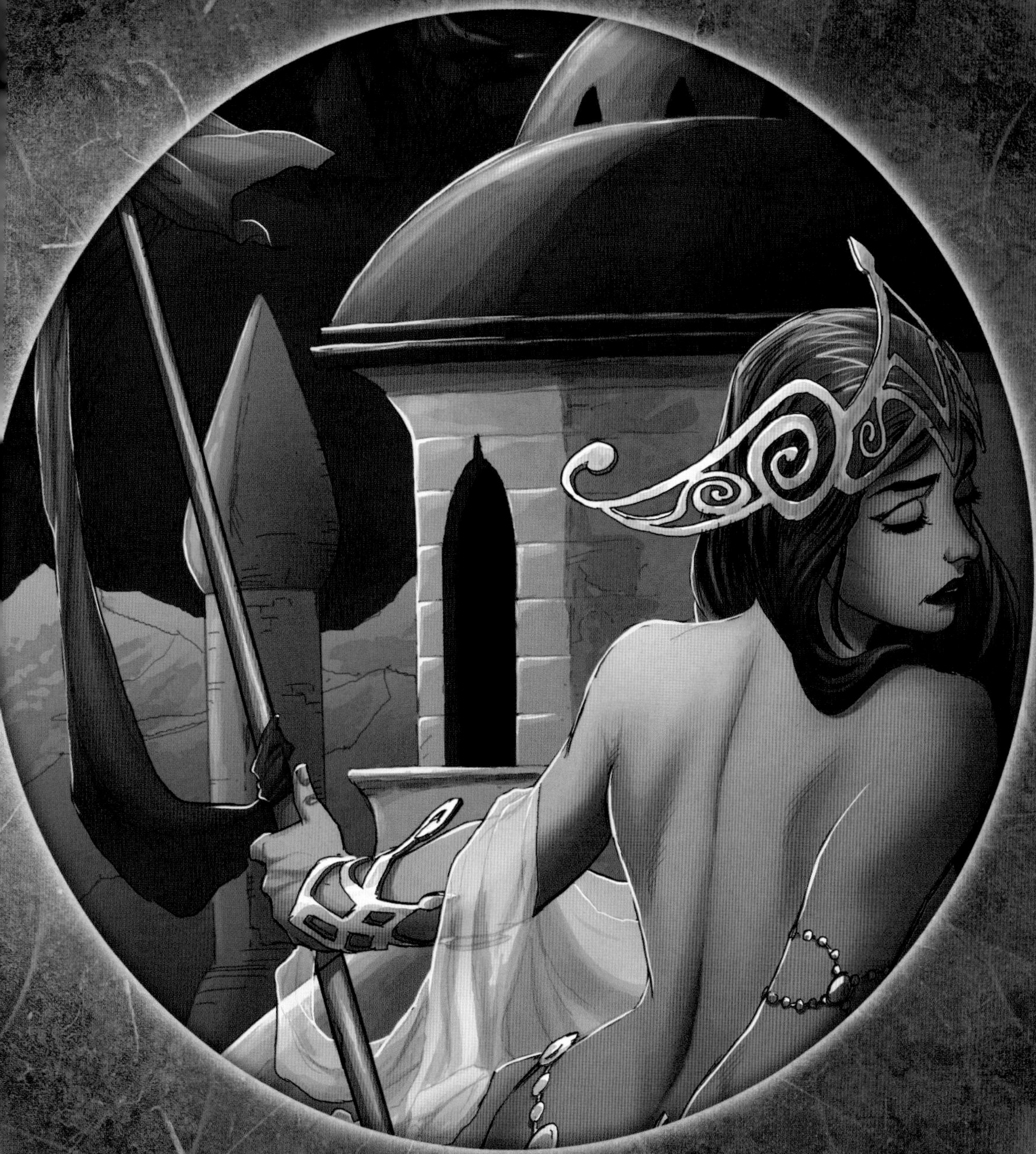

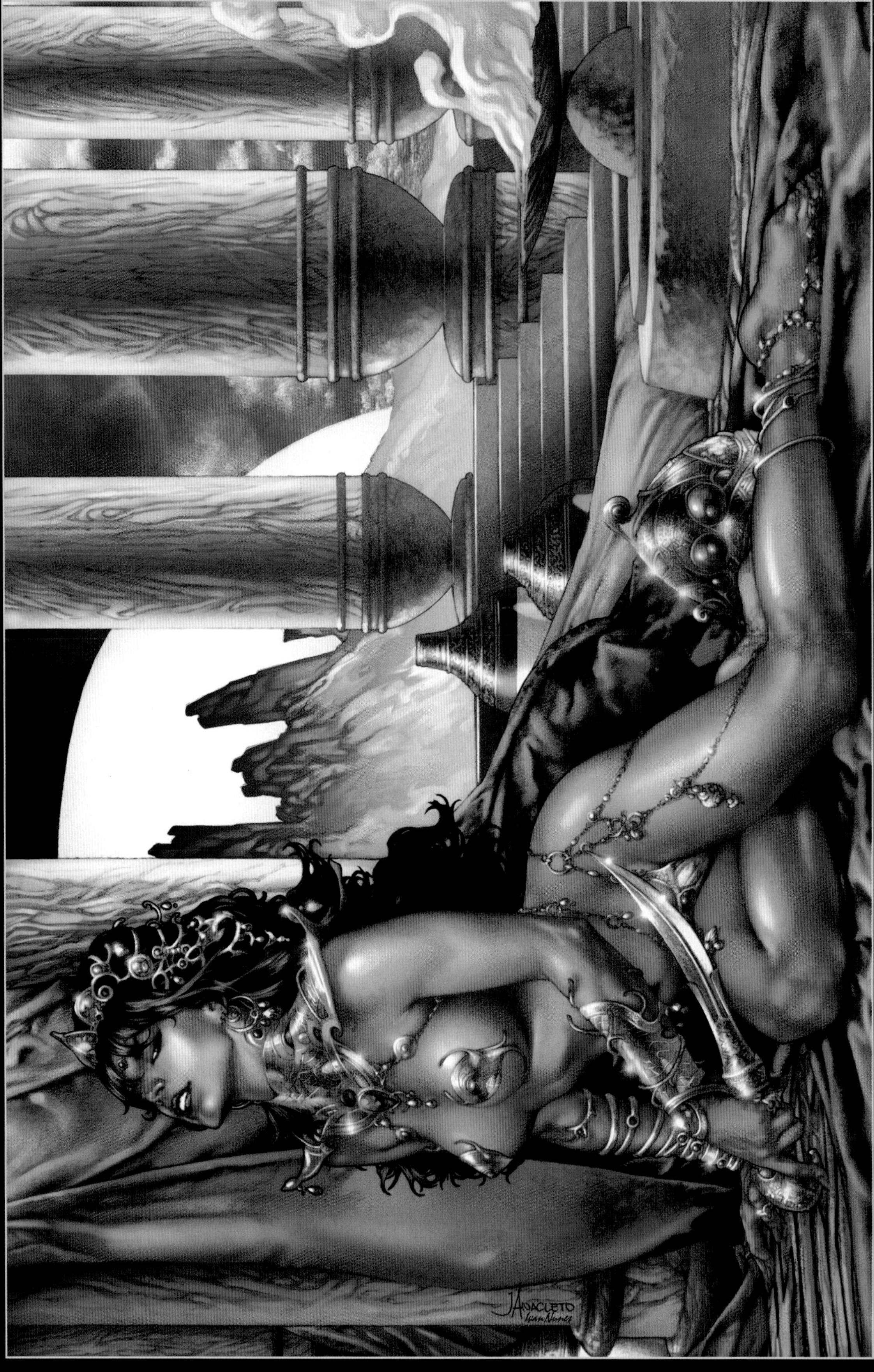
J ANACLETO
Ivan Nunes

issue #5 cover by **JAY ANACLETO**
colors by **IVAN NUNES**

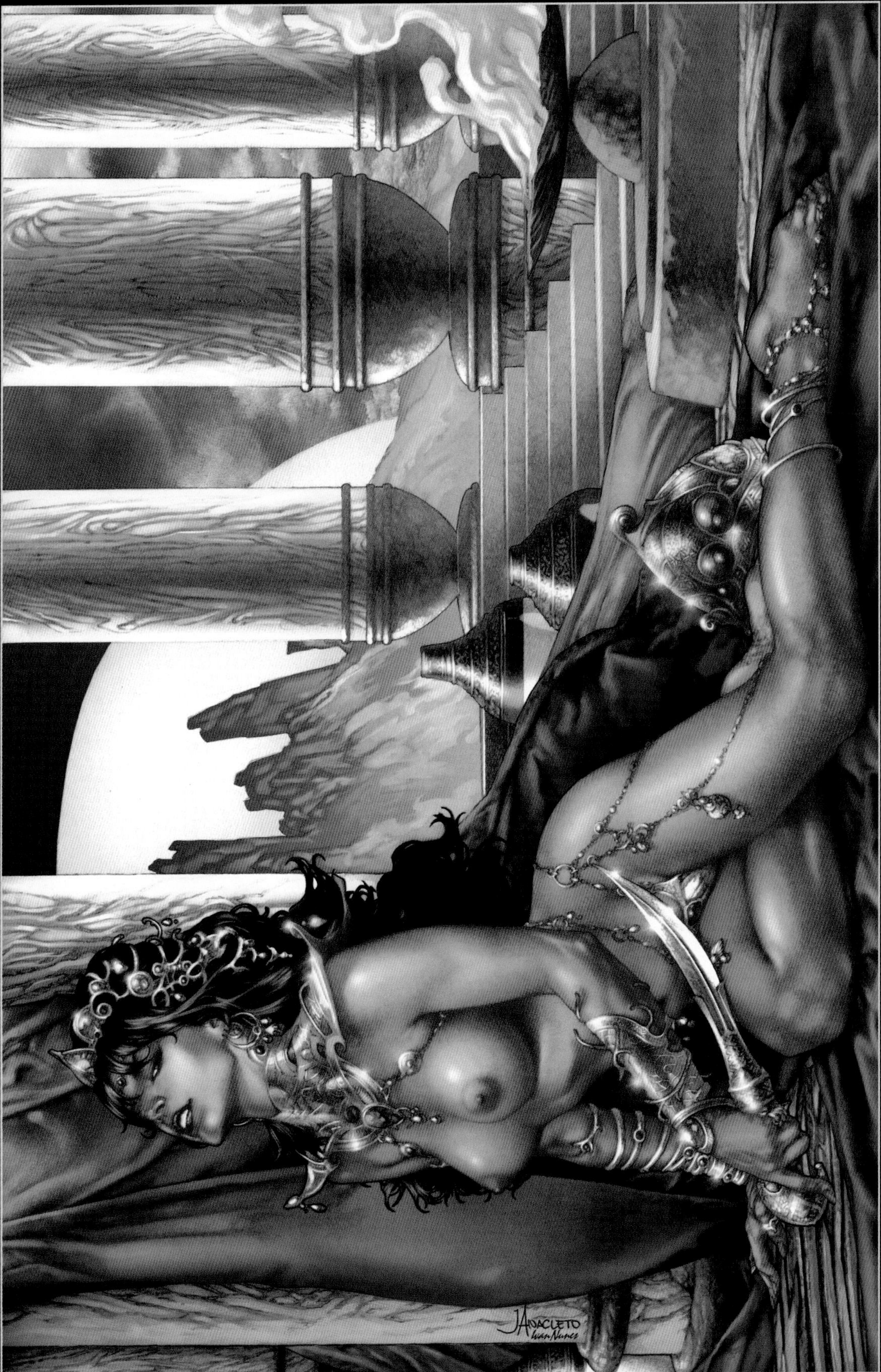

issue #5 risqué cover by **JAY ANACLETO**

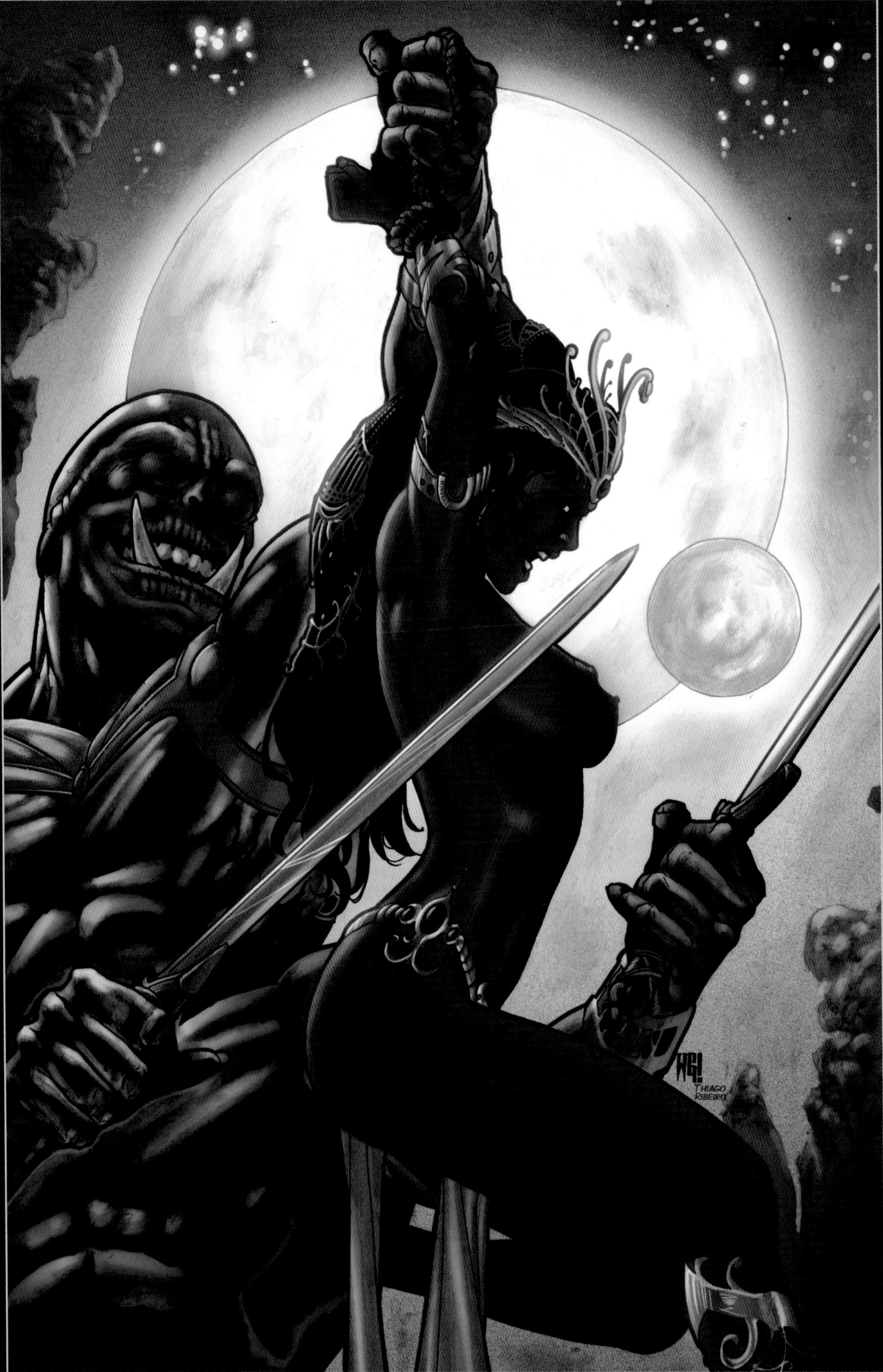
WG!
THIAGO RIBEIRO

issue #5 risqué cover by **WALTER GEOVANI**
colors by **THIAGO RIBEIRO**

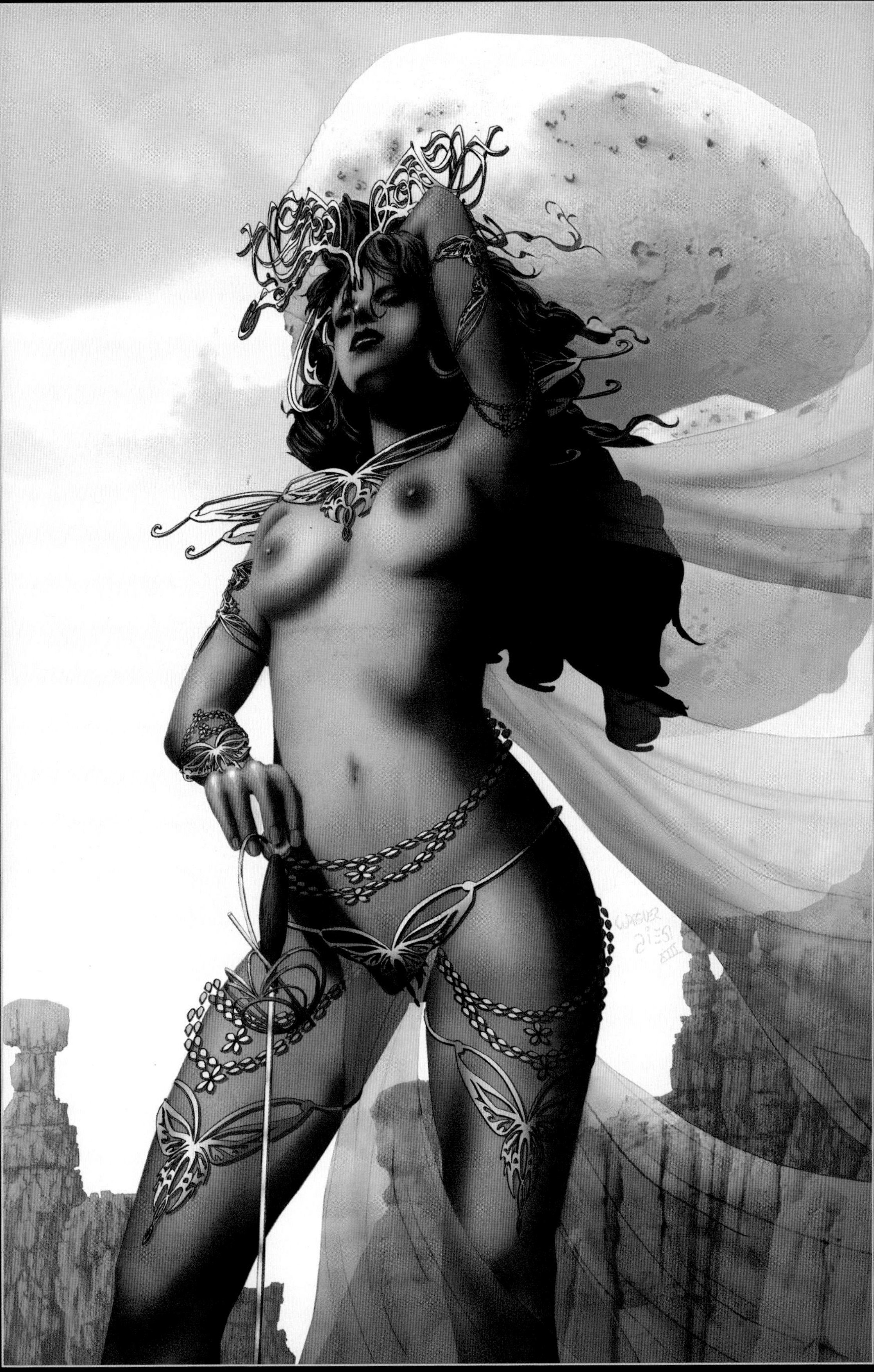

issue #5 risqué cover by **WAGNER REIS**

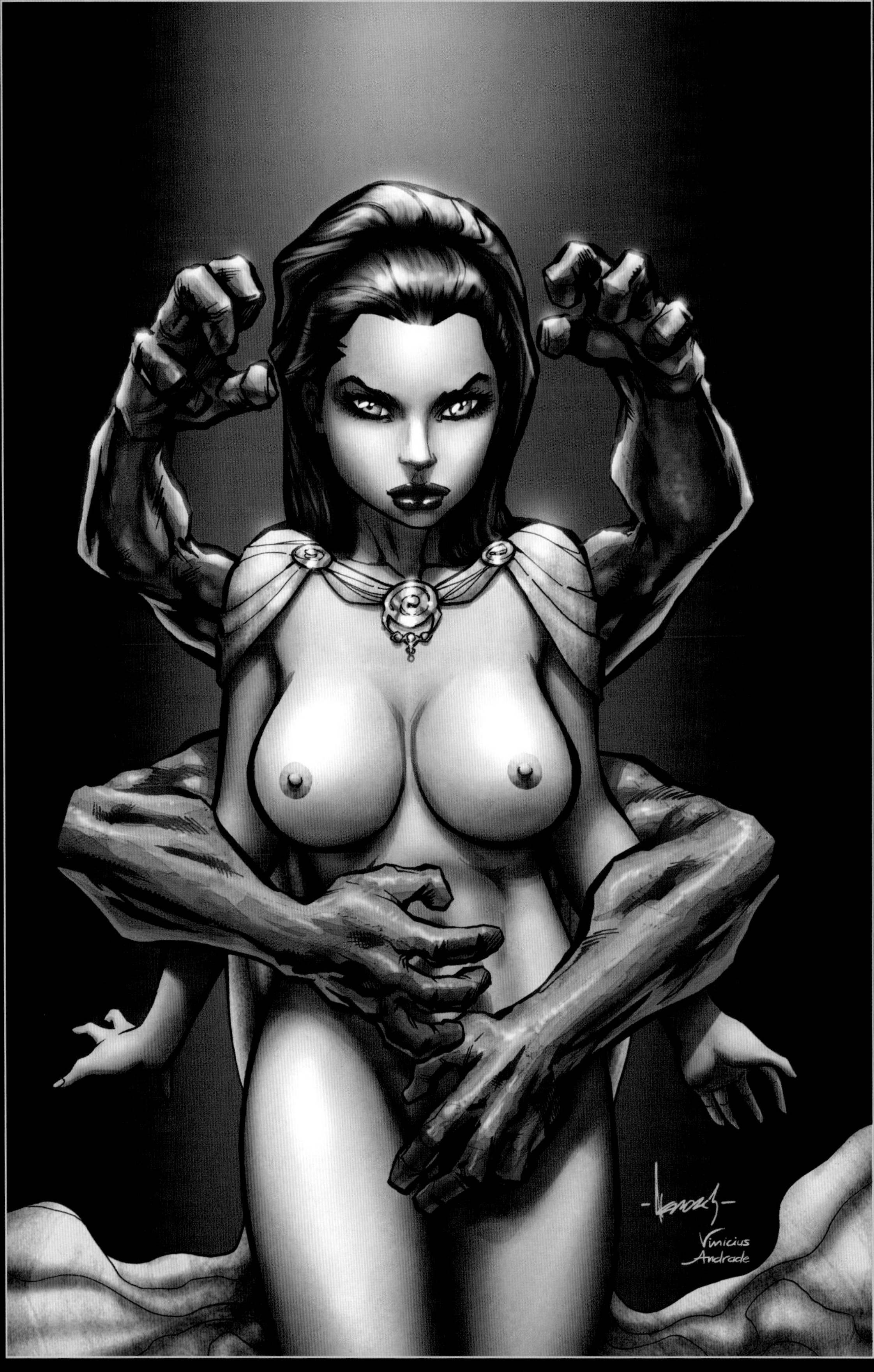
Vinicius
Andrade

issue #5 risqué cover by **ALÉ GARZA**

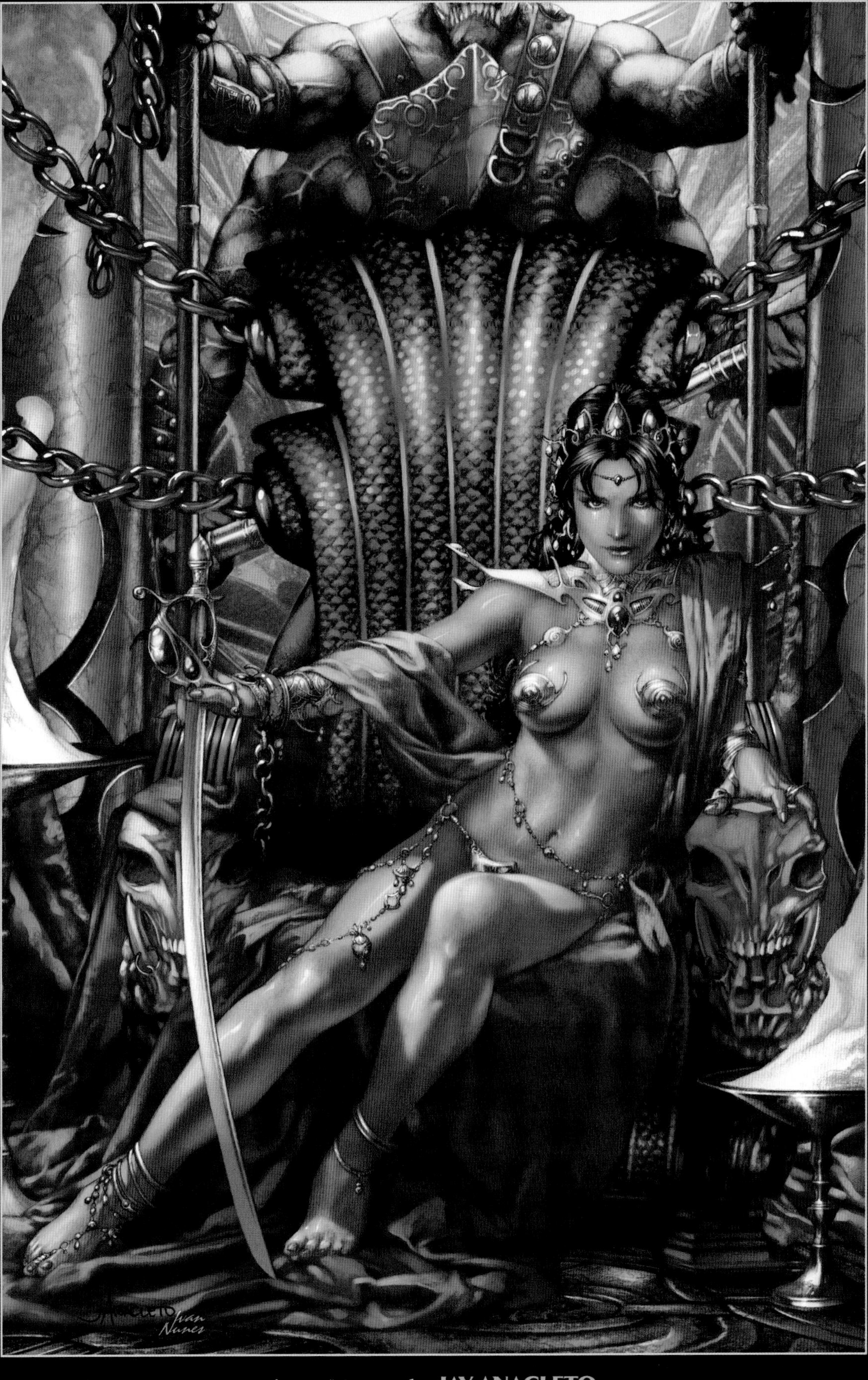

issue #6 cover by **JAY ANACLETO**
colors by **IVAN NUNES**

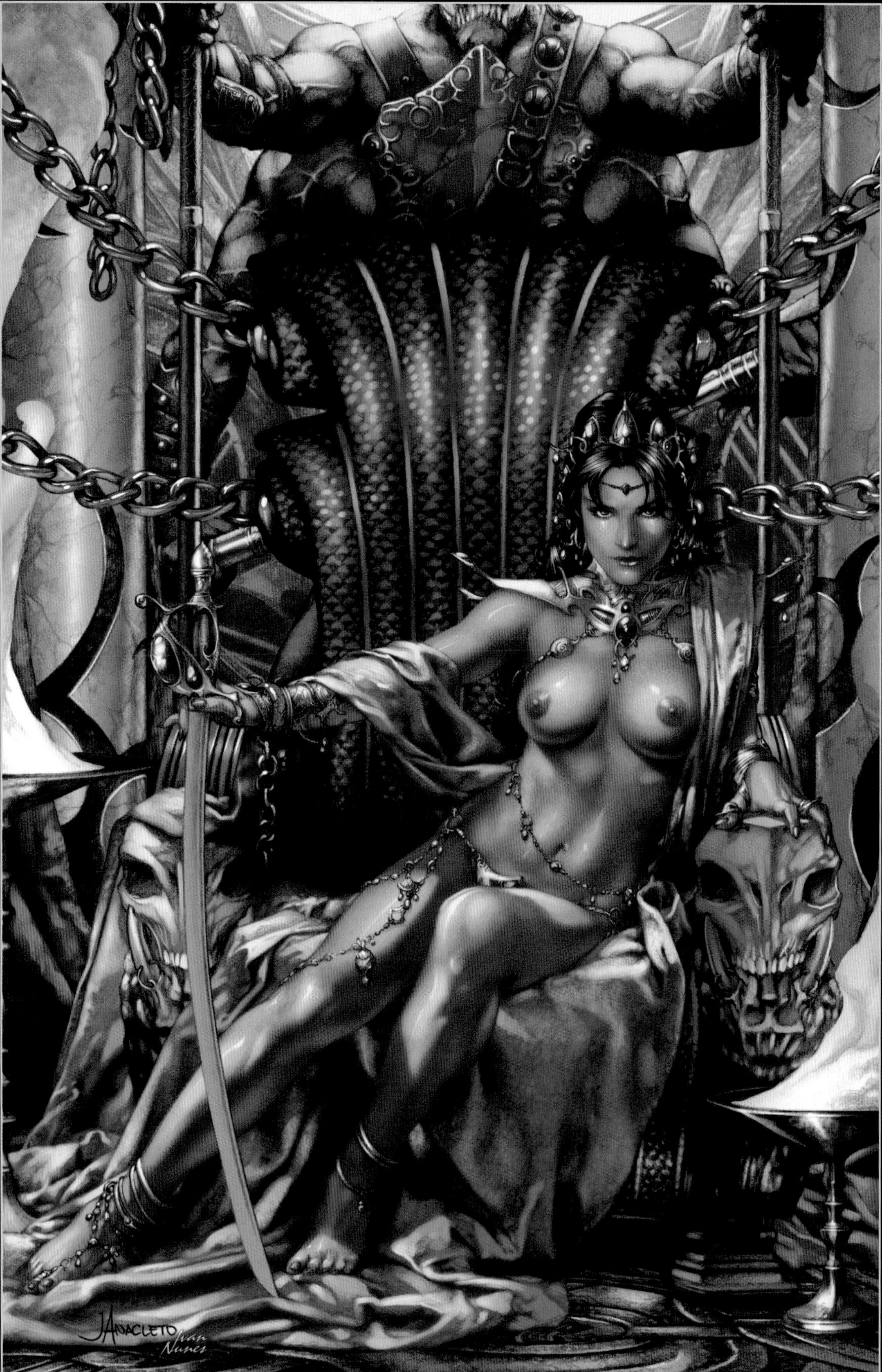
JANACLETO
Ivan Nunes

issue #6 risqué cover by **JAY ANACLETO**

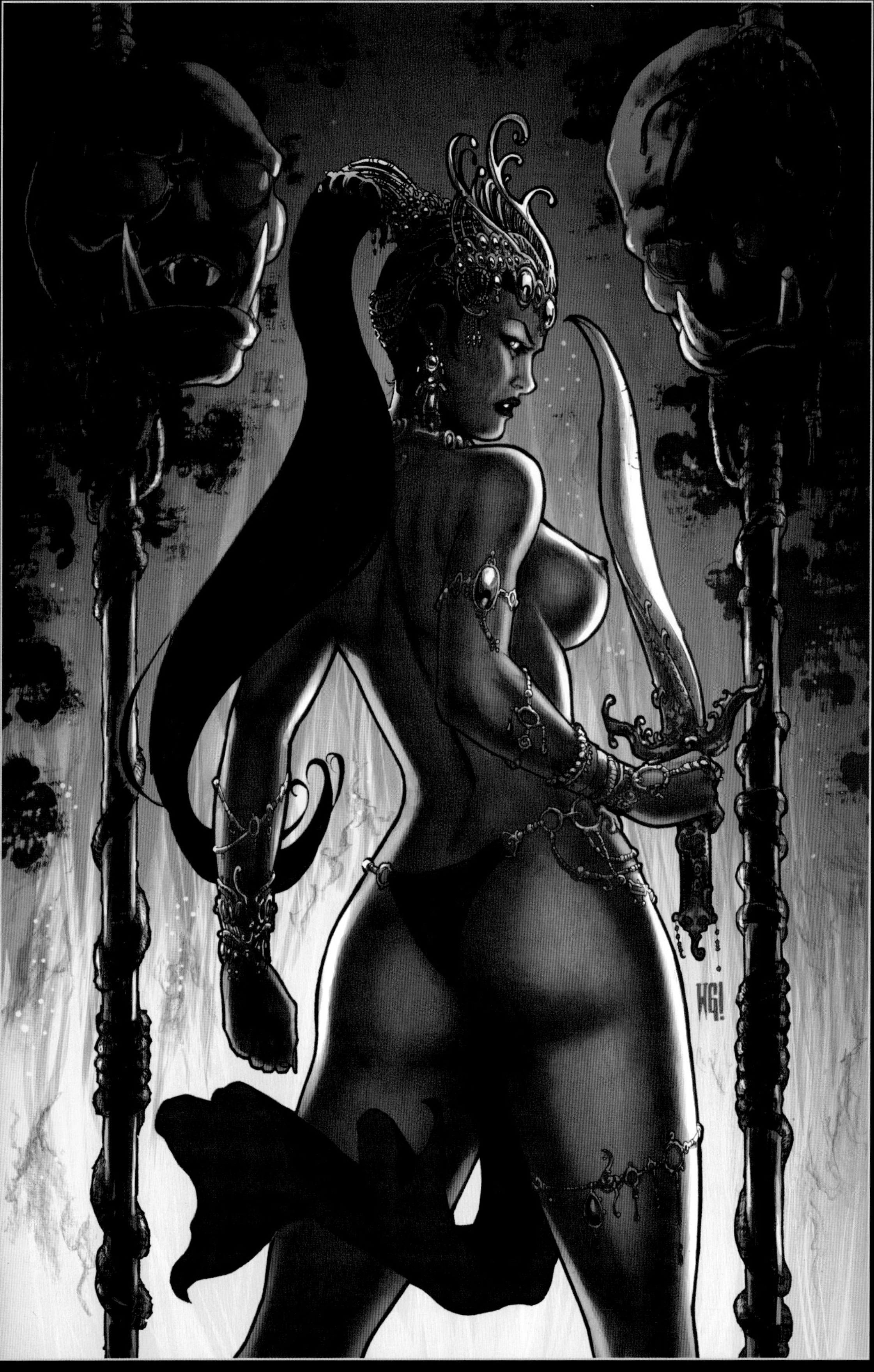
WG!

issue #6 risqué cover by **WALTER GEOVANI**

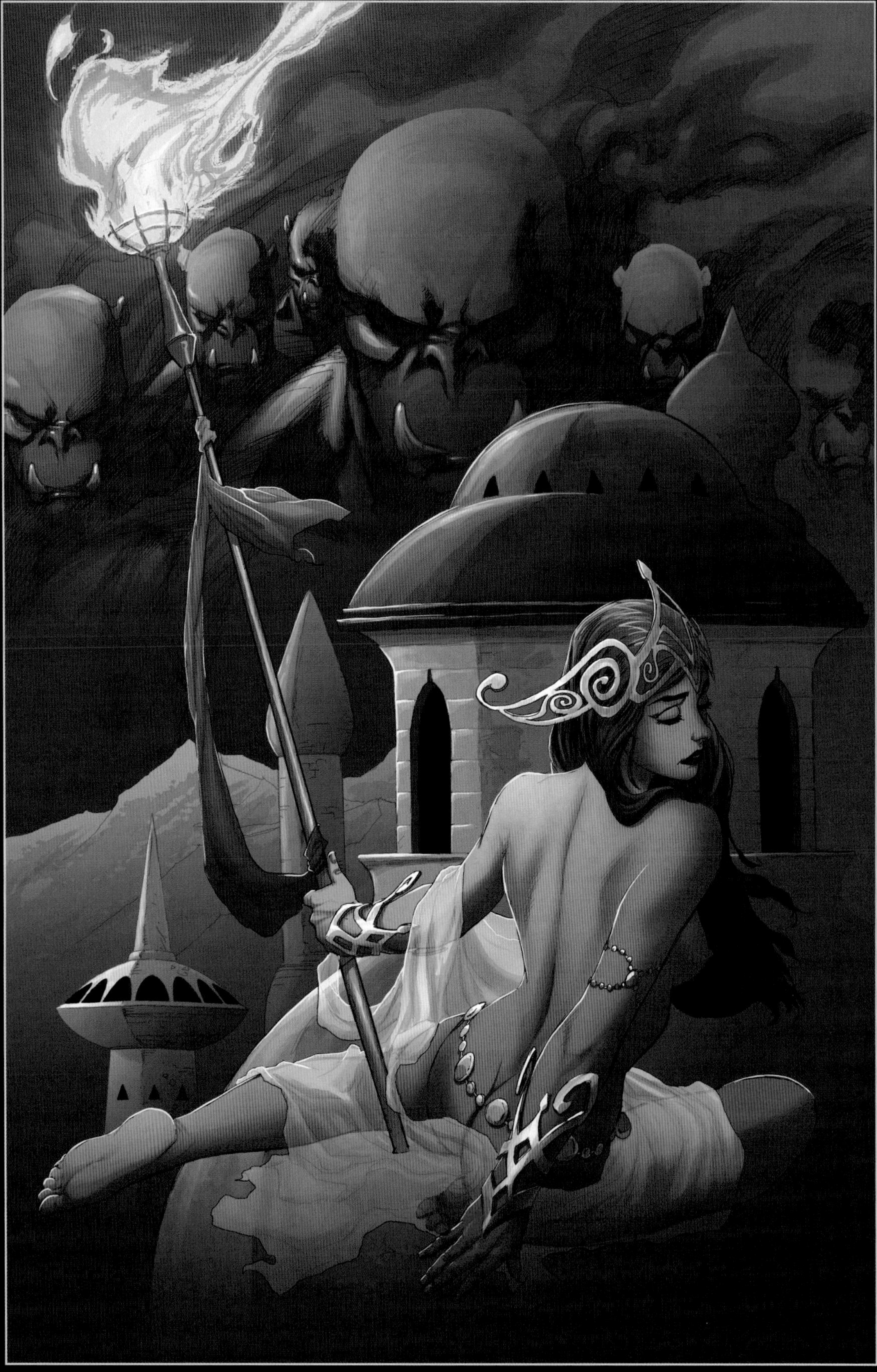

issue #6 risqué cover by **MEL RUBI**

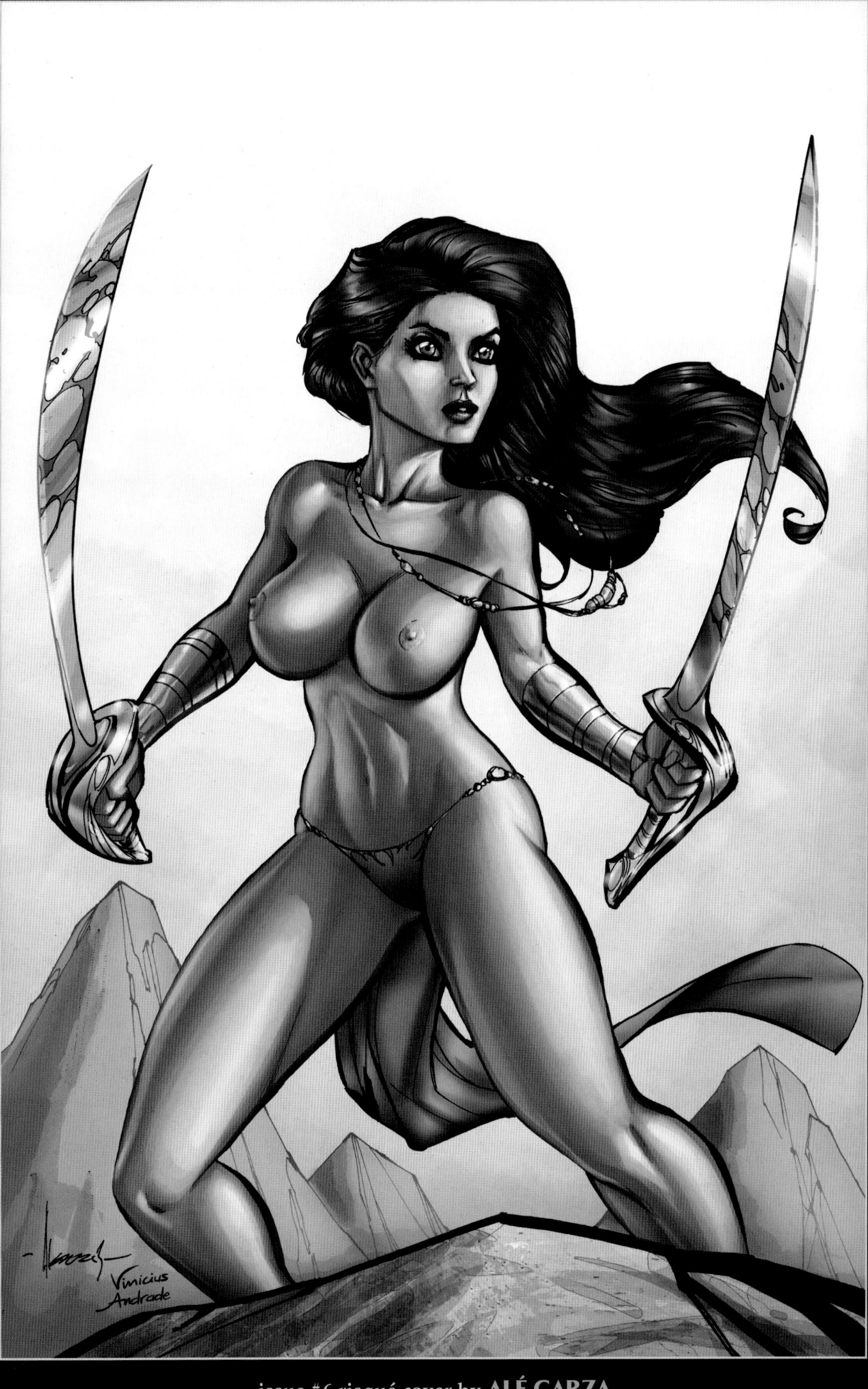
Vinicius Andrade

issue #6 risqué cover by **ALÉ GARZA**
colors by **VINICIUS ANDRADE**

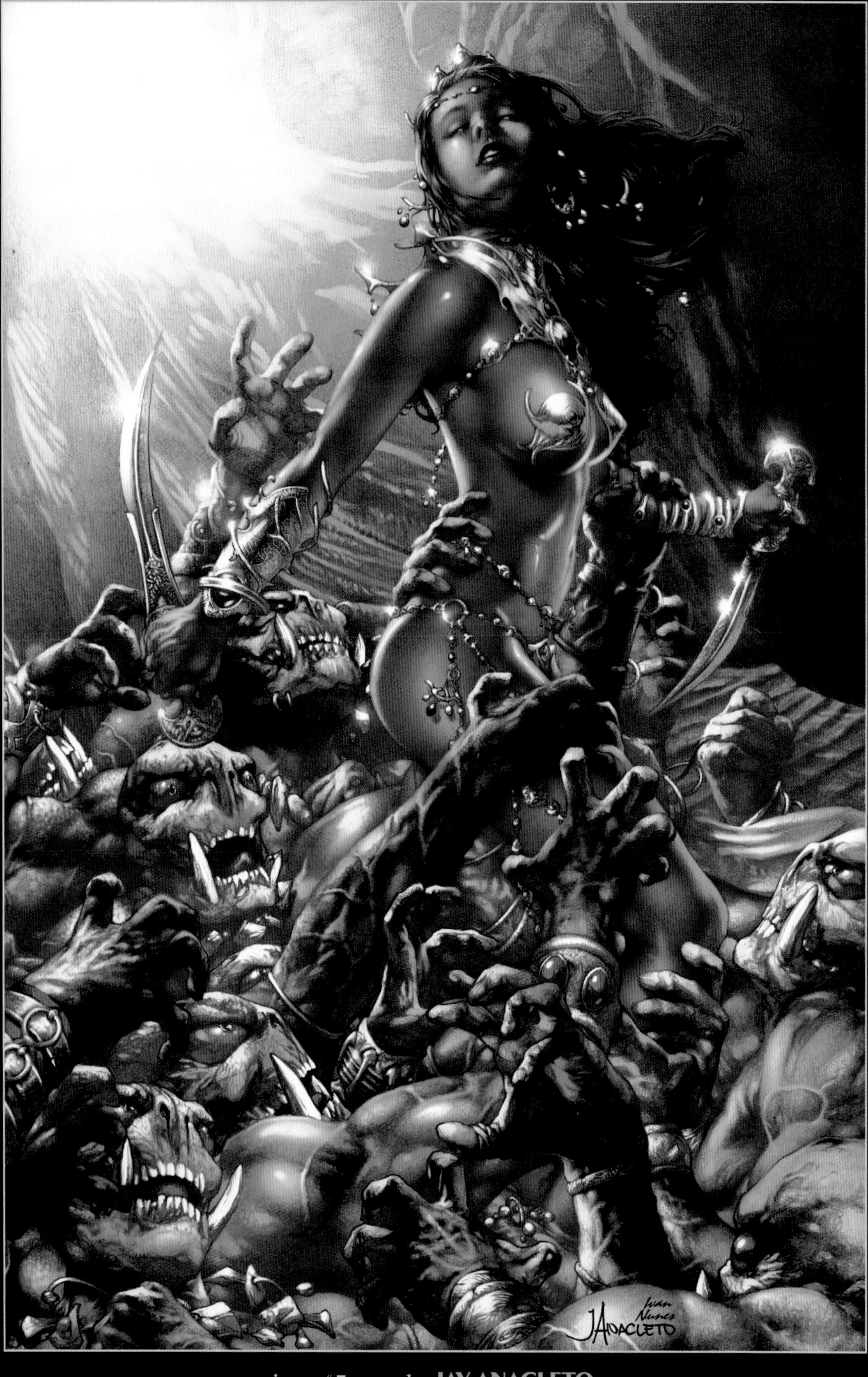
Ivan Nunes
J Anacleto

issue #7 cover by **JAY ANACLETO**
colors by **IVAN NUNES**

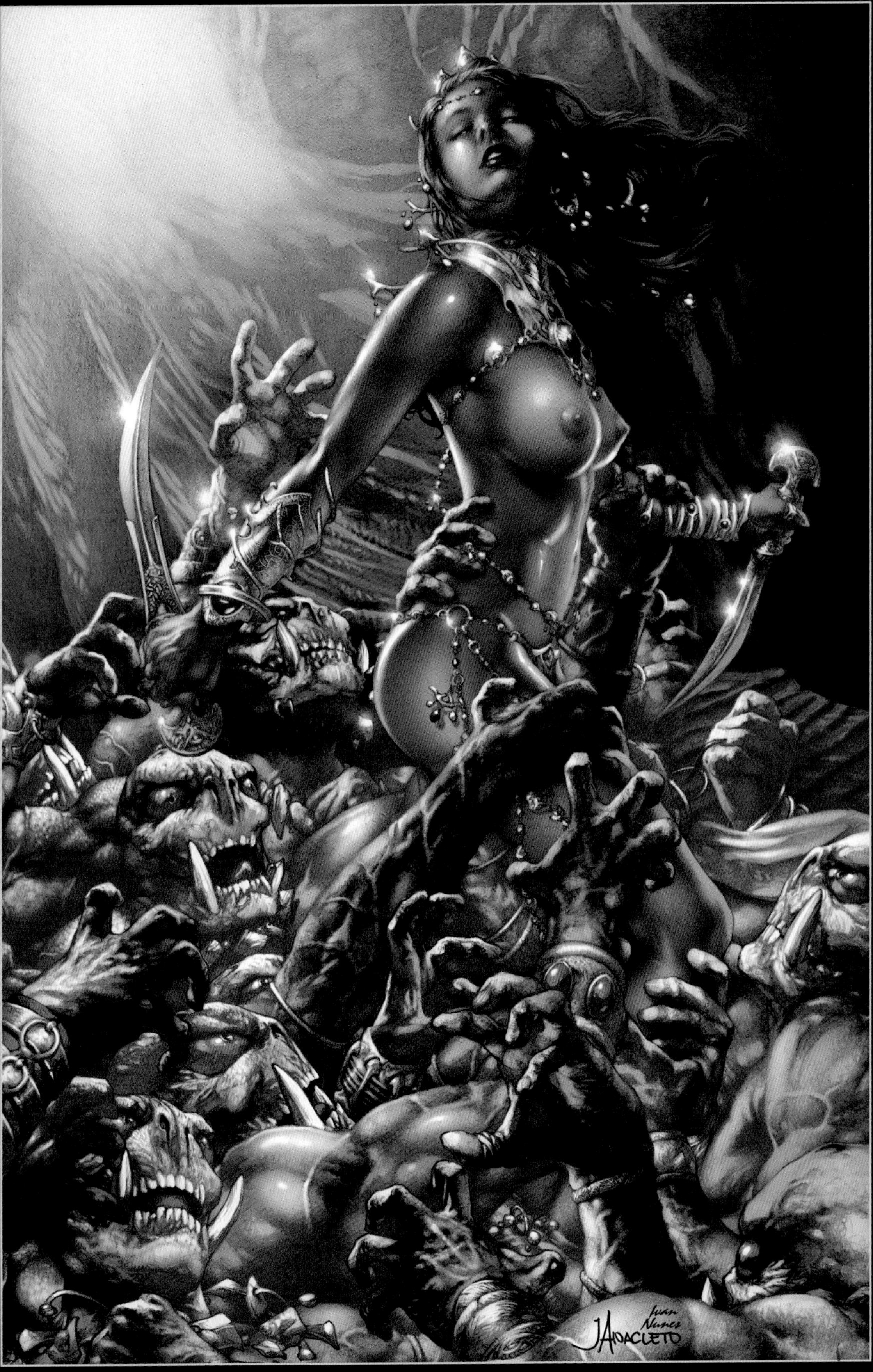

issue #7 risqué cover by **JAY ANACLETO**

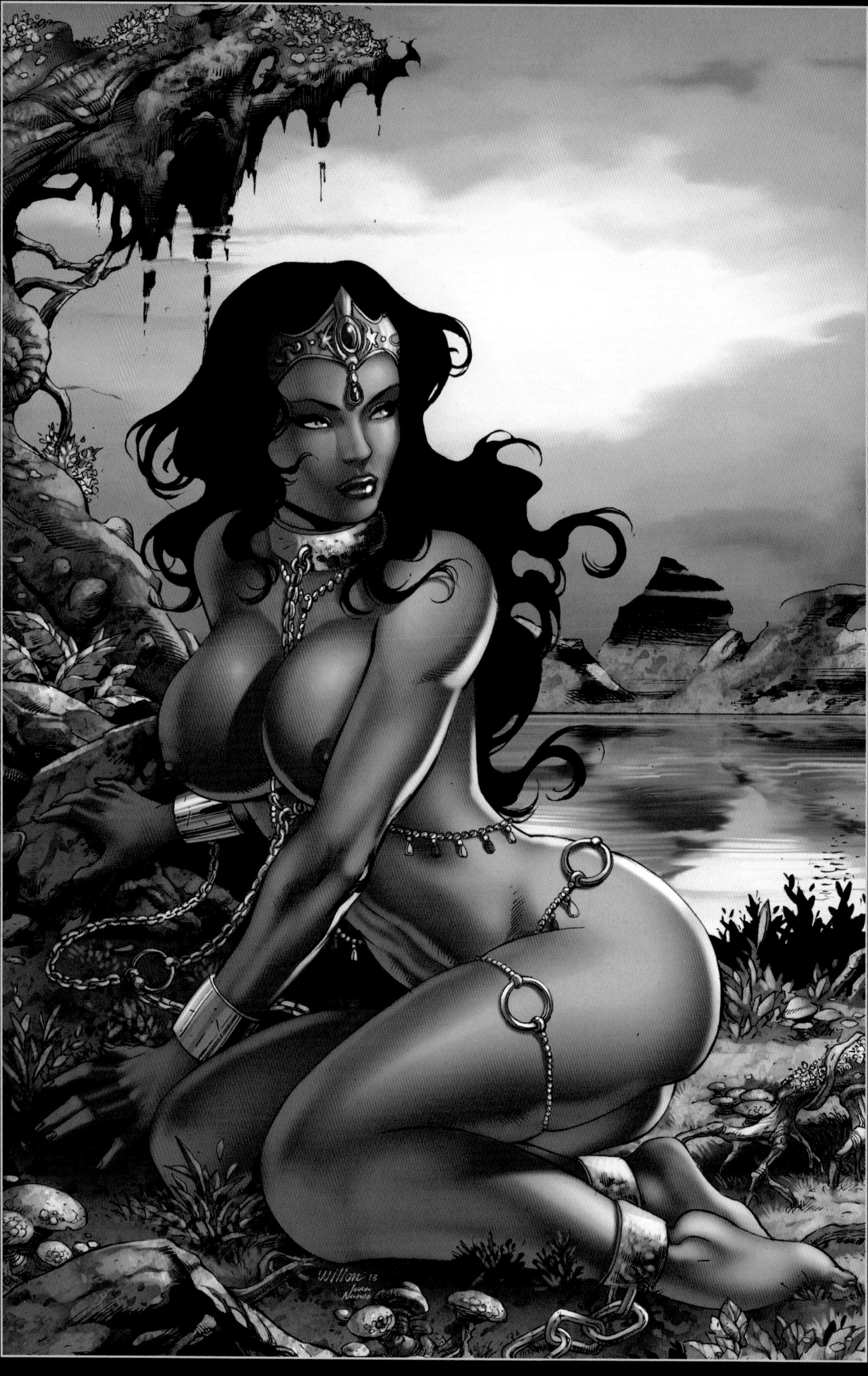

issue #7 risqué cover by **MILTON ESTEVAM**

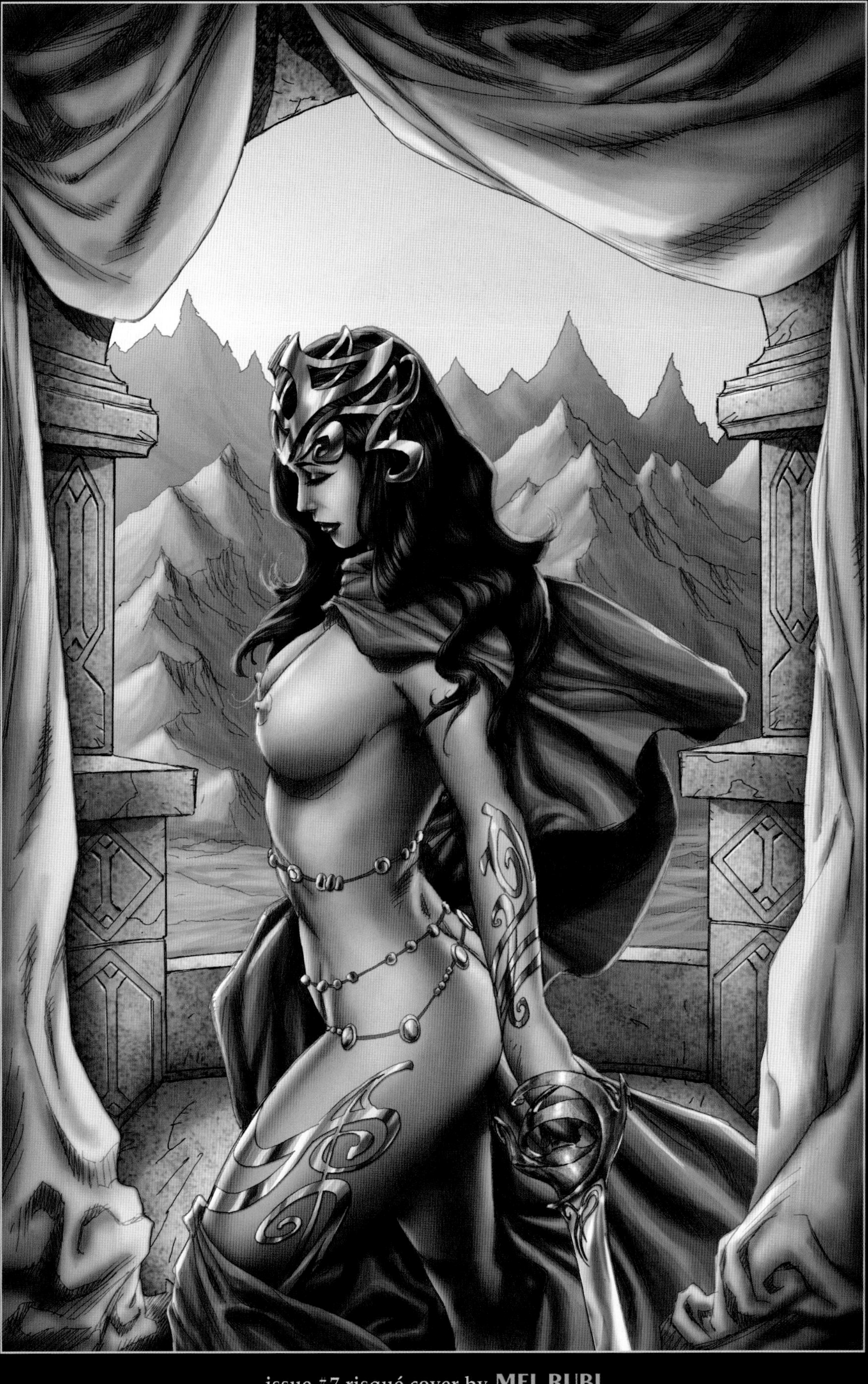

issue #7 risqué cover by **MEL RUBI**
colors by **VINICIUS ANDRADE**

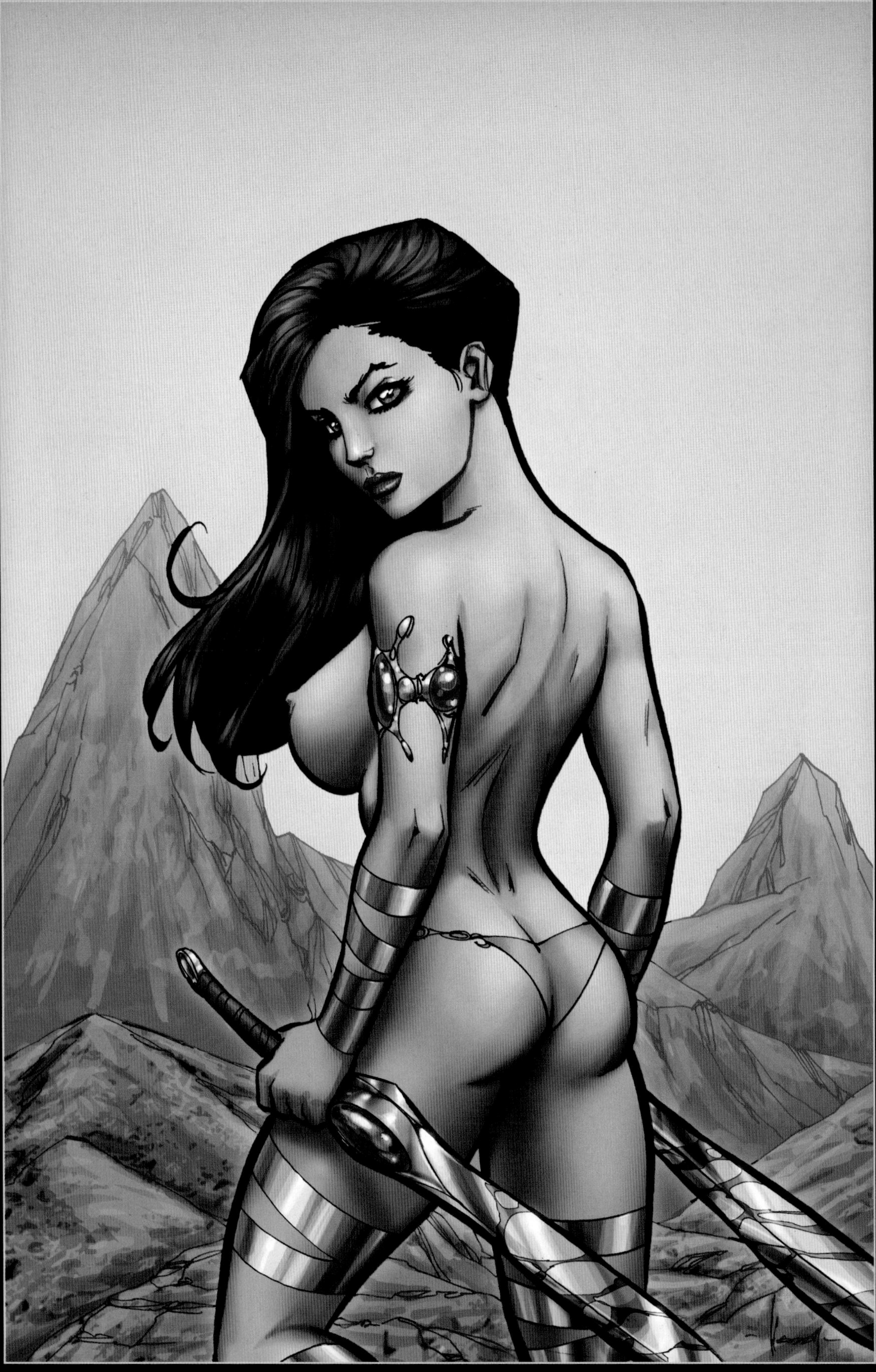

issue #7 risqué cover by **ALÉ GARZA**

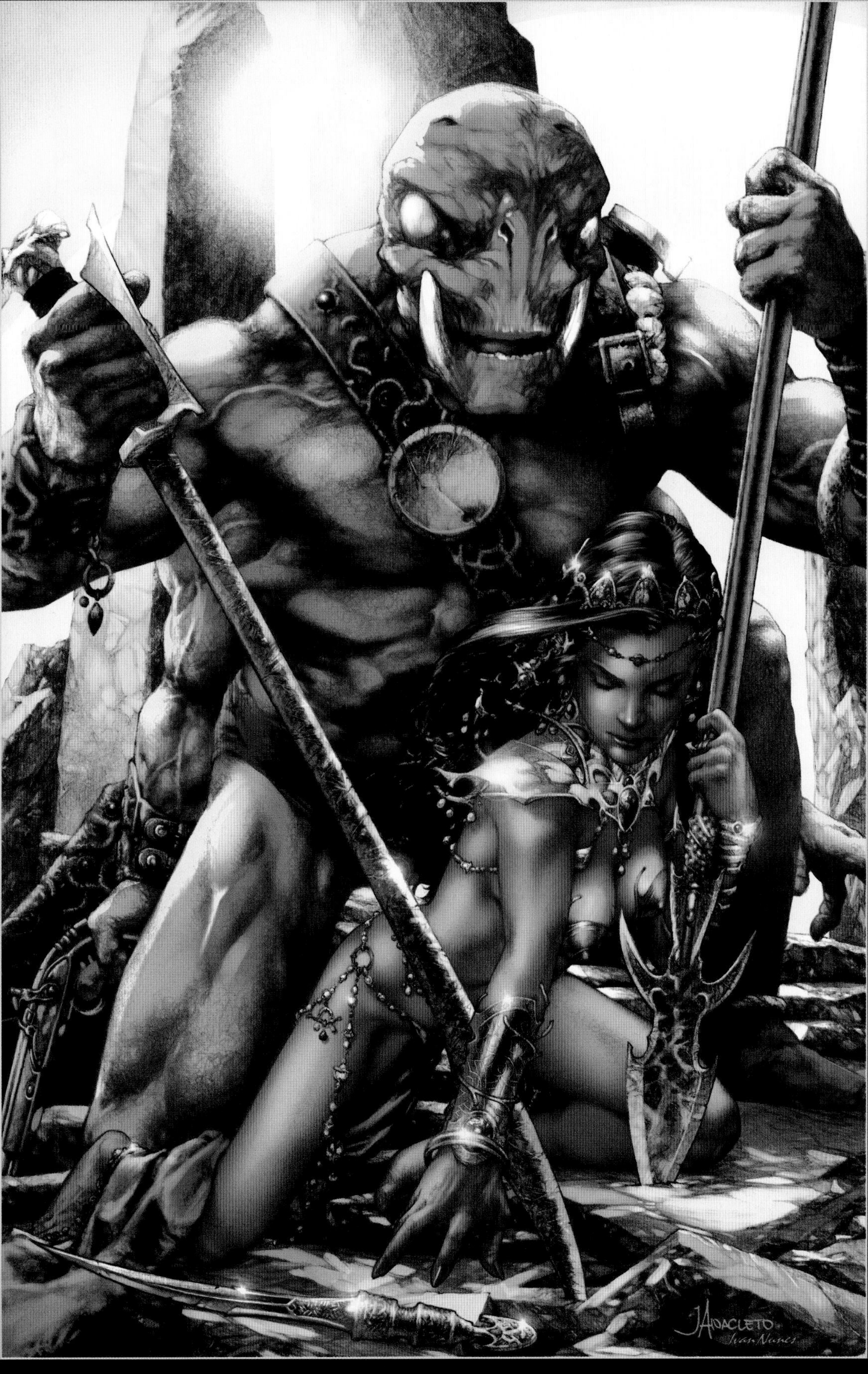
J ANACLETO
Ivan Nunes

issue #8 cover by **JAY ANACLETO**
colors by **IVAN NUNES**

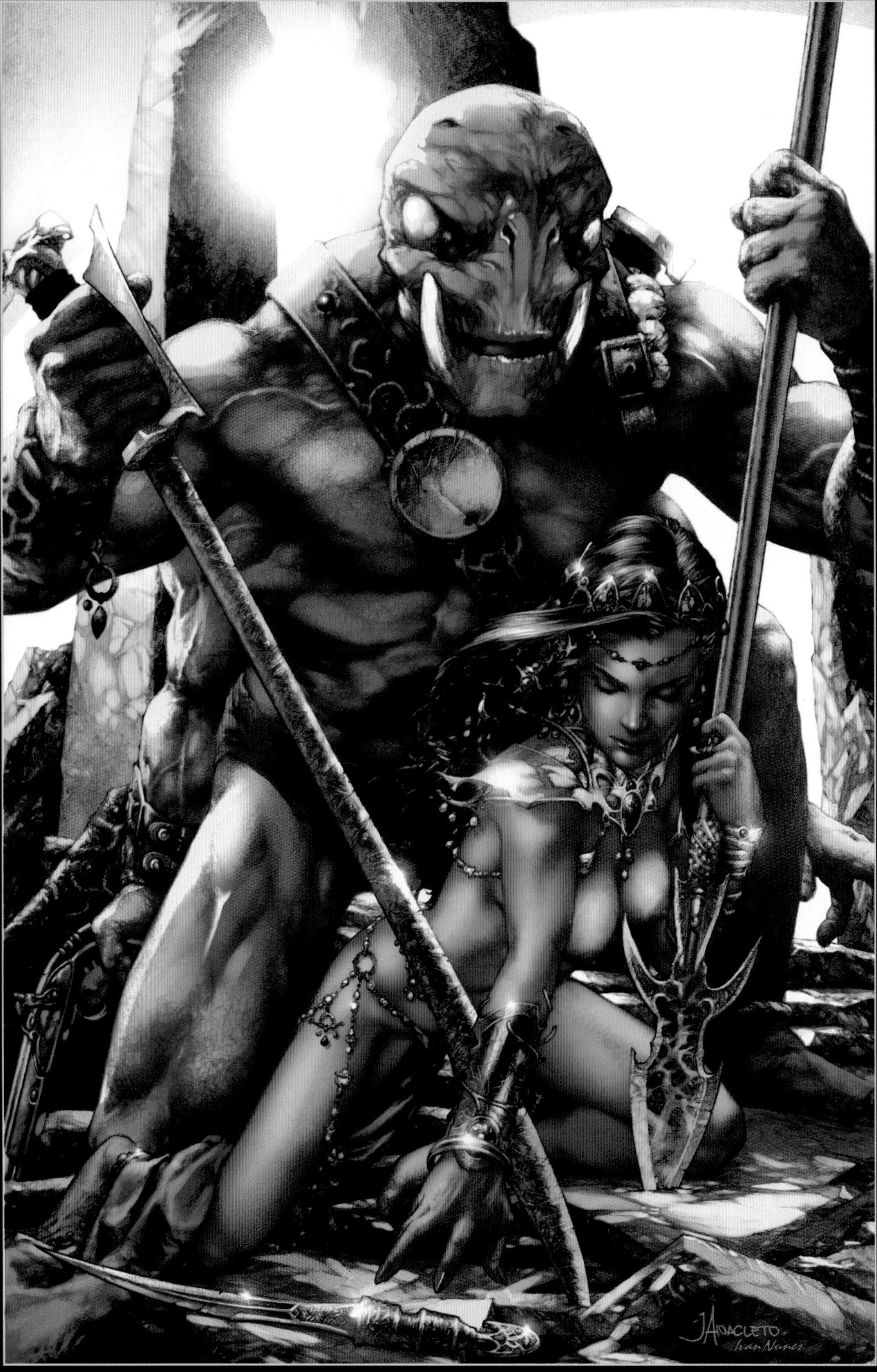
J ANACLETO
Ivan Nunes

issue #8 risqué cover by **JAY ANACLETO**

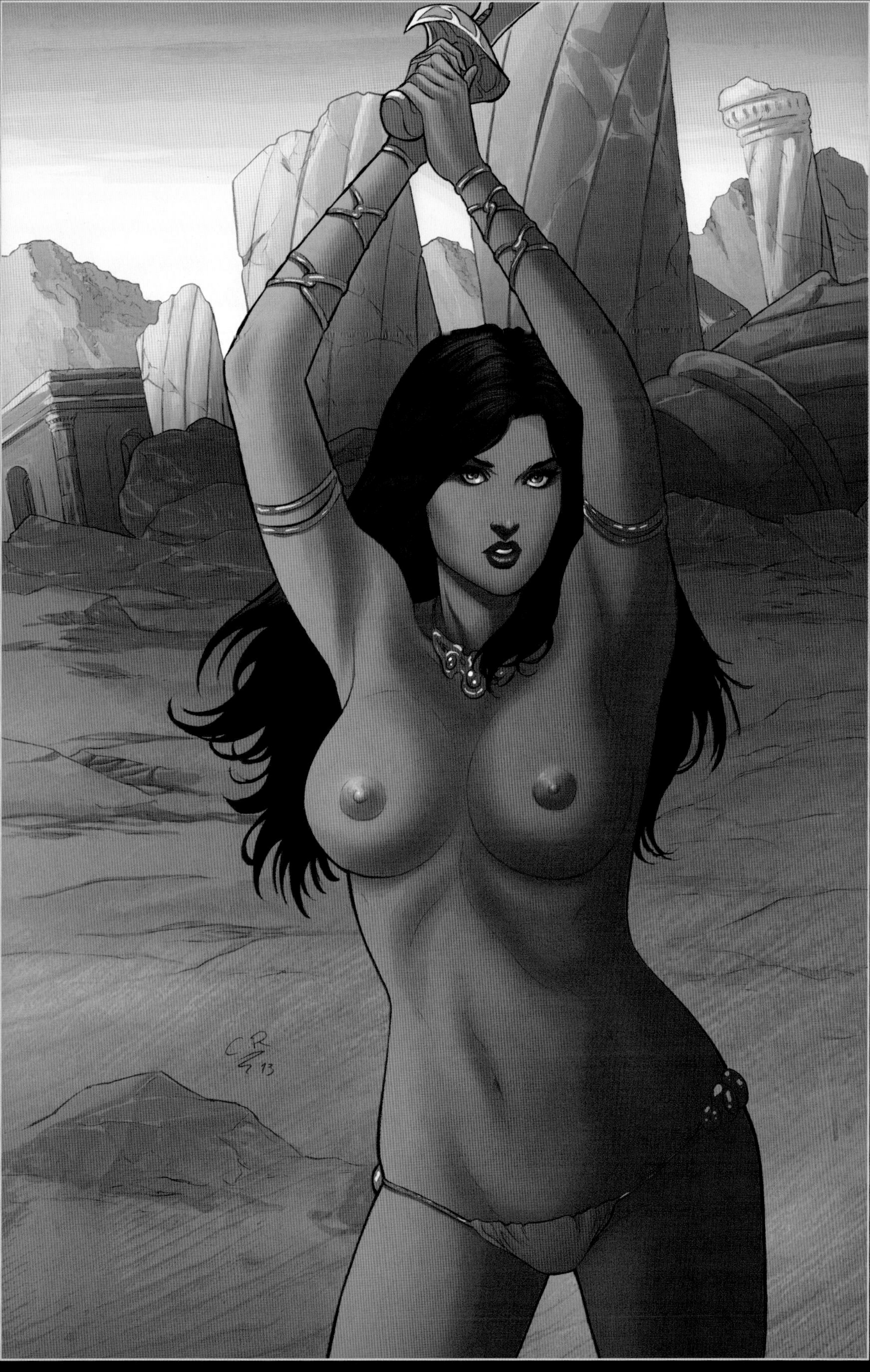

issue #8 risqué cover by **CARLOS RAFAEL**

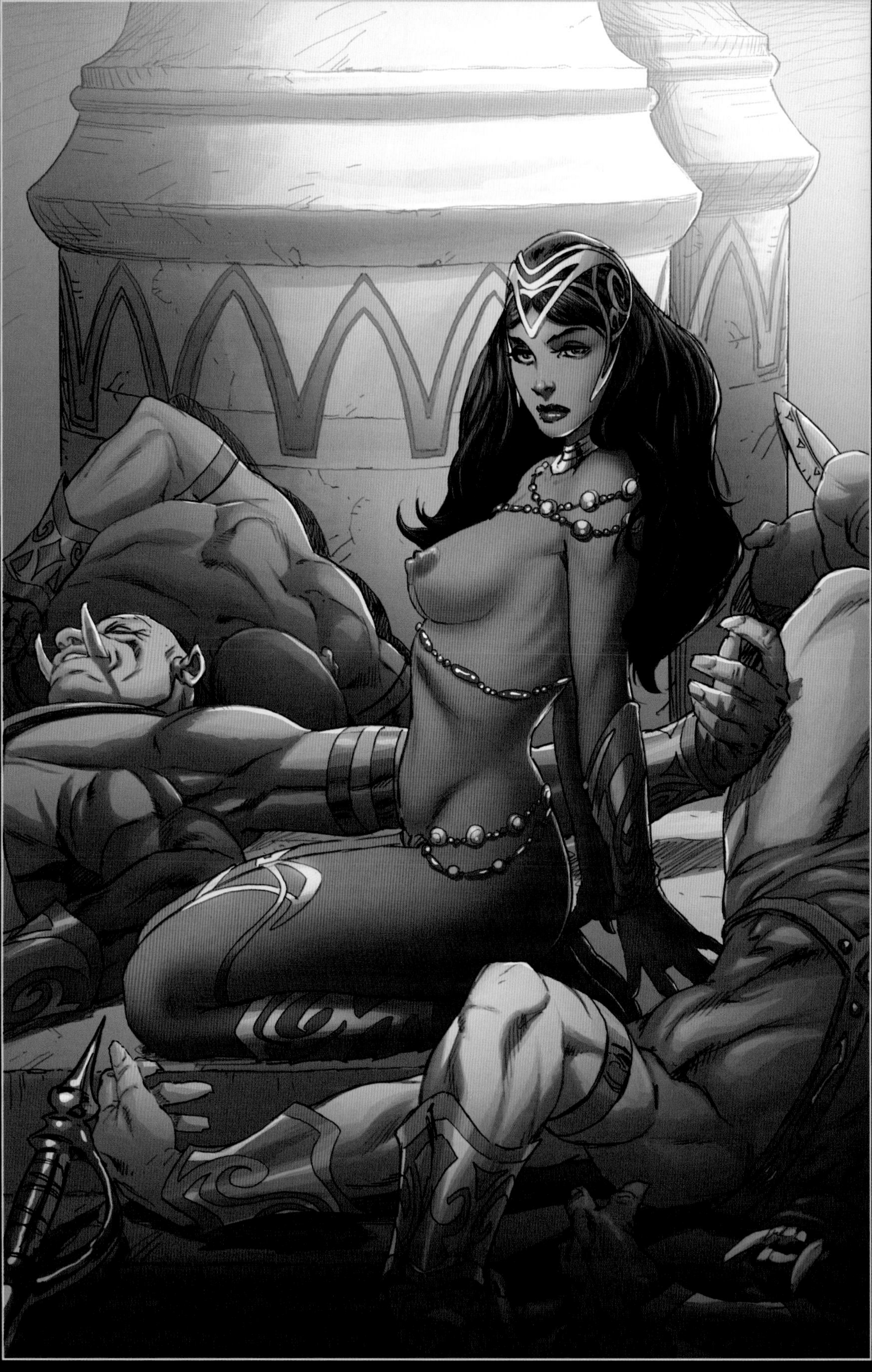

issue #8 risqué cover by **MEL RUBI**

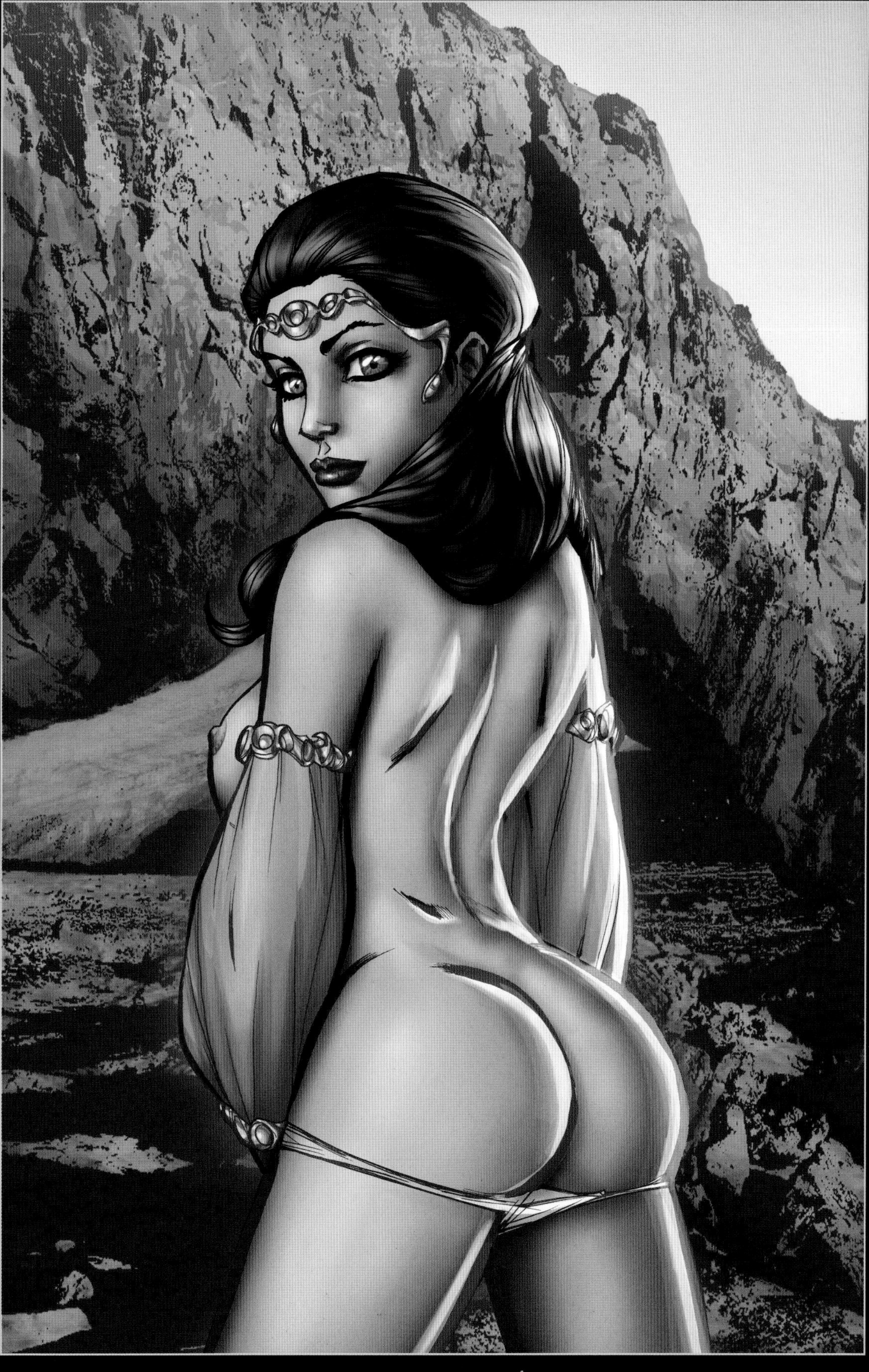

issue #8 risqué cover by **ALÉ GARZA**

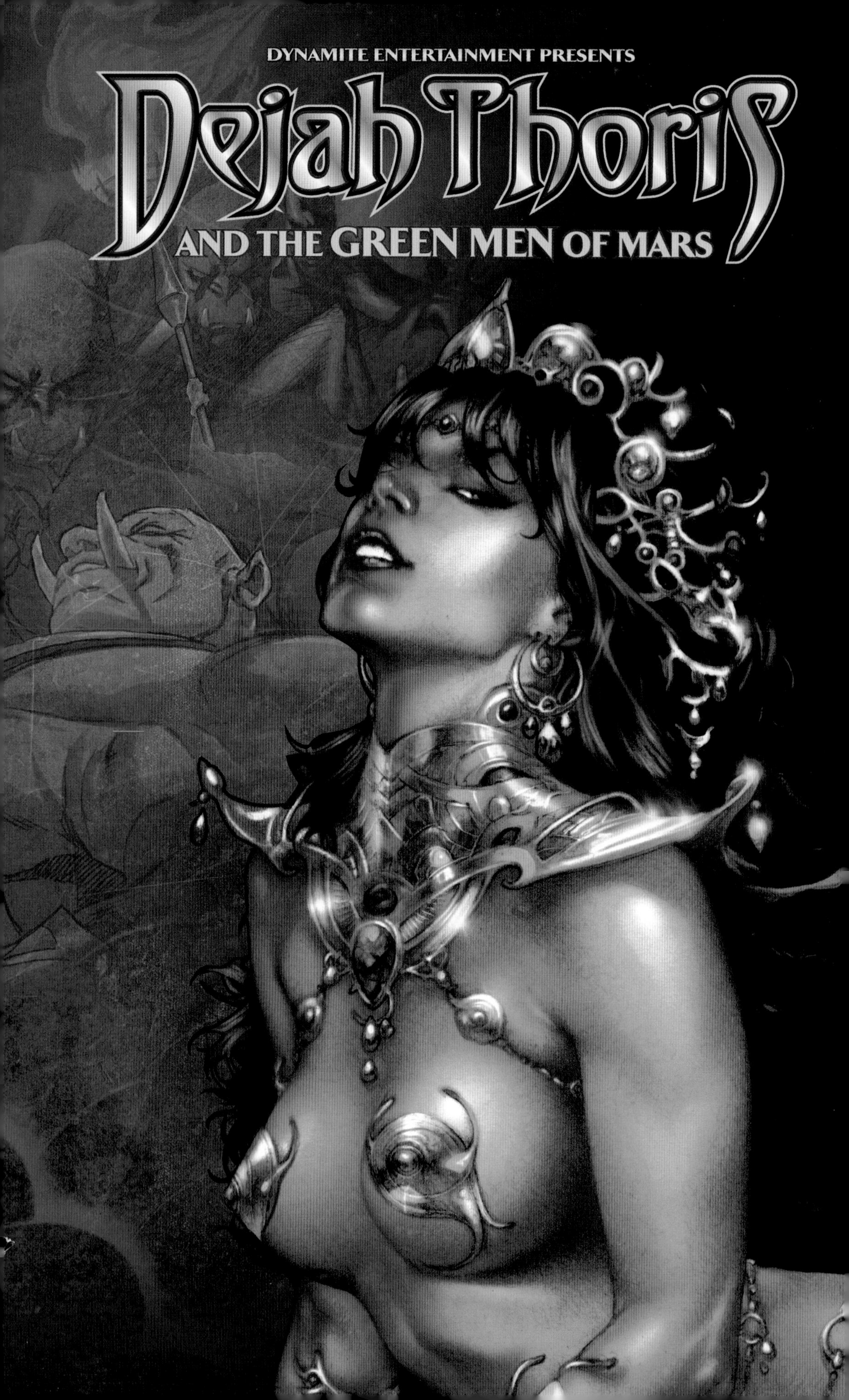
DYNAMITE ENTERTAINMENT PRESENTS
Dejah Thoris
AND THE GREEN MEN OF MARS